READINGS ON

MARK TWAIN

OTHER TITLES IN THE GREENHAVEN PRESS LITERARY COMPANION SERIES:

AMERICAN AUTHORS

Nathaniel Hawthorne
John Steinbeck

BRITISH AUTHORS

The Tragedies of William Shakespeare

THE GREENHAVEN PRESS
Literary Companion
TO AMERICAN AUTHORS

READINGS ON

MARK TWAIN

David Bender, *Publisher*
Bruno Leone, *Executive Editor*
Scott Barbour, *Managing Editor*
Katie de Koster, *Book Editor*

Greenhaven Press, San Diego, CA

Library of Congress Cataloging-in-Publication Data

Readings on Mark Twain / Katie de Koster, book editor.
    p.   cm. — (Greenhaven Press literary companion to American authors)
    Includes bibliographical references and index.
    ISBN 1-56510-471-4 (lib. bdg. : alk. paper).— ISBN 1-56510-470-6 (pbk. : alk. paper)
    1. Twain, Mark, 1835–1910—Criticism and interpretation.
I. de Koster, Katie, 1948-   . II. Series.
PS1338.R43   1996
818'.409–dc20   95-51236
                                                                              CIP

Cover photo: UPI/Bettmann

No part of this book may be reproduced or used in any form or by any means, electrical, mechanical, or otherwise, including, but not limited to, photocopy, recording, or any information storage and retrieval system, without prior written permission from the publisher.
Every effort has been made to trace the owners of copyrighted material.

Copyright ©1996 by Greenhaven Press, Inc.
PO Box 289009
San Diego, CA 92198-9009
Printed in the U.S.A.

TO

JOHN SMITH,

WHOM I HAVE KNOWN IN DIVERS AND SUNDRY PLACES ABOUT THE WORLD, AND WHOSE MANY AND MANIFOLD VIRTUES DID ALWAYS COMMAND MY ESTEEM, I

DEDICATE THIS BOOK.

It is said that the man to whom a volume is dedicated, always buys a copy. If this prove true in the present instance, a princely affluence is about to burst upon

THE AUTHOR.

Mark Twain,
The Celebrated Jumping Frog of Calaveras County and Other Sketches

The difference between the *almost right* word and the *right* word is really a large matter—'tis the difference between the lightning-bug and the lightning.

Mark Twain

Contents

Foreword	11
Mark Twain: A Biography	13
The First Continental American Literature (1946) *by Bernard De Voto*	45

The new heartland culture—exemplified by Mark Twain and Abraham Lincoln—grew up in disregard of European culture. Twain, with his midcontinental upbringing and his deep and varied experience of American life, marks the beginning of a continental American literature.

Lessons in Extravagance at the Comstock Lode (1978) *by Warren Hinckle and Fredric Hobbs*	55

The fabulous riches being wrested from the silver Comstock Lode created in Virginia City a fantastic setting of ostentation, extravagance, and exaggeration—which precisely suited the style of reporter Samuel Clemens. Dan De Quille, Clemens's colleague at the Virginia City *Territorial Enterprise*, had a strong effect on his developing style, and it was here that Clemens first used his most famous pseudonym, Mark Twain.

An Interpreter of American Character (1897) *by Charles Miner Thompson*	62

Mark Twain's childhood, deprived of the advantages of a good education and refined surroundings, prevents him from achieving greatness as a literary artist. He is not a skillful writer or a great humorist, nor has he created eternal characters in his work. His real gift is for expressing himself. Twain is the prototype of the typical American; since his characters reflect his own life, his writing interprets the national character.

Mark Twain as Prospective Classic (1898) *by Theodore de Laguna*	69

Those who most enthusiastically applaud Twain's work do not suspect him of greatness; he simply seems unpretentious, one of their own kind. Yet although his diction offends the educated taste, his humor is common clay, and his powers of sustained narrative are seriously questioned, his charm is irresistible. Mark Twain has given to the world one great character: his own—and the world should be grateful.

A Call to Authorship (1896) *by Joseph Twichell*	76

When the Civil War shut down the Mississippi River, riverboat pilot Sam Clemens (Mark Twain) lost his livelihood. He tried a variety of occupations but succeeded best at newspaper work. Assorted inhibitions—among them the lack of a literary education—kept him from conceiving of himself as an "author" until well after he had become one. He has read and studied widely to repair the deficiencies in his education.

Pure American English (1920) *by Brander Matthews*   83
Although Mark Twain is known for his characters' vernacular language, he was very precise in his use of words. He spoke and wrote American English—distinct from British English—yet he used language so pure that the English have no trouble understanding him.

A Serious Humorist (1910) *by Simeon Strunsky*   88
Because Mark Twain was an incomparable humorist, people paradoxically insist on praising him as a philosopher. Twain did indeed have a serious side, but this was a result of his being a humorist: the aftermath of much laughter is a rebound toward grief.

An Unfulfilled Genius (1920) *by Van Wyck Brooks*   91
Mark Twain's pessimism and cynicism, made light of by his contemporaries, actually expressed a deep malady of his soul. Although he had the talent and ability to become a great creative force, Twain failed to realize his genius. This feeling of failure explains the sadness and bitterness of his old age.

Who Owns the Uncrowned King? (1925)   98
by Upton Sinclair
Although Mark Twain was treated like an uncrowned American king, he was bitterly unhappy because his genius was repressed. He allowed the repression of both his style and his ideas. In order to be successful, he wrote to appeal to the bourgeois dictates of the ruling classes, which were in conflict with his liberal sympathies.

The Great Critical Controversy (1958) *by Philip S. Foner*   107
When Van Wyck Brooks published *The Ordeal of Mark Twain* in 1920, he set off a major controversy. Using the new psychoanalytical tools of Freudianism, Brooks charged that several psychological and social factors had derailed Twain from realizing his full potential as a social satirist. His analysis was met head-on by Bernard De Voto, whose *Mark Twain's America* attacked Brooks's thesis, assumptions, and conclusions. Most Twain criticism written since 1920 has been affected by this controversy.

Twain's Inescapable Disillusionment (1935)   115
by Owen Wister
Twain's tempestuous nature helped him escape for a while the dread of the Calvinist creed he grew up with. But the seeds of that creed, along with a new understanding of history, his disillusioning experience of America following the Civil War, personal grief, and perhaps illness—all combined to nurture the bitterness of his later years.

Using the Vernacular for Humor (1962)   121
by Henry Nash Smith
Mark Twain's work was shaped by two opposing forces: he used native humor to emphasize the contrast between rural

simplicity and empty elegance and refinement. Since the characters' speech is the main method used to distinguish between "straight" and "low" characters, the term "vernacular" is used to refer not only to the language of rustic characters but also to the values and ethical assumptions they represent.

Mark Twain, H.L. Mencken, and "The Higher Goofyism" (1964) *by C. Merton Babcock* 124

Although Mark Twain and H.L. Mencken shot humor at many of the same targets, Twain's warm style helped people laugh at themselves while Mencken's acerbic wit poked a harsher brand of fun. Mencken, who shared with Twain the belief that human life is basically a comedy, was one of the few critics of his time who understood that Twain was "America's greatest humorist."

Twain's Twinning (1989) *by Susan Gillman* 131

A recurring theme in Twain's work is that of duality, of identities borrowed and exchanged. This fascination with the double personality appears in many works, including *Tom Sawyer, Huckleberry Finn, The Prince and the Pauper,* and *Pudd'nhead Wilson*—as well as in the author's own dual persona as Samuel L. Clemens and Mark Twain.

A Short Summary of Some of Twain's Sources (1961) 136
by Edward Wagenknecht

Mark Twain drew from many sources, both fictional and real, for his characters and settings. He made the material taken from his sources part of himself and through this assimilation transformed it into his own creations.

A Turning Point in American Literature (1991) 143
by Gerald Parshall

Although *The Adventures of Huckleberry Finn* has been found objectionable by some ever since it was published in 1885, others call it not only "the great American novel" but also "one of the world's best books."

Three Coherent Elements in *Huckleberry Finn* (1962) 145
by Henry Nash Smith

The Adventures of Huckleberry Finn follows interweaving threads of adventure, social satire, and the developing character of Huck. The basic coherence of these interrelated parts indicates that Twain had all three in mind as he began writing, although they become deeper and richer in the later sections of the book. The exploration of Huck's psyche is the book's ultimate achievement.

The River Controls *Huckleberry Finn* (1950) *by T.S. Eliot* 151

Only one natural force can completely control the course of a human journey: a river. In *The Adventures of Huckleberry Finn*, the River gives the novel its form; it also controls the voyage of Huck and Jim. The end of the novel reflects the

connection between Huck and the River: Huck, like the
River, has neither beginning nor ending.

Huckleberry Finn and Censorship (1995)   155
by Lance Morrow
Attempts have been made to deprive children of the right to
read *The Adventures of Huckleberry Finn* on the grounds that
it is a racist tract. The book is a rich, deep text on many
important issues, including violence, child abuse, and alcoholism. At the same time, it is an inventory of essential values. The book should be thoroughly studied, and read in
conjunction with works on the reality of slavery and the similarities between Huck and Mark Twain's many black friends.

Appendix: The Ruckus over Huckleberry Finn: A variety of
critical objections to the novel have been made over the century since it was published, but some of the arguments have
changed over time.

A Classic of American Reform Literature (1958)   168
by Charles L. Sanford
In *A Connecticut Yankee in King Arthur's Court*, Mark Twain
both symbolically reenacted the American Revolution and
examined the "utopian" character of the industrial revolution. His hero, Hank Morgan, is intended as an archetype of
"hard, unsentimental common sense," but Twain suggests
that the mechanical blessings of material progress have
deprived Americans of imagination and a sense of heart.
A Connecticut Yankee (1888) is compared with Edward
Bellamy's *Looking Backward* (1887), a utopian novel concerned with industrial reform.

Clemens, Twain, and Morgan Are Not the Same   174
Man (1993) *by Lewis A. Lawson*
In *A Connecticut Yankee in King Arthur's Court*, a complex
superstructure built around Hank Morgan's tale of his visit
to Arthurian England and other, internal clues suggest that
Mark Twain did not endorse his hero or his hero's ideas—
and that Sam Clemens remained yet a further step removed
from Morgan.

The Power of the Mysterious in *A Connecticut*   180
Yankee (1976) *by Kurt Vonnegut Jr.*
The ending of *A Connecticut Yankee in King Arthur's Court*
suggests some secrets about its author, Mark Twain.

Camelot's Castle in Connecticut (1964) *by Hamlin Hill*   183
In *A Connecticut Yankee in King Arthur's Court*, Hank
Morgan wakes up to the sight of a knight and soon spies a
castle—yet he believes he is still in Connecticut. Twain's contemporaries would have understood: P.T. Barnum, the
famous circus showman, had built a castle in Bridgeport,
Connecticut, and stocked it with colorful circus leftovers.

The Absurdity of Man-Made Differentials (1959)   185
by Langston Hughes
> In *Pudd'nhead Wilson,* Twain's basic theme is a serious treatment of slavery—and of the absurdity of any artificial differentiation made between people. In presenting Negroes as developed human beings, Twain stands above most writers of his time. That he was ahead of his time is also shown by his use of fingerprinting in his story and his understanding of the principles of behavioristic psychology.

Chronology	192
Works by Mark Twain	198
For Further Research	203
Index	206

Foreword

*"'Tis the good reader that
makes the good book."*

Ralph Waldo Emerson

The story's bare facts are simple: The captain, an old and scarred seafarer, walks with a peg leg made of whale ivory. He relentlessly drives his crew to hunt the world's oceans for the great white whale that crippled him. After a long search, the ship encounters the whale and a fierce battle ensues. Finally the captain drives his harpoon into the whale, but the harpoon line catches the captain about the neck and drags him to his death.

A simple story, a straightforward plot—yet, since the 1851 publication of Herman Melville's *Moby-Dick*, readers and critics have found many meanings in the struggle between Captain Ahab and the whale. To some, the novel is a cautionary tale that depicts how Ahab's obsession with revenge leads to his insanity and death. Others believe that the whale represents the unknowable secrets of the universe and that Ahab is a tragic hero who dares to challenge fate by attempting to discover this knowledge. Perhaps Melville intended Ahab as a criticism of Americans' tendency to become involved in well-intentioned but irrational causes. Or did Melville model Ahab after himself, letting his fictional character express his anger at what he perceived as a cruel and distant god?

Although literary critics disagree over the meaning of *Moby-Dick*, readers do not need to choose one particular interpretation in order to gain an understanding of Melville's novel. Instead, by examining various analyses, they can gain numerous insights into the issues that lie under the surface of the basic plot. Studying the writings of literary critics can also aid readers in making their own assessments of *Moby-Dick* and other literary works and in developing analytical thinking skills.

The Greenhaven Literary Companion Series was created with these goals in mind. Designed for young adults, this unique anthology series provides an engaging and comprehensive introduction to literary analysis and criticism. The essays included in the Literary Companion Series are chosen for their accessibility to a young adult audience and are expertly edited in consideration of both the reading and comprehension levels of this audience. In addition, each essay is introduced by a concise summation that presents the contributing writer's main themes and insights. Every anthology in the Literary Companion Series contains a varied selection of critical essays that cover a wide time span and express diverse views. Wherever possible, primary sources are represented through excerpts from authors' notebooks, letters, and journals and through contemporary criticism.

Each title in the Literary Companion Series pays careful consideration to the historical context of the particular author or literary work. In-depth biographies and detailed chronologies reveal important aspects of authors' lives and emphasize the historical events and social milieu that influenced their writings. To facilitate further research, every anthology includes primary and secondary source bibliographies of articles and/or books selected for their suitability for young adults. These engaging features make the Greenhaven Literary Companion Series ideal for introducing students to literary analysis in the classroom or as a library resource for young adults researching the world's great authors and literature.

Exceptional in its focus on young adults, the Greenhaven Literary Companion Series strives to present literary criticism in a compelling and accessible format. Every title in the series is intended to spark readers' interest in leading American and world authors, to help them broaden their understanding of literature, and to encourage them to formulate their own analyses of the literary works that they read. It is the editors' hope that young adult readers will find these anthologies to be true companions in their study of literature.

MARK TWAIN: A BIOGRAPHY

A word of warning is in order for those who wish to know The Truth about Mark Twain: He wrote autobiographical fiction and fictional autobiography—and he is the primary source of information about his own life. The life of Mark Twain is a story told by Samuel Langhorne Clemens, and the events, dates, and embellishments he gave are all, so to speak, subject to verification and clarification. When Twain was writing his autobiography, he made it plain: "I don't believe these details are right but I don't care a rap. They will do just as well as the facts."

Fortunately for those who value facts over a more artistic truth, Twain wrote prolifically in notebooks and in letters to family and friends—and many of these writings have survived. Researchers have painstakingly studied these "private" manuscripts for indications of "what really happened," combining them with reminiscences of his family, friends, and business associates to "set the record straight." What follows is, therefore, a fairly straight record of the life of Mark Twain . . . always subject to later verification.

FLORIDA, MISSOURI

> I was born the 30th of November, 1835, in the almost invisible village of Florida, Monroe County, Missouri. . . . The village contained a hundred people and I increased the population by 1 per cent. It is more than many of the best men in history could have done for a town. It may not be modest in me to refer to this but it is true.
>
> Autobiography of Mark Twain

The baby who would grow up to be Mark Twain was christened Samuel Langhorne Clemens when he was born in that tiny hamlet in Missouri. His parents, John Marshall and Jane Lampton Clemens, both originally of Virginia families, had met in Kentucky. (John, who had become the male head of his family at the age of seven, had gone to Kentucky to relieve financial pressures in Virginia—a pattern that would be repeated often.) When they married in Lexington in 1823, Jane was twenty and John twenty-four or -five, and "neither of them had an overplus of property. She brought him two or three negroes but nothing else, I think," reported Sam. Although they were not wealthy, they were considered "gentry." The couple moved to Tennessee, pausing in a couple of towns before landing in the small settlement of Jamestown, in the eastern hills of Tennessee. There John, with his law schooling and his "ancestors" (including, it was said, one of the judges who sentenced England's King Charles I to death), became the leading citizen. Jane's family claimed elevated connections, too; they believed they were related to the Lambtons of England, earls of Durham.

Ancestors notwithstanding, John Clemens was a poor businessman. A steady decline in the Clemenses' situation led them to look for better opportunities in the West. The family sold all they had (except for thousands of acres of undeveloped Tennessee land and their one remaining slave) and began the hard journey to Missouri in the spring of 1835. Jane later told her granddaughter, Annie Moffett, that the family had intended to settle in St. Louis. Just before they arrived, a Negro boy was lynched by burning, and cholera was plaguing the town when they got there—so they moved on, to Florida, Missouri. While some Twain biographers believe Jane was already pregnant with Sam before the family left Kentucky, biographer Bernard De Voto—deducing, perhaps, from the statement that Sam was a "seven-months baby"—believes he was conceived on that April journey. In any case, Sam was traveling before he was born, and he never really stopped.

John Clemens brought his family to a two-room frame house with a lean-to kitchen in Florida. It must have been crowded: The Clemens family already included Orion (born 1825; the family pronounced his name with the accent on the first syllable), Pamela (born 1827), Margaret (1830), and Benjamin (1832). There would be one more son after Sam— Henry, born in 1838. (Pamela remembered another son, Pleasants Hannibal, who had died in Tennessee at the age of three months.)

Florida was a town with "prospects." Located on the Salt River, surrounded by rich land, already the location of flour mills, a sawmill, and distilleries, it seemed to need only vision and development to make it a bustling commercial town. Missouri was filled with such progressive ideas. For example, in 1833, a group of businessmen had surveyed land on both sides of the Missouri River, planning a city to compete with the older river towns for the lucrative trade between East and West; originally named Westport, that town is now known as Kansas City. With similar dreams, John Clemens threw himself into the civic life of Florida, leading the efforts to improve the Salt River to allow steamboat navigation and to bring a railroad to the town. But the country suffered a financial crash in 1837, and the envisioned improvements for Florida never happened. John was always a better visionary than a businessman; once again his own business—a store—was failing. In the fall of 1839, soon after Sam's sister Margaret died at the age of nine from "bilious fever," John traded his holdings in Florida for land and buildings in nearby Hannibal, Missouri, on the Mississippi River, and moved his household again.

Hannibal, Missouri

Although the family's fortunes continued to decline, the next few years gave young Sam the childhood that would later be chronicled (with a few changes, of course) in *The Adventures of Tom Sawyer* and *The Adventures of Huckleberry Finn*. The Clemenses had moved to Missouri to be near Jane's sister, Patsy, and her family. Jane's brother-in-law, John Quarles, was a successful farmer, respected and popular, and—unlike Sam's rather austere father—genial and generously good-natured. "I have not come across a better man than he was," wrote Sam many years later. Sam began spending the summers at the Quarles farm, and his memories of that time as recorded in his autobiography are rich and splendid:

> It was a heavenly place for a boy, that farm of my uncle John's. The house was a double log one, with a spacious floor (roofed in) connecting it with the kitchen. In the summer the table was set in the middle of that shady and breezy floor, and the sumptuous meals—well, it makes me cry to think of them. Fried chicken, roast pig; wild and tame turkeys, ducks and geese; venison just killed; squirrels, rabbits, pheasants, partridges, prairie-chickens; biscuits, hot batter cakes, hot buckwheat cakes, hot "wheat bread," hot rolls, hot corn pone; fresh corn boiled on the ear, succotash, butter-beans, string-beans, tomatoes, peas, Irish potatoes, sweet potatoes; buttermilk, sweet milk, "clabber"; watermelons, muskmelons, cantaloupes—all fresh from the garden; apple pie, peach pie, pumpkin pie, apple dumplings, peach cobbler—I can't remember the rest.

The farm, with its orchards, barns, stables, wandering brook with forbidden (and therefore irresistible) swimming pools, and slave quarters (where Sam became friends with several of the slaves), played a role in the later literature of Mark Twain: "In *Huck Finn* and in *Tom Sawyer, Detective*, I moved it down to Arkansas," he recalled. "It was all of six hundred miles but it was no trouble; it was not a very large farm—five hundred acres, perhaps—but I could have done it if it had been twice as large."

The generous summer lifestyle, which probably began

when Sam was seven or eight, may have contributed to his survival. He had been a sickly child—he said he "lived mainly on allopathic medicines during the first seven years" of his life. As Twain biographer John Lauber points out, "Merely to live was an accomplishment for such a child, demonstrating unexpected toughness at a time when, according to a Hannibal paper, 'one quarter of the children born die before they are one year old; one half die before they are twenty-one.'" The Clemenses had already lost Margaret at the age of nine (and, according to Pamela, the infant Pleasants Hannibal). Benjamin would die when he was ten, in 1842.

But Sam seemed to survive against all odds, even when he made the odds longer against himself. In 1845, when he was about the same age Margaret and Benjamin had been when they died, Hannibal was hit with an epidemic of measles that killed many of its children. "There was a funeral almost daily and the mothers of the town were nearly demented with fright," he recalled. Jane Clemens went to extraordinary lengths to keep Pamela, Henry, and Sam away from contagion, with the result that Sam was constantly in fear that he had caught the deadly disease. He finally decided he could live in suspense no longer, and snuck into bed with a seriously ill friend, Will Bowen. It took two tries—he was caught the first time and hustled out of the sickroom—but he managed to get "a good case of measles" that took him "within a shade of death's door." Years later, when asked to write about a "turning point" in his life, he settled on that trip almost to death as his theme.

Sam was growing up, by all reports an energetic and mischievous boy, gathering adventures and characters that would serve Mark Twain as a mother lode of ideas. He attended school, reluctantly; he excelled in the weekly competitive spelling bees, but did not otherwise distinguish himself—especially in deportment, his brother Henry's forte. He later wrote, "My mother had a good deal of trouble with me but I think she enjoyed it. She had none at all with my brother Henry, who was two years younger than I, and I think that the unbroken monotony of his goodness and truthfulness and obedience would have been a burden to her but for the relief and variety which I furnished in the other direction." Henry virtuously reported Sam for his many misdeeds, such as going swimming (Sam "nearly drowned" several times while growing up). When Sam had been particularly bad, his mother would send him to attend Sunday evening church services, but he recollected that he frequently detoured to play with his friends instead.

The "relief and variety" Sam furnished his mother included such daredevil escapades as the time (about 1849, he said later) when he and a friend, Tom Nash, went skating on the frozen Mississippi River one night, "probably without permission. I cannot see why we should go skating in the night unless without permission, for there could be no considerable amusement to be gotten out of skating at midnight if nobody was going to object to it." The river began to break up while the two were about a half mile from shore, and they began to race for safety. The next hour was spent anxiously negotiating patchy moonlight and floating ice cakes. Although Sam made it to shore safely, Tom fell into the freezing water when he had nearly reached solid ground. He crawled out, but his icy bath led to "a procession of diseases," ending in scarlet fever, which left him completely deaf—a fate that, if it had happened to Sam, might well have prevented the birth of "Mark Twain" some fourteen years later.

A Darker Side of Hannibal

Although Missouri would officially side with the North during the Civil War (1861–65), under the terms of the Missouri Compromise of 1820 (an attempt to prevent the issue of slavery from tearing the nation apart) it had entered the Union as a slave state. Sam Clemens thus grew up with slaves. His family's decline had been charted by the sales of their slaves over the years; finally, having none of their own, they rented slaves by the year from neighbors. He later recalled:

> In my schoolboy days I had no aversion to slavery. I was not aware that there was anything wrong about it. No one arraigned it in my hearing; the local papers said nothing against it; the local pulpit taught us that God approved it, that it was a holy thing and that the doubter need only look in the Bible if he wished to settle his mind—and then the texts were read aloud to us to make the matter sure.

Sam Clemens would be an adult before he came to an understanding of slavery as "a bald, grotesque and unwarrantable usurpation." But he did relate to the slaves he knew as people: "All the negroes were friends of ours, and with those of our own age we were in effect comrades. I say in effect, using the phrase as a modification. We were comrades and yet not comrades; color and condition interposed a subtle line which both parties were conscious of and which rendered complete fusion impossible." The subtle line maintained by a slaveholding society remained, but his empathy for his slave friends was awakened by his mother:

> We had a little slave boy whom we had hired from some one, there in Hannibal. He was from the eastern shore of Maryland and had been brought away from his family and his friends halfway across the American continent and sold. He was a cheery spirit, innocent and gentle, and the noisiest creature that ever was, perhaps. All day long he was singing, whistling, yelling, whooping, laughing—it was maddening, devastating, unendurable. At last, one day, I lost all my temper and went raging to my mother and said Sandy had been singing for an hour without a single break and I couldn't stand it and *wouldn't* she please shut him up. The tears came into her eyes and her lip trembled and she said something like this:
>
> "Poor thing, when he sings it shows that he is not remembering and that comforts me; but when he is still I am afraid he is thinking and I cannot bear it. He will never see his mother again; if he can sing I must not hinder it, but be thankful for it. If you were older you would understand me; then that friendless child's noise would make you glad."
>
> It was a simple speech and made up of small words but it went home, and Sandy's noise was not a trouble to me any more.

In Hannibal, separating and selling the members of a slave family "was a thing not well liked by the people and so it was not often done, except in the settling of estates," he remembered. But the rare sight of a dozen black women and men chained together, awaiting shipment to the southern slave market, left him with a memory of "the saddest faces I have ever seen." Another memory was seeing a Negro man killed by a white man "for a trifling little offence"; everybody seemed indifferent about the slave's fate, feeling only sympathy for the owner who had lost valuable property.

Violent death was a danger not only for slaves in that nearly frontier town. Sam suffered nightmares after witnessing several other tragedies: the shooting of an old man "in the main street at noonday" by a wealthy businessman who just walked away, unmolested, after taking this revenge for a slight; the stabbing of a young California emigrant by a drunken comrade; attempted murder by two brothers who held down their uncle and tried to kill him with a revolver that would not fire; the death of another drunken California emigrant who threatened a widow and her daughter and was answered by a chest full of slugs shot from an old musket. Sam's penchant for absorbing guilt found an early opportunity when he saw a tramp in the street who would be arrested for public drunkenness. Feeling generous, Sam found him some matches so he could smoke his pipe. Later that night, the tramp was burned to death in the village jail. The young, sensitive Sam, trying to make sense of the Calvinist teachings about God and Providence, found in each of these incidents a personal lesson intended "to beguile me to a better life." His guilt simply increased when he felt himself fail to maintain his repentance for all his self-perceived flaws.

THE DEPTHS OF POVERTY

Meanwhile his father's lifelong pattern of a steady decline in fortunes, interrupted by brief flashes of prosperity, continued. Hannibal would have something of the future John Clemens had envisioned for Florida—over the first ten years after the family moved there, its population would grow from a few hundred to nearly three thousand—but Sam's father never managed to profit from his dreams of glory. John Lauber writes that "things went badly for the Clemenses in Hannibal. Creditors pressed them hard, they moved frequently, there was a sheriff's sale in 1843 and another ordered in December 1846—but the sheriff found nothing left to seize. . . . Orion was apprenticed to a printer in St. Louis—much against his will, for he felt that he was a gentleman's son and deserved a profession." In 1846, the Clemenses were reduced to sharing quarters with another family, for whom Jane cooked.

According to the family tradition, the 1846 calamity was the result of John's "going security for" (co-signing) a large note for a man named Ira Stout, who then declared bankruptcy and left the Clemenses ruined by the liability to pay the entire note. Their fortunes were about to turn around again the next year, they believed, when the ultimate disaster hit:

> When my father died, in 1847, the disaster happened—as is the customary way with such things—just at the very moment when our fortunes had changed and we were about to be comfortable once more after several years of grinding poverty and privation. . . . My father had just been elected clerk of the Surrogate Court. . . . He went to Palmyra, the county-seat, to be sworn in about the end of February. In returning home horseback twelve miles[,] a storm of sleet and rain assailed him and he arrived at the house in a half-frozen condition. Pleurisy followed and he died on the 24th of March.
>
> Thus our splendid new fortune was snatched from us and we were in the depths of poverty again.

Sam wrote little about his father, perhaps because John died when Sam was young, perhaps because he felt more of an affinity with his fun-loving mother. Unlike Jane, John was precise in his use of English. In 1845 he enrolled in a series of twenty lectures on Grammar, and shared the lessons with his children. (He wrote Orion in St. Louis, sending copies of his lecture notes and warning him not to show them to anyone else, since he had permission to share the lectures only with members of his immediate family.) This careful attention to the language was part of his legacy. There was more, whether of heredity or of environment. John and Sam shared a strong intellect and a deep integrity; dreams of wealth and a desire for success; independent thinking, shaded by a strain of pessimism; involvement in the affairs of their communities (which, for Sam, would become the world community); and an abiding sense of justice, of right and wrong.

Samuel Charles Webster, a grandson of Sam's sister Pamela, wrote that "Mark Twain inherited his humor, his temperament, and his red hair from his mother's side. His accuracy in workmanship he got from his father. His accuracy in facts he never got from anybody."

"NEWSPAPER COLLEGE"

When John Clemens died, Orion—having temporarily reconciled himself to the printing trade—was sending a portion of his wages to his mother. Pamela moved to another town and was supporting herself teaching piano and guitar lessons. Although he later said he had been taken from school immediately upon his father's death, recent research has shown that Sam continued to attend school at least part-time for two more years. But in his fourteenth year, it was time for him to begin to support himself, and he was apprenticed to Joseph Ament, publisher of the weekly Hannibal *Courier*. He was to board with his master, learn the printing trade, and receive two suits of clothing a year (he got just one—Ament's oversized castoffs). He soon graduated to setting type, and to making mischief with his fellows. One journeyman, Wales McCormick, stayed in his memory for his "limitless and adorable irreverence"—a trait Mark Twain would carry to new heights.

In the nineteenth century, printing was "the poor man's college." Newspapers were consciously "literary," offering poems and essays from both classical and contemporary authors, and liberally borrowing the best pieces from one another. Setting type letter by letter required attention to the words; an apt mind would soon learn to distinguish good writing from bad, and absorb a sense of style. The lad who had been an unenthusiastic schoolboy now became an eager reader, and began the self-education that would continue throughout his life.

After the discovery of gold in California in 1848, the papers were filled with news from the goldfields. A route to the West passed through Hannibal, and Sam and his friends caught the fever, going downriver a few miles on Saturdays to "dig for gold," enviously watching as at least eighty of Hannibal's townsfolk left for California.

Although Sam did not succumb to gold fever just yet, the emigration west did affect the Clemens family. The editor of the Hannibal *Journal* joined the gold rush, and Orion decided the time was ripe to start his own paper in Hannibal. Perhaps borrowing on his prospects (the Tennessee land their father had bought before Sam was born), Orion began the weekly *Western Union*, and offered his brother Sam $3.50 per week plus board to join him. Since that was $3.50 more than the *Courier* paid, Sam accepted the offer. Pamela also returned home, and the Clemenses were together again.

Orion was a lousy businessman, and the promised pay failed to materialize more often than not. But he did offer Sam something the *Courier* had not: an opportunity to get into print.

THE FIRST NEWSPAPER WRITINGS

Sam's first published work was "A Gallant Fireman," a one-paragraph anecdote in the January 16, 1851, *Western Union*. It describes the reactions of the paper's "printer's devil," Jim Wolf, to a fire in the grocery store next door to the newspaper office. The young man, "seeing us somewhat excited, concluded he would perform a noble deed, and immediately gathered the broom, an old mallet, the wash-pan and a dirty towel, and in a fit of patriotic excitement, rushed out of the office and deposited his precious burden some ten squares off, out of danger." The fire had long been out when he returned an hour later, "thinking he had immortalized himself."

In May of the following year, Sam's work gained a much larger audience. "The Dandy Frightening the Squatter," a humorous tale of moderate length, appeared in the Boston *Carpet-Bag* on May 1, 1852. Exactly a week later, the Philadelphia *American Courier* printed Sam's description of the town he would later make famous as Tom Sawyer and Huck Finn's St. Petersburg: "Hannibal, Missouri."

By fall 1852, Sam was on a roll. "A Family Muss," a report on a drunken man's assaults on family and friends livened by the use of a comic Irish dialect, appeared with Sam's pseudonymous byline "W. Epaminondas Adrastus Perkins" on September

9 in the Hannibal *Journal*. (Orion had purchased a second paper and combined them; the publication was now known by this name.) The following week, Sam entered his first journalistic feud. Orion had complained about stray barking dogs in an August issue, and the editor of the rival Hannibal *Tri-Weekly Messenger*, J.T. Hinton, had responded sarcastically. Orion did not respond to Hinton's sally; Sam did. His September 16 answer to the affront, "'Local' Resolves to Commit Suicide," was accompanied by a crude woodcut showing Hinton as a dog-headed man. The artwork, wrote Sam, "caught the gentleman's countenance as correctly as the thing could have been done with the real *dog*-gerytype apparatus." (Daguerreotypes, an early form of photographs, had been popular since they were brought to the United States by Samuel F.B. Morse and John W. Draper in December 1839.) Hinton's response to this insult ("low and contemptible," "obscene and despicable") was met on September 23 by a pair of woodcuts with captions under the heading "'Pictur' Department"—accompanied in the same issue by Orion's attempts to smooth over the controversy.

Sam had been given the chance for the September 16 effort by Orion's absence (he had gone to Tennessee in a vain attempt to sell the land left by their father). In charge of the paper for the first time, Sam filled several columns with features by "W. Epaminondas Adrastus Blab" (the alias had a new last name). "Historical Exhibition—A No. 1 Ruse" was an early attempt to make a story out of local events and real people. It tells of a practical joke played on a succession of people who refuse to share their hard-won knowledge of the punchline with other potential dupes.

But W. Epaminondas was, as far as the *Journal* was concerned, a one-month wonder. In the September 23 issue, Blab noted that "it is customary, nowadays, for a man, as soon as he gets his name up, to take a 'furrin' tour, for the benefit of his health; or, if his health is good, he goes without any excuse at all." He then announced his intention to retire from public life to Glasscock's Island (a bit of land in the Mississippi that Mark Twain would make famous as Jackson's Island in *Tom Sawyer* and *Huckleberry Finn*).

By May 1853 the *Journal* was struggling to survive; Orion turned it into a daily and even gave Sam his own column in the May 23 issue. That month Sam tried out a host of new pen names: A Son of Adam, Peter Pencilcase's Son, Rambler, Grumbler, John Snooks. The spate of writing may have signaled Sam's need to spread his wings—or perhaps it was just spring fever. In any case, Sam was soon off on his first travels. By late May or early June, he had set off for New York (although he told his family he was headed for St. Louis, to keep them from worrying—or perhaps from trying to stop him).

BREAKING AWAY

An accomplished typesetter could find work in almost any town. Sam did stop in St. Louis for a few weeks to earn money for the rest of his journey; then he headed for New York City. Arriving in late August 1853, he was soon employed by a printing house and writing long letters home. His family had apparently heard the lurid tales of what could happen to a young man when he went to the big city; in one of his letters, Sam wrote: "You ask me where I spend my evenings. Where would you suppose with a free printer's library containing more than 4,000 volumes within a quarter of a mile of me, and nobody at home to talk to?" (Free public libraries were still relatively rare; most libraries were founded for a defined group of people—printers, sailors, merchants—or were subscription libraries, charging a fee.)

The free reading was about all Sam could afford; his pay was poor, and by October he had moved on to Philadelphia, where he worked for the *Inquirer*. His hours were odd but the

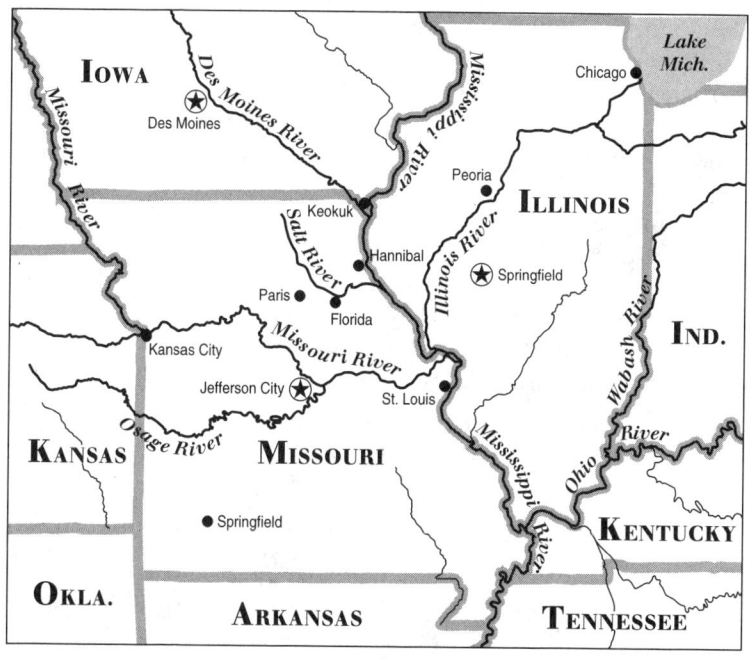

pay was better, allowing him to enjoy his spare time seeing the sights, and even take a quick trip to Washington, D.C. But the novelty was beginning to wear off, and he set his sights on going back to St. Louis. In late summer 1854, he briefly returned "home," which was now Muscatine, Iowa. Orion, Henry, and Jane were living there, where Orion published the Muscatine *Tri-Weekly Journal.* Arriving early in the morning, he decided to wait at a hotel instead of going directly to the Clemens home. While there he picked up a book of portraits of the monarchs of England and amused himself by memorizing the dates of their reigns. This, he later reported, stimulated an interest in English history that would eventually express itself in *A Connecticut Yankee in King Arthur's Court* and *The Prince and the Pauper.*

After a brief visit, Sam went back to St. Louis, where he worked as a printer for less than a year. The recently married Orion moved to Keokuk, Iowa, and opened a printing shop, the Ben Franklin Book and Job Office, with his brother Henry. Sam, who wanted to be a riverboat pilot, asked a wealthy St. Louis relative for help in achieving his goal but was turned down. In midsummer 1855, he moved to Keokuk to join his brothers in the new venture, on the promise of $5.00 per week plus board. Here he stayed for about a year and a half, working with his brothers, reading voraciously but apparently doing little writing for publication, discovering a talent for public speaking. He also began keeping a notebook—the earliest to survive, and possibly the first one he kept regularly. Along with laundry lists, French lessons, his signature in various decorative styles, and the occasional note on people he met, he recorded a few pages on phrenology (a method of describing character according to the configuration of the skull) and descriptions of the four "temperaments." He was, he decided, "sanguine"—cheerfully optimistic, confident—while Orion was "nervous."

On November 1, 1876, in response to a letter from an old friend, J.H. Burrough, he recalled himself at that time:

> As you describe me I can picture myself as I was 22 years ago. The portrait is correct. You think I have grown some; upon my word there was room for it. You have described a callow fool, a self-sufficient ass, a mere human tumble-bug, stern in air, heaving at his bit of dung and imagining he is re-molding the world and is entirely capable of doing it right. Ignorance, intolerance, egotism, self-assertion, opaque perception, dense and pitiful chuckle-headedness—and an almost pathetic unconsciousness of it all. That is what I was at 19–20.

MAKING HIS FORTUNE, PART I

As usual, Orion's business was not doing well. He had made Sam a partner, who would share the "profits" instead of drawing a salary. Sam could tell this was no way to get ahead. Having been stymied in his attempt to achieve his first goal, becoming a riverboat pilot, sanguine, irrepressible Sam was soon working on a new scheme for making his fortune. "I had been reading Lieutenant Herndon's account of his explorations of the Amazon and had been mightily attracted by what he said of coca," he reported in his autobiography. "I made up my mind that I would go to the head-waters of the Amazon and collect coca and trade in it and make a fortune." He wrote to his brother Henry of his plans in August 1856, remarking that although Orion had promised him "fifty or a hundred dollars in six weeks" for this new venture, he doubted he would get it. He also confided, "I believe that the secret of Ma's willingness to allow me to go to South America lies in the fact that she is afraid I am going to get married! Success to the hallucination."

Sam spent the winter of 1856–57 in Cincinnati, working at the printing office of Wrightson & Company to earn money for his passage to South America. Perhaps the most noteworthy aspect of this period was a friendship he struck up with a fellow boarder, a Scotsman named Macfarlane. Little is known about him—not his occupation or even his first name—but he said he was a self-educated man, and he had developed his own philosophy, which impressed the young typesetter who was half his age. Sam spent many evenings with Macfarlane that winter, listening to him explain his reasoning. His theory of evolution, propounded some fifteen years before Charles Darwin published *The Descent of Man*, made a particularly strong impact on Sam:

> Macfarlane considered that the animal life in the world was developed in the course of eons of time from a few microscopic seed germs, or perhaps one microscopic seed germ, . . . and that this development was progressive upon an ascending scale toward ultimate perfection until man was reached; and that then the progressive scheme broke pitifully down and went to wreck and ruin!
>
> He said that man's heart was the only bad heart in the animal kingdom; that man was the only animal capable of feeling malice, envy, vindictiveness, revengefulness, hatred, selfishness, . . . the sole animal in whom was developed the base instinct called *patriotism*, the sole animal that robs, persecutes,

oppresses and kills members of his own immediate tribe, the sole animal that steals and enslaves the members of any *tribe*.

Whether Macfarlane planted seeds that blossomed later in Mark Twain or simply found a soul already compatible with his philosophy, those who read the writings of Mark Twain's last years will recognize in them the same bitter pessimism as expressed in the Scotsman's ideas.

By springtime, Sam had saved enough to pay his way to New Orleans on the steamer *Paul Jones*. He planned to set sail for the Amazon from that port, but on the way south he met one of the boat's pilots, Horace Bixby, whom he soon persuaded to help him become a riverboat pilot. Bixby agreed to teach Sam the Mississippi River from St. Louis to New Orleans for five hundred dollars—one hundred dollars in advance. Sam borrowed the advance from William Moffett, who had married his sister Pamela, and began to learn the snags, curves, and hidden obstacles of the great river.

Mark Twain wrote of his life on the Mississippi, with a certain amount of literary license, in the book called, appropriately, *Life on the Mississippi*. Being a pilot was much more than adventure and travel. Riverboat pilots were respected, almost revered. Once the boat left shore, they were in supreme command—not even subject to orders from the captain. Piloting required intense attention to details, which had to be committed to memory—an admirable trait for an author-to-be to develop. The job was lucrative: A master pilot could expect the same income as the vice president of the United States. The confidence that came from the sense of command and the income eventually led Sam to take over the role of head of the family from the feckless Orion. It was now Sam who found employment for their brother Henry.

Sam was a cub pilot on the *Pennsylvania* in June 1858, working under William Brown, master pilot and petty tyrant. Henry was working as third (or mud) clerk on the same boat when Brown accused him of insubordination and attacked him with a lump of coal. Sam sprang to his brother's defense—the only recorded time he resorted to physical violence.

As it turned out, this episode may have saved Sam's life, but it led to yet another lifelong feeling of guilt. Because of the altercation Sam left the ship in New Orleans, but Henry stayed aboard. At six o'clock on the morning of June 13, 1858, the *Pennsylvania*'s four boilers exploded. The boat had just won a race with a rival steamer and was preparing to race another; the boilers (one of which was known to leak badly) had been fired up to the limit. At least two hundred people died immediately; many others—including Henry—later succumbed to their injuries. Sam, who was traveling north as a passenger on the *A.T. Lacey*, arrived in time to be with his brother and watch as he took six days to die. He blamed himself for Henry's having been on the *Pennsylvania*. The guilt he felt was only made worse by those who congratulated him on his luck for not having been aboard.

The accident did not drive Sam from the river, although he did take a month off—and continued to be lucky by thus missing an epidemic of yellow fever in New Orleans. On April 5, 1859, he received his pilot's license. A respected gentleman now, he decided that chewing tobacco was no longer appropriate for his new position in life, and he quit for good. He began to dress with style. He apparently made friends readily, and there was no shortage of young women to dance with at fancy parties. The slightly built man whose head seemed a little too large for his body, with his red curly hair and his blue-green eyes and "a Roman nose, which greatly improves the beauty of his features" (according to his daughter Susy, in the biography she wrote when she was thirteen), had found a career he planned to follow until the end of his days.

The Civil War intervened.

THE CIVIL WAR

In his autobiography, Mark Twain did not dwell on the war:

> I was in New Orleans when Louisiana went out of the Union, January 26, 1861, and I started North the next day. Every day on the trip a blockade was closed by the boat [it was the last one allowed to go north], and the batteries at Jefferson Barracks (below St. Louis) fired two shots through the chimneys the last night of the voyage. In June I joined the Confederates in Ralls County, Missouri, as a second lieutenant under General Tom Harris and came near having the distinction of being captured by Colonel Ulysses S. Grant. I resigned after two weeks' service in the field, explaining that I was "incapacitated by fatigue" through persistent retreating.

This offhanded treatment does not reveal the difficulties Sam had in deciding what side to take in this conflict of brother against brother. The Clemens family had owned slaves, and Sam had grown up with "the Peculiar Institution." Orion, however, was a staunch abolitionist. Missouri was a border state; although it stayed in the Union, many of its citizens fought for the Confederacy (including Frank and Jesse James, who polished their robbing and looting skills as part of a bloodthirsty pro-Confederate guerrilla group, the infamous Quantrill's Raiders).

"The Private History of a Campaign That Failed," written by Mark Twain in 1885, tells more about the choice Sam Clemens made. (Although the details may be fictionalized, family members who visited the troop and other Rangers who later wrote their reminiscences verify that the overall picture was accurate.) It is a story that recalls the differences between Tom Sawyer and Huckleberry Finn. Sam and several of his friends from Hannibal got together one night and formed a military company. They dubbed themselves the Marion Rangers and made almost everyone an officer; Sam was second lieutenant. Setting out on an "expedition" in a Tom Sawyer spirit of horseplay and fun, they basically went on a prolonged campout, playing at military drills on occasion. When rumor of an approaching enemy force reached them, the council of war (everyone in the troop) agreed that the main concern was that they not retreat *toward* the enemy. A losing battle with a farmer's dogs was followed by several scares about Union troops searching for Confederates to hang. The frequent rumors soon lost their force, so that one night, after another report of an approaching enemy, it was a surprise when a lone horseman did appear. Sam fired on him and, when no other troops appeared, the Rangers crept out of hiding to approach their foe.

> When we got to him the moon revealed him distinctly. He was lying on his back, with his arms abroad; his mouth was open and his chest heaving with long gasps, and his white shirt-front was all splashed with blood. The thought shot through me that I was a murderer; that I had killed a man—a man who had never done me any harm. That was the coldest sensation that ever went through my marrow. I was down by him in a moment, helplessly stroking his forehead; and I would have given anything then—my own life freely—to make him again what he had been five minutes before. And all the boys seemed to be feeling in the same way.... They had forgotten all about the enemy; they thought only of this one forlorn unit of the foe. ... He muttered and mumbled like a dreamer in his sleep, about his wife and his child; and I thought with a new despair, "This thing that I have done does not end with him; it falls upon them too, and they never did me any harm, any more than he."
>
> In a little while the man was dead. He was killed in war; killed in fair and legitimate war; killed in battle, as you may say; and yet he was as sincerely mourned by the opposing force as if he had been their brother.... It soon came out that mine was not the only shot fired; there were five others,—a division of the guilt which was a grateful relief to me.

A Huckleberry Finn heart could devastate one who had

been playing Tom Sawyer. In his notes for *Huckleberry Finn*, Twain wrote, "A sound heart and a deformed conscience come into collision, and conscience [i.e., the standards and dictates of society] suffers defeat." Like Tom Sawyer, who in *Huckleberry Finn* indulged in fantasy games to "free" Jim even though he knew he was unnecessarily risking Jim's life, Marion's Rangers were playing at the "adventure" of war. Like Huck, who defied his conscience and indulged his heart to help Jim escape slavery, Sam finally refused to play that popular game.

Some of Marion's Rangers went on to become efficient, effective soldiers, but Sam had had enough of war. After falling back with his fellows a few more times, he (along with about half the troop) set out for home.

HEADING WEST

Although his sympathies were on the Union side, Orion no more wished to fight than Sam did. Orion had campaigned for Abraham Lincoln, and an old friend of his, Edward Bates, was Lincoln's attorney general. This fortunate combination resulted in Orion's appointment as secretary of the Nevada Territory, which had been created on February 28, 1861, from land taken from Mexico. Like California with its gold, Nevada with its Comstock Lode of silver (discovered in June 1859) was considered vital to the Union, so officials were dispatched to the new territory quickly. Orion could not afford the fare, but Sam (who had been supporting Orion and his family since he began earning a pilot's wages) had an idea: He would become the unofficial secretary to the new secretary, and pay the way for both of them. (Orion's wife, Mollie, and daughter, Jennie, would remain in Iowa temporarily.) The brothers went up the Missouri River to St. Joseph and, on July 26, 1861, they were off by stagecoach to Carson City. They reached that new capital of the Nevada Territory on August 14, after a journey evocatively described in Mark Twain's *Roughing It*.

MAKING HIS FORTUNE, PART II

It was not long before Sam had ventured out of Carson City. He and a friend staked a timber claim in the nearby countryside (the silver mines needed timber to shore up tunnels), but their campfire got out of control and burned down their prospective profits. He turned to mining for a while, the prospect of unlimited riches being irresistible, but found it a hard life, again with no profit. He was still writing letters home, some of which were published in a Keokuk paper, and he began sending humorous letters (signed "Josh") to the Virginia City *Territorial Enterprise*, Nevada's leading newspaper. Just as he was beginning to feel desperate about his financial situation, the *Enterprise* offered him a job as a full-time reporter for $25.00 a week. It was not the millions he had been planning to make, but he accepted, and set out for Virginia City.

With its new millionaires, its rough population struggling to become the *next* millionaires, and its frontier conditions, Virginia City seemed a model of the "wild and woolly West." In its "anything goes" atmosphere Sam's extravagant style found plenty of room to grow. For the first time, writing was a vocation for Sam (although he continued to speculate in silver). Here he found colleagues whose examples helped develop his talent—especially the *Enterprise*'s Dan De Quille (called "Dandy Quille" by his friends, his real name was William Wright) and Clement T. Rice of the rival Virginia City *Union*, whom Sam dubbed "The Unreliable" and with whom he carried on a wild and friendly literary rivalry. In this circle of peers he found a masculine fellowship.

Twain analyst Bernard De Voto describes Sam in the Washoe (as the Nevada Territory was called then):

> The frontier was American energy in its highest phase.... Great wealth in hard rock and speculative stocks, the chaos of frontiersmen seeking it, the drama of their conflicts, the violence of their life, the spectacle of their pleasures, and above all the rhythm of destiny shaping the national experience—there seems no reason to deplore this....
>
> One may say, at least, that Washoe perfectly satisfied and agreed with the compositor-pilot-prospector who here came into his heritage. It was Washoe that matured Sam Clemens, that gave him, after three false apprenticeships, the trade he would follow all his life, and that brought into harmony the elements of his mind which before had fumbled for expression. In the desert air a writer grew to maturity....
>
> He went about this gorgeous spectacle completely enraptured.... Nurtured on the drama of frontier life, deeply dramatic in his own impulses, he found this Western drama infinitely absorbing. The *Enterprise* was a nerve center of the spectacle. He had constantly the pride of being privy to Washoe's secrets. The paper had enormous power; he took his share in it, intoxicated. His pulse beat in time with the feverish pulse of the Comstock....
>
> His writing expressed the Comstock. Expressed it—and enraptured it. Fantastic, male, fortissimo. "The Empire City Massacre" and "The Petrified Man" carried his name eastward and westward, and deepened Washoe's pride in him. The jovial war

Petrified Man

One must assume that those who accepted as true this tall tale of Twain's failed to pay careful attention to the placement of the hands.

A petrified man was found some time ago in the mountains south of Gravelly Ford. Every limb and feature of the stony mummy was perfect, not even excepting the left leg, which has evidently been a wooden one during the lifetime of the owner—which lifetime, by the way, came to a close about a century ago, in the opinion of a savan[t] who has examined the defunct. The body was in a sitting posture, and leaning against a huge mass of croppings; the attitude was pensive, the right thumb resting against the side of the nose; the left thumb partially supported the chin, the fore-finger pressing the inner corner of the left eye and drawing it partly open; the right eye was closed, and the fingers of the right hand spread apart. This strange freak of nature created a profound sensation in the vicinity, and our informant states that by request, Justice Sewell or Sowell, of Humboldt City, at once proceeded to the spot and held an inquest on the body. The verdict of the jury was that "deceased came to his death from protracted exposure," etc. The people of the neighborhood volunteered to bury the poor unfortunate, and were even anxious to do so; but it was discovered, when they attempted to remove him, that the water which had dripped upon him for ages from the crag above, had coursed down his back and deposited a limestone sediment under him which had glued him to the bed rock upon which he sat, as with a cement of adamant [extremely hard stone], and Judge S. refused to allow the charitable citizens to blast him from his position. The opinion expressed by his Honor that such a course would be little less than sacrilege, was eminently just and proper. Everybody goes to see the stone man, as many as three hundred having visited the hardened creature during the past five or six weeks.

Mark Twain, "Petrified Man," Virginia City *Territorial Enterprise*, October 4, 1862.

---

of editors, familiar enough in Missouri journalism, here acquired the Western drawl, derisive and extravagant. The boys assaulted each other in columns of wonderful abuse; they then joined arms and sang the night away at one palace or another.

It was here, on February 2, 1863, that "Mark Twain" was born. This new pseudonym was clearly taken from his steamboat days. "Mark twain" is the cry of the leadsman announcing that the boat is in two fathoms (twelve feet—the minimum for safety) of water. Depending on the direction the boat is traveling, it signals either relief or warning: the boat has just reached safe water or it has traveled into *barely* safe water. (Some biographers speculate that Sam had also used the term in bars, telling the bartender to mark him down for a second drink on credit, but there is little hard evidence to prove or disprove the suggestion.) Of course, Twain had his own explanation:

> I was presently sent down to Carson City to report the legislative session. I wrote a weekly letter to the paper; it appeared Sundays, and on Mondays the legislative proceedings were obstructed by the complaints of members as a result. They rose to questions of privilege and answered the criticisms of the correspondent with bitterness, customarily describing him with elaborate and uncomplimentary phrases, for lack of a briefer way. To save their time, I presently began to sign the letters, using the Mississippi leadsman's call, "Mark Twain" (two fathoms—twelve feet) for this purpose.

Sam—now becoming known as Mark Twain—had restless feet, so it is unlikely that he would have remained in Nevada for long. By the spring of 1864, he wrote in *Roughing It*, "I wanted to see San Francisco. I wanted to go somewhere. I wanted—I did not know what I wanted. I had spring fever and wanted a change, principally, no doubt." Perhaps his spring fever made him more reckless in writing than usual; he managed to annoy and insult quite a few people, among them James Laird, publisher of the *Union*. (He later said that the piece that had gotten him in trouble this time was not meant to be published, but had been picked up for printing by an overzealous copy boy while he was at dinner.) Egged on by colleagues at their respective papers, Laird and Twain soon found themselves committed to a duel. Dueling was illegal, and some of those he had insulted were threatening to bring other charges against him. On May 29 prudence (and restlessness) prevailed; he took the stagecoach to San Francisco.

CALIFORNIA

Mark Twain had been a good-sized frog in a smallish pond in Nevada and, judging from his reports of his activities there, the *Enterprise* did not overwork him. In these respects California was a bit of a letdown. He complained, "After leaving Nevada I was a reporter on the *Morning Call* of San Francisco. I was more than that—I was the reporter. There was no other. There was enough work for one and a little over, but not enough for two—according to Mr. Barnes's idea, and he was the proprietor and therefore better situated to know about it than other people." The workday began at nine with an hour at the police court and ended at eleven at night after visits to "the six theaters, one after the other: seven nights in the week, three hundred and sixty-five nights in the year. We remained in each of those places five minutes," he said, and then tried "to find something to say about those performances which we had not said a couple of hundred times before." He did not even sign his stories; the paper had hired someone to cover the city, not "Mark Twain."

He was writing with "a torpid heart," but one day he witnessed an incident that brought fire back to his feelings. He had watched hoodlums "chasing and stoning a Chinaman who was heavily laden with the weekly wash of his Christian customers, and I noticed that a policeman was observing this performance with an amused interest—nothing more. He did not interfere." Twain wrote up the story "with considerable warmth and holy indignation," believing that what he had produced was "literature." He was humiliated and angry when Barnes declined to publish it because the paper's readers, he said, hated the Chinamen. From disinterest in the job, Twain's feelings turned to active distaste.

Finally persuaded that there was too much work for one, Barnes agreed to hire an assistant, Smiggy McGlural, for half wages. The new hire worked so energetically that at the end of McGlural's first month on the job, Barnes advised Twain to resign.

Twain was not totally without resources; he had been writing contributions for the San Francisco *Californian* (at twelve dollars apiece, he was their highest-paid contributor). The *Californian* had a knowing, sophisticated tone, and Twain's writing was becoming more consistently satirical and less crude. Bret Harte, whom he came to know after Barnes gave him his leisure, thought Twain's work for the paper was comparable to the best of Charles Dickens's sketches. In his connection with Harte, then a promising young writer, and the other writers for the *Californian*, Twain began to see himself as a writer, rather than a journalist.

Depressed in San Francisco and somewhat at odds with the local authorities (perhaps because he put up bail for a friend who then left town), Twain went with a friend to an old mining camp in Tuolumne, California, on Jackass Hill. To pass the time in the frequently bad weather, Twain again began keeping a notebook, making notes on local characters and on the stories they told. One of those stories, with a few Twain embellishments, would later become "The Celebrated Jumping Frog of Calaveras County."

On February 20, 1865, Twain headed out of camp and back toward San Francisco on foot, arriving on February 26. There he found a letter from Artemus Ward, a famous Western humorist he had met in Nevada, inviting him to write a sketch for Ward's new book. Twain had been gone too long; it was too late to get a story to Ward. He returned to newspaper writing, in effect a freelancer, contributing to several local journals, the *Enterprise* in Virginia City, local papers back home, and occasionally New York papers.

Orion had lost his position in Nevada (because of an overabundance of integrity, according to his brother). Will Moffett, Pamela's husband, died that year, leaving her with two children. Thus Twain's self-imposed family responsibilities made his poverty seem even more desperate. He had once told Orion that he would never return home until he had made his fortune; it seemed that would never happen. He considered going back to the river as a military pilot. But even as he was touching bottom, his efforts were slowly beginning to pay off. East Coast journals picked up his writings from Western papers, and began to notice this bright new humorist called Mark Twain. In September, the New York *Round Table* called him "the foremost among the merry gentlemen of the California press"; in November, the New York *Weekly Review*, a prestigious journal, said he was "one of the cleverest of the San Francisco writers." These responses heartened the humorist, and he threw himself into his work once again, writing daily letters for the Virginia City *Enterprise* and reviews for the San Francisco *Chronicle*, making enough to begin to get out of debt. And he finally wrote down the story of "Jim Smiley and His Jumping Frog" (in a later title Celebrated as being from Calaveras County).

Artemus Ward's book had been delayed, so he again asked Twain for a contribution. Twain sent the "Frog." When it arrived too late for the book, Ward sent it on to the New York *Saturday Press* instead. Its appearance in that paper's issue of November 18, wrote the San Francisco *Alta California*'s Eastern correspondent, "set all New York in a roar." Widely reprinted, it made its author a minor national celebrity.

Tired of San Francisco and heartened by his growing reputation on the East Coast, Twain began planning his escape. He would write a book; he would collaborate with Bret Harte on one or another joint project . . . he would become a travel correspondent.

THE SANDWICH ISLANDS

The steamer *Ajax* made its first voyage to the Sandwich Islands, as Hawaii was then called, in January 1866. Twain had been invited to join the select group of passengers, but had said no because of his commitment to the *Enterprise*. He soon regretted having passed up the opportunity, and persuaded the Sacramento *Union* to send him on the *Ajax*'s March 7 voyage to Honolulu, promising to send them "twenty or thirty letters" at twenty dollars apiece.

He spent four months in the islands, writing for the *Union*'s readers informative, humorous, picturesque descriptions of what he saw and what he learned. He gave himself a fictional companion, Brown, to provide a vulgar counterpart to the genteel observations of Mark Twain—making Twain a fictional character, too. By a stroke of luck, he was in Honolulu when the survivors of the *Hornet*, an American clipper ship that had burned at sea, arrived in port. He wrote all night so he could send the story out by a ship leaving for the mainland at nine the next morning, thus providing the *Union* with a major scoop, a front-page story that was widely reprinted. (Not only did the scoop add to his fame; on his return to California he demanded a three-hundred-dollar bonus for the three-column story . . . and got it.)

Returning to San Francisco on August 13, he found himself restless again. In order to take advantage of the favorable press he was getting, he needed to go back to "the states," preferably to New York; otherwise, he would never be more than a regional phenomenon. But, while his finances had stabilized (and the Civil War was over), he still could not afford passage to the other side of the continent. Thomas McGuire, who owned several theaters, advised him: "Now was the time to make my fortune—strike while the iron was hot—break into the lecture field. I did it." His first San Francisco lecture, based on his tour of the Sandwich Islands, was a smashing success: Not only did the audience love him, he netted nearly three months' salary for ninety minutes on the stage. He had found the medium that would, time and again, help him dig out from financial woes.

After a triumphal tour of California and Nevada towns, followed by a "farewell" tour in various venues in and around San Francisco, Twain finally had enough money and confidence to return to his family with pride intact. The *Alta California* proudly claimed him as its travel correspondent, who would tour the world and write about it for its readers. On December 15, 1866, he left San Francisco on the steamer *America*.

A Pause for Reflection

Twain scholar Bernard De Voto wrote that the seeds of all that Mark Twain would become could already be found in him at this point in his life:

> In California, through the two and a half years following May, 1864, Mark's work grew surer and grew, also, broader in scope. It is possible to discover, or perhaps to imagine, an acceleration in both developments after the interlude at Jackass Hill. If not imaginary, this acceleration may have been due to the success of "The Jumping Frog." Be that as it may be, all the rest of Mark Twain's books are embryonic in what he had written by December, 1866, when he went east. These casual pieces outline the future: the humorist, the social satirist, the pessimist, the novelist of American character, Mark Twain exhilarated, sentimental, cynical, angry, and depressed, are all here. The rest is only development.

Making His Fortune, Part III

After a horrendous voyage, Twain arrived in New York in mid-January 1867. The city had changed in the thirteen years since young Sam Clemens had been there, and he was not comfortable with its new "frenzied energy." He wrote about its "attractions" for his California readers, but by March he was ready for a visit with his mother and sister in St. Louis. While there, he supplemented his income by lecturing in several area towns, to gratifying response. Back in New York, he found an old California acquaintance, Charles Webb, to publish his first book, *The Celebrated Jumping Frog of Calaveras County and Other Sketches*, which had moderate sales even though it was ignored by reviewers. He also had some success in giving his Sandwich Islands lecture a few times—a notable accomplishment since there was considerably more competition for the public's entertainment dollar in New York than there had been for his earlier lectures in the West and Midwest. But he remained sanguine; he was about to make good on the *Alta California*'s promise of a "world correspondent." On June 8, 1867, he embarked on the first pleasure cruise to sail from an American port, a five-month voyage to the Mediterranean and the Holy Land on the *Quaker City*, an adventure whose stories would be told in his book *Innocents Abroad*.

It was on this voyage that Twain met Mary Mason Fairbanks, the intelligent and cultivated wife of the publisher of the Cleveland *Herald*; she would become a lifelong friend and "civilizing influence" (and would also vouch for him to his future mother-in-law). Even more momentous was his first glimpse of a woman who was not even there. "I saw her first in the form of an ivory miniature in her brother Charley's stateroom in the steamer *Quaker City* in the Bay of Smyrna, in the summer of 1867, when she was in her twenty-second year. I saw her in the flesh for the first time in New York in the following December." It had taken just that one look at her portrait, Twain said, for him to fall in love with Olivia Langdon, daughter of a wealthy coal magnate of Elmira, New York.

It was not until February 2, 1870, that Livy Langdon finally married Mark Twain. (She really married Sam Clemens, of course; but if he had not been Mark Twain, he would not have had the necessary prospects of wealth and position to consider such a marriage.) She had properly (for a Victorian woman) refused to consider him a suitor for many months; she finally said yes on February 4, 1869. Her family seems to have reacted at first with some horror at the idea that this rough upstart, without firm prospects or connections, would take away their cherished and pampered Livy. But the length of the courtship also reflected Twain's determined effort to make a name and fortune for himself that would make him acceptable to the Langdons: His tours on the lecture circuit made courtship in person an occasional indulgence, and much of their relationship in the years between meeting and wedding was conducted by mail.

By all accounts—those of their intimate friends as well as their own—the two were extremely happy with each other. It was a marriage of contrasts, and they delighted in their differences. Livy called her husband "Youth," recognizing his eternally young nature. She tried to dust him off and make him presentable, and he enjoyed her efforts to do so. He could exasperate her sense of propriety on occasion, but having her as a balance in his life seemed to help him curb (or at least keep private) many of the rash eruptions that had in the past made "moving on" to another place so frequently a wise decision.

Once the decision to marry was made, the Langdons accepted Twain with generosity, if occasionally tinged with condescension. Their wedding gift to the couple (a complete surprise to their new son-in-law) was a large house, fully furnished and staffed, in Buffalo, New York, where Twain had purchased a one-third share in the Buffalo *Express*. (Jervis Langdon, Livy's father, had advanced him the twenty-five-thousand-dollar purchase price—one reason the lucrative lecture tours had to continue.) The income from Livy's funds would be about forty thousand dollars a year; along with Twain's income, which was growing quite respectably, the newlyweds were able to live very handsomely.

While they were happy in each other, there were griefs and tragedies almost from the beginning of their marriage. Jervis Langdon died of cancer on August 6, 1870, just months after the wedding. Livy had spent weeks nursing her father and suffered a nervous collapse when he died. Mrs. Langdon went to Buffalo to be with her daughter and son-in-law, and soon another visitor, a friend of Livy's, stopped by on her way to Detroit. The friend, Emma Nye, contracted typhoid fever and on September 29, after the Clemenses had nursed her for a month, she died in their bed.

Twain was trying to work—he had promised *Roughing It* to the publisher by January—but more difficulties intervened. Livy nearly had a miscarriage in October. On November 7 Langdon Clemens was born, tiny (four and a half pounds), frail, sickly, at least a month premature. Complications of childbirth nearly killed Livy, and her convalescence was agonizingly slow.

Buffalo was understandably not a happy home for the young family. They decided to sell the house and visit Quarry Farm, Livy's adopted sister's summer home in the hills above Elmira. (They found healing there, and would return to spend many summers at the farm.) In the fall of 1871 they moved to a rented home in Hartford, Connecticut. On March 19, 1872, their second child, Olivia Susan (Susy), was born. But Langdon never did become robust; Mark Twain's only son died on June 2, of diphtheria. In some convoluted way, Twain blamed himself for the death.

A rotten start for a marriage, but things finally began to improve. They became devoted to Susy, who seems to have been somewhat precocious (even allowing for the fond memories of her father, who was an unparalleled biography-enhancer). As she grew, she seemed more like her father than did her two sisters (Clara, born June 8, 1874, and Jean, born July 26, 1880). Their devotion to Susy would make her death from meningitis at the age of twenty-four a nearly unbearable blow to her parents.

MAKING HIS FORTUNE, PART IV

The quarter-century after his marriage was a relatively prolific period for Mark Twain. His literary stature grew, even though he had chosen to publish most of his books by the subscription method: A publishing company would send out salesmen to contract with individual readers to buy a book when it was published. The book would not be printed until the subscription sales promised sufficient profit. Rarely was "good literature" published this way, and the newspaper and magazine critics haughtily ignored subscription books. But it was much more lucrative than sales that depended on bookstores for distribution. Twain was piqued at the critics who refused to consider his work for review, but he considered the profits worth it. Eventually, critics did recognize his work, led by William Dean Howells, editor of the *Atlantic*, who later became one of Twain's closest friends. Yet in spite of (or perhaps because of) the critics' disdain, Twain's readership among "ordinary people" grew steadily over the years.

But books were not Twain's only plan for profit. He was an inventor, and was perennially interested in new technology. Unfortunately, he seemed to have inherited the Clemens style of investment: buy high, sell low. He was an easy touch for almost any inventor with a new way to make things work. He was "burned" many times, though, so when a young agent asked him to buy stock in a new invention called the telephone—"as much as I wanted for five hundred dollars"—he declined. (His Hartford home was, however, the first private house in the nation to have a telephone.)

The Paige typesetting machine, an invention whose value he felt confident in assessing since he had been a typesetter, was to prove a catastrophic investment. In 1880 he invested two thousand dollars on hearing a description of the machine, then another three thousand after seeing a prototype at work at the Colt factory in Hartford, Connecticut. Soon he took on the burden of supporting the machine and its inventor, James W. Paige, while Paige tried to make the typesetter "perfect." By 1885 he was pouring money into the invention, often to the point of having to curtail his family's expenses; he later figured he had spent $190,000 on the machine.

While he was spending himself into a hole with the typesetter, another investment, Webster & Company publishing house, was costing considerably more than it made—a grave annoyance, since it was counted on to provide income by publishing Twain's work. Along with other bad investments and a financial downturn that wiped out Livy's yearly income from coal stocks, Mark Twain was eventually brought to the point of bankruptcy. Ironically—since his father had been left holding the bag by a bankrupt man—he did not take advantage of the bankruptcy laws that would have allowed him to pay his creditors pennies on the dollar. His friend Henry H. Rogers told him, "Business has its laws and customs and they are justified; but a literary man's reputation is his life; he can afford to be money poor but he cannot afford to be character poor; you must earn the cent per cent and pay it." Livy concurred. Rogers, a wealthy, shrewd businessman, a chief strategist for Standard Oil, offered to take over management of Twain's bankruptcy and his finances, to which Twain gratefully agreed. In July 1895, at the age of fifty-nine, Mark Twain embarked on a world lecture tour and in less than five years made enough to repay all his creditors in full.

A Darker Side of Mark Twain

Many critics and biographers have speculated on the cause of Mark Twain's increasingly bitter pessimism in the last decade or so of his life. Although he lived very well in some years, he never was able to feel secure, and he had the Clemens dreams of great wealth. The Tennessee land bought by John Clemens gradually changed hands in transactions that seemed to bring no profit to the family; once Orion scuttled a potentially lucrative sale of part of it because the buyer wanted to plant vineyards there, and that day Orion was a teetotaler. (An untimely new dedication to abstinence from alcohol was also blamed for helping him lose his position in Nevada.) The legacy of land, which John Clemens had confidently expected would make his children wealthy, was instead a curse to Mark Twain:

> With the very kindest intentions in the world toward us he laid the heavy curse of prospective wealth upon our shoulders. He went to his grave in the full belief that he had done us a kindness. It was a woeful mistake but fortunately he never knew it. . . .
>
> It kept us hoping and hoping during forty years and forsook us at last. It put our energies to sleep and made visionaries of us—dreamers and indolent. We were always going to be rich next year—no occasion to work. It is good to begin life poor; it is good to begin life rich—these are wholesome; but to begin it poor and *prospectively* rich! The man who has not experienced it cannot imagine the curse of it.

Twain had expected to make millions from the Paige typesetter; instead, it helped bankrupt him while he supported its inventor for years. Paige, like Orion, seemed to have a penchant for snatching defeat from the jaws of victory: At least once when the machine seemed to be working well and customers were ready to buy, he decided it must have another embellishment—which never worked.

Twain's bitterness was always entwined with a sense of guilt he could occasionally shake but never completely escape. The Calvinist beliefs of his family and boyhood neighbors—he was raised a Presbyterian—were harsh indictments of sinful man. Although he did not subscribe to the religion of his family, its stern pronouncements delivered while he was young had a strong effect in nurturing his perpetual sense of guilt. He blamed himself for the deaths of the tramp to whom he had given matches; his brother Henry for whom he had found employment; his son, Langdon, whom he had taken for a carriage ride on a cold day; his daughter Susy, who became ill in Connecticut while he and Livy were in Europe (trying to recoup their fortune) and died before they could reach her. He does not seem to have blamed himself for Livy's death—she had been a near-invalid for years before he met her. But the fact that during the many months of her final illness his presence was considered so disturbing that he was not allowed to see her at all for weeks at a time, and only for a few minutes when he was allowed into the sickroom, could not have made a guilt-prone man happy.

A free spirit who disliked authority, he nevertheless accepted the burden of responsibility for his mother, brothers, and sister, supporting them more or less consistently throughout his life. That sense of responsibility made his bankruptcy and its disruptive effects on their lives as well as on his wife and daughters' lives even more crushing a blow. On their silver wedding anniversary, after twenty-five years of marriage, he had nothing to offer Livy but a silver five-franc piece. The bankruptcy, of course, would have threatened the confidence of most people; Twain felt special anger because he believed that many people—inventors and publishers headed the list—had been cheating or otherwise taking advantage of him.

The theft of his works by foreign publishers fed his bitterness. He often had to go to England to attend the publication of his books, since an author had to be in the country at the time of publication in order to receive any copyright protection. Nevertheless, many publishers around the world made money selling the works of Mark Twain without paying him a penny in royalties. (He fought for copyright reform in the United States to prevent similar unfairness for foreign authors; he hoped, of course, that the law would become international.)

He had traveled the world and found much to disturb him in the global community as well as in the personal one. He found war abhorrent, tyranny unforgivable, imperialism unjustified. The more he saw of the world, the more the pessimistic philosophizing of the Scotsman Macfarlane seemed borne out. And in his role as an international celebrity, he saw more of the world's problems—and frauds—than most of his fellows did, because people frequently asked for his support for one cause or another, presenting their pleas with the direst evidence of need.

Mark Twain had seen plenty of death all his life, but as he grew older, so did his friends and family. Jane Clemens died in 1890; so did Livy's mother. Pamela's son-in law, Charles L. Webster (who had run the Webster publishing house) died in 1891. Pamela died in 1894, as did Orion's wife, Mollie. Susy died in 1896. Orion died in 1897. Livy died in 1904, and his life was thrown out of balance forever. Pamela's son, Samuel (named after his uncle), died in 1908. Twain's benefactor, Henry H. Rogers, died in 1909. In September 1909 Clara married and moved to Europe, and Twain settled down with his third daughter, Jean, in Redding, Connecticut. On Christmas Eve, Jean suffered an epileptic seizure and drowned in her bath.

Mark Twain's frequent bouts of pessimism do not seem to present an unsolvable mystery.

HALLEY'S COMET

Although much has been made of Twain's pessimism, his dark view of human nature in his later years, there was still evidence of sanguine Sam. His writings tended to be dark, but his sense of humor was irrepressible. He was still "Youth," and still loved cats and children. He corresponded with and occasionally entertained a coterie of girls, whom he called his "angelfish." He enjoyed their fresh views on life, their innocence, their sense of fun, and they brought back to him his happy days with his own young daughters. He was not perpetually miserable, but he was tired and his life was running out.

When Sam was born in 1835, Halley's Comet was visible on its regular return visit toward the sun. He had often said he expected to die when the comet made its next appearance—in 1910. In 1909 he told his official biographer, Albert Bigelow Paine:

> I came in with Halley's comet in 1835. It is coming again next year, and I expect to go out with it. It will be the greatest disappointment of my life if I don't go out with Halley's comet. The Almighty has said, no doubt: "Now here are these two unaccountable freaks; they came in together, they must go out together."

On April 20, Halley's comet reached its perihelion—its closest approach to the sun—and then began its journey back out into the solar system. On April 21, 1910, at about midday he told his daughter Clara, "Goodbye dear, if we meet," and then fell into a doze. Around sunset, he died.

ABOUT THIS BOOK

Mark Twain was a prolific journalist and author with a writing career that spanned nearly sixty years, and his critics, analysts, biographers, and reviewers have had nearly a century and a half to offer their insights into his life and work. Delving into works by and about Mark Twain thus offers a fascinating opportunity to learn not only about the author and his works, but about the changing fashions in social issues, literature, and literary analysis.

The various parts of this book cast light on different aspects of the man and his work. The biographical sketch focuses on how Samuel Langhorne Clemens became Mark Twain; his early years, with their formative influences and events, provide the bulk of the information. The essays discuss Mark Twain as an author and examine his works. Since Twain wrote so much autobiographical fiction, they illuminate his life as well as his art. The chronology offers an overview of major historical events of Mark Twain's lifetime and situates him and his work within this larger context; it is supplemented by the chronological listing of the author's works. This listing and the bibliography of works about Twain open doors to almost unlimited opportunities for further research.

The essays offer insights not only into Twain and his work; the essays themselves show how literary taste and literary analysis have changed over the past century. Literary criticism was relatively new and much less sophisticated when Twain was alive; he even tried his hand at it himself, most notably in "Fenimore Cooper's Literary Offenses." Early criticism of the work of Mark Twain seemed to focus on whether he was a humorist or a philosopher; a humorist or a "real" author; a harmless humorist or an unwholesome influence; a happy humorist or a bitter pessimist. As the works of Sigmund Freud became known, scholars searched Twain's writings, both published and unpublished, for signs of Freudian influences in his life (the pernicious effects of women found a leading role in their analyses). A backlash developed against the most extreme of the Freud-followers, and for a while examining the "intrinsic values" of the works themselves became fashionable. In recent years, attention has focused on one word that appears frequently in Twain's work—"nigger"—which has triggered debates on whether Twain was racist or just the opposite, his works a danger to young readers who might be hurt by the word or a good way to defuse racism and heal wounds.

The work as literature, the work as social commentary, the work as a tool for change—all wrapped in an astonishingly entertaining package. The sheer entertainment value of Twain's work has kept it popular through all the controversies. This book helps examine what lies under the entertainment.

The First Continental American Literature

Bernard De Voto

In the 1800s, America's center of gravity shifted westward with new settlers. While the literature of the Atlantic states had divorced itself from Europe, it was still consciously an heir to its European ancestors. In contrast, the new heartland culture—exemplified by Mark Twain and Abraham Lincoln—grew up in disregard of Europe. Twain, with his midcontinental upbringing and his deep and varied experience of American life, marks the beginning of a continental American literature.

The first truly American literature grew out of the tidewater [seacoast] culture of the early republic. It was the culture of a people who, whatever their diversity, were more homogeneous in feeling and belief than Americans as a people have ever been since then. We have come to think of the literature whose greatest names are Ralph Waldo Emerson and Edgar Allan Poe, Henry David Thoreau and Herman Melville, Nathaniel Hawthorne and Walt Whitman, as our classic period, and in a very real sense the republic that shaped their mind was classical. It felt a strong affinity for the Roman Republic, it believed that Roman virtues and ideas had been expressed in the Constitution, it gave us a great architectural style because it identified its own emotions in the classic style. When sculptor Horatio Greenough let a toga fall from Washington's naked shoulders he was not out of tune with contemporary taste: Washington seemed a kind of consul, so did Jefferson, and in the portraits of them which our stamps and coins preserve they have a Roman look. This classical republican culture was at its most vigorous when our classic writers were growing up. But there is an element of anachronism in all

---

Excerpted from editor's Introduction to *The Portable Mark Twain*, edited by Bernard De Voto. Copyright © 1946, © 1968, renewed 1974 by The Viking Press, Introduction, notes, and compilation. All rights reserved. Reprinted by permission of Viking Penguin, a division of Penguin Books USA, Inc.

literature, and while these men were themselves in full vigor American culture entered a new phase.

The American Heartland Produces a New Culture

The culture of the early republic crossed the Alleghenies in two streams, one Southern, the other mainly New England; but they were more like each other than either was like the one which their mingling presently helped to produce. For beyond the mountains people found different landscapes, different river courses, different relationships of sky and wind and water, different conceptions of space and distance, different soils and climates—different conditions of life. Beyond still farther mountains lay Oregon and California—and they were implicit in the expanding nation as soon as the treaty that gave us Louisiana was signed—but first the United States had to incorporate the vast expanse between the eastern and the western heights of land. That area is the American heartland. Its greatest son was to call it the Egypt of the West because nature had organized it round a central river and it touched no ocean, but it came into the American consciousness as the Great Valley. When the tidewater culture came to the Great Valley it necessarily broke down: new conditions demanded adaptations, innovations, new combinations and amplifications. The new way of life that began to develop there had a different organization of feeling, a different metabolism of thought. It was no more native, no more "American," than that of the first republic, but it was different and it began to react on it.

The heartland was midcontinental and its energies were oriented toward the river at its center—and were therefore turned away from Europe, which had been a frontier of the early republic. And life in the heartland, with its mingling of stocks, its constant shifting of population, and its tremendous distances, led people in always increasing numbers to think continentally. Both facts were fundamental in the thought and feeling of the new culture.

Lincoln Embodies the Heartland Culture

The American littoral [coastal region] came only slowly, with greater slowness than the fact demanded, to realize that the nation's center of gravity was shifting westward. It tragically failed to understand one consequence of that shift, thirty years of contention between the Northeast and the South to dominate the Great Valley or at least achieve a preferential linkage with it. The failure to understand was in great part a failure to think continentally—as was made clear at last when the Civil War demonstrated that no peaceful way of resolving the contention had been found. Even now too many Americans fail to understand that the war, the resolution by force, only made explicit the organization of our national life that is implicit in the geography which the Great Valley binds together. Abraham Lincoln understood our continental unity; he argued it persistently down to the outbreak of the war and from then on. And Lincoln was a distillation of the heartland culture.

PREDICTING MARK TWAIN?

The first part of Alexis de Tocqueville's famous study of the new American nation, Democracy in America, *was published in 1835—the year Sam Clemens was born.*

The Americans have not yet, properly speaking, got any literature. Only the journalists strike me as truly American. They certainly are not great writers, but they speak their country's language and they make themselves heard. I should class the others as foreigners. They stand to the Americans much as the imitators of the Greeks and Romans stood to ourselves at the time of the Renaissance—objects of curiosity, but not of general sympathy. They are entertaining, but they do not affect mores. . . .

As things are, I am sure that they will have a literature in the end. But it will have a character peculiarly its own, different from the American literature of today. No one can guess that character beforehand. . . .

By and large the literature of a democracy will never exhibit the order, regularity, skill, and art characteristic of aristocratic literature; formal qualities will be neglected or actually despised. The style will often be strange, incorrect, overburdened, and loose, and almost always strong and bold. Writers will be more anxious to work quickly than to perfect details. Short works will be commoner than long books, wit than erudition, imagination than depth. There will be a rude and untutored vigor of thought with great variety and singular fecundity. Authors will strive to astonish more than to please, and to stir passions rather than to charm taste.

Alexis de Tocqueville, *Democracy in America*, 1835.

Lincoln's feeling for the continentalism of the American nation was so intense that it almost transcended the transcendent facts. It was a deposit in the very cells of his bones from the soil of the Great Valley. He was, as his biographer William Henry Herndon rightly says, one of the limestone men, the tall, gaunt, powerful, sallow, saturnine men who appear in quantity enough to constitute a type when the wilderness on both sides of the Ohio comes under the plow. His radical democracy was wrought from the experience of the Great Valley. In his ideas and beliefs as in the shadowed depths of his personality there is apparent a new articulation of American life. His very lineaments show it. When you turn from the Jefferson nickel to the Lincoln penny as when you turn from Jefferson's first inaugural address to any of Lincoln's state papers, in the flash of a total and immediate response you understand that you have turned from one era to a later one. You have turned from the tidewater republic to the continental empire.

Lincoln expressed a culture and brought a type to climax. Similarly, when that culture found major literary expression it did so from a rich and various, if humble, literary tradition. As always, the literary expression was the later one; the economic, social, and political impact was felt much earlier. The lag, however, was not so great as Walt Whitman thought. Whitman was sixty when in 1879 he traveled across the Great Valley to its western limit, where the Front Range walls it off. He traversed it with a steadily growing conviction that here in the flesh were the people whose society he had envisioned in so many rhapsodies, Americans who had been fused, annealed, compacted (those are his words) into a new identity. He felt that literature had not yet spoken to these prairie people, "this continental inland West," that it had not yet spoken for them, that it had not made images for their spirit.

The poet supposed that he was speaking of things still to come but he was already wrong by a full ten years. The thing had happened. And the first notification that it had happened can be dated with an exactness not often possible in the history of literature. That notification came in 1869 with the appearance of a book of humorous travel sketches by Samuel Langhorne Clemens, who, faithful to the established tradition, signed it with a pen name, Mark Twain.

A CONSCIOUS INDIFFERENCE TO EUROPE

Innocents Abroad was greeted with an enthusiasm that made Mark Twain a celebrity overnight, and with too much misunderstanding of a kind that was to persist throughout his career. It was a funny book and a cardinal part of its fun was its disdain of European culture. This disdain, the mere fact of making humor of such disdain, and its frequent exaggeration into burlesque all produced an effect of shock—in most ways a delightful shock but in some ways an uneasy one. Yet the point was not the provinciality of such humor, though it was frequently provincial, and not its uncouthness, though it was sometimes uncouth, but the kind of consciousness it implied. Again it is absurd to speak of this as the first American literature that was independent of European influences, for our literature had obediently divorced itself from Europe as soon as Emerson ordered it to. The humorous core of *Innocents Abroad* was not independence of Europe, but indifference to it. Thoreau and Emerson and Poe were detached from Europe but completely aware of being heirs to it, but here was a literature which had grown up in disregard of Europe—which had looked inward toward the Mississippi and not outward beyond the Atlantic. Failure to appreciate the implications of this difference was one reason, no doubt the weightiest one, why for two full generations literary critics thought of Mark Twain as no more than a clown. But the same identity, the same organization of personality, that made Lincoln the artificer of our continental unity was what made Mark Twain a great writer.

There are striking affinities between Lincoln and Mark Twain. Both spent their boyhoods in a society that was still essentially frontier; both were rivermen. Both absorbed the midcontinental heritage: fiercely equalitarian democracy, hatred of injustice and oppression, the man-to-man individualism of an expanding society. Both were deeply acquainted with melancholy and despair; both were fatalists. On the other hand, both were instinct with the humor of the common life and from their earliest years made fables of it. As humorists, both felt the basic gravity of humor; with both it was an adaptation of the mind, a reflex of the struggle to be sane; both knew, and Mark Twain said, that there is no humor in heaven. It was of such resemblances that William Dean Howells was thinking when he called Mark Twain "the Lincoln of our literature."

A Legacy of Restlessness and Hope

Samuel Clemens was born at Florida, Monroe County, Missouri, on November 30, 1835, a few months after his parents reached the village from Tennessee. His father was a Virginian, his mother a Kentuckian, and as a family they had made three moves before this one. Florida was a handful of log cabins only two hundred miles east of the Indian Country and in the earliest stage of frontier economy.... Sam could retain little conscious memory of the chinked-log, open-fireplace hamlet with its woods-runners and movers; mostly it would mean the immediacy of nature, the infinity of the forest, the ease of escape into solitude and an all-encompassing freedom. He was still short of four when the Clemenses made their last move, this time eastward. They seem to have been movers by force of circumstance, not instinct; it was always the pressure of poverty and the hope of betterment that impelled them on. But they bequeathed restlessness to their son.

The final move brought them to Hannibal, an older settlement than Florida and perhaps four times as large but still short of five hundred inhabitants. Hannibal is the most important single fact in the life of Samuel Clemens the person and Mark Twain the writer. It too was lapped round by forest; it maintained the romantic mystery, the subliminal dread, and the intimacy with nature that he had been born to; but it had passed the pioneering stage. It must be seen as a later stage that characterized all our frontiers east of the great plains, after the actual frontier of settlement had pushed westward, after the farms had been brought in and functional communities had been established, but while the frontier crafts and values and ways of thinking lingered on, a little mannered perhaps, a little nostalgic, but still vital. The frontier thugs had passed to other fields or degenerated to village loafers and bullies. There were a few Indians near by and sizable numbers not too far away but they were a spectacle, not a threat. A few hunters and trappers ranged the woods but they were relics, brush folk, not of the great race. There were as many frame houses as log cabins; if the schoolhouse had a puncheon [split log] floor, the squire's wife had a silk dress from St. Louis. Caste lines were almost nonexistent. Hannibal was a farmers' market village. More than half of its inhabitants were Southerners, but Southerners modified by the Great Valley. Its slaves were servants, not gang laborers.

THE PARADOX ON THE MISSISSIPPI

But also Hannibal was on the Mississippi. Here enters the thread of cosmopolitanism that is so paradoxically interwoven with the extreme provincialism of this society. Steamboats bore the travelers and commerce of half a continent past the town wharf. Great rafts of logs and lumber—it was the latter kind that Huck and Jim traveled on—came down from Wisconsin. A population of freighters, movers, and mere drifters in shanty boats, keelboats, broadhorns, mackinaws, and scows added pageantry. Other types and other costumery came down from the lakes and northern rivers: voyageurs, trappers, winterers, Indians of the wilderness tribes always seen in ceremonial garments on their way to make treaties or collect annuities. All these belonged to the rapidly widening movement of the expanding nation. Moreover, Hannibal was within the aura of St. Louis, eighty miles away, and St. Louis was the port through which the energies of a truly imperial expansion were moving toward Santa Fe, Oregon, and California. Perhaps dimly but quite permanently any river town so near St. Louis would give even the most local mind an awareness of the continental divide, the Columbia, the Pacific, the Southwest. A town that may have never heard of Zebulon Pike or John Ledyard or Jonathan Carver nevertheless felt the national will that had turned them westward. The year of Mark's birth, 1835, may properly be taken as the year when the final phase of our continental expansion began. And the fruitfulness of Hannibal for Mark's imagination may reasonably be said to have stopped with his tenth year, just before that final phase raised up the irrepressible conflict.

For two things remain to be said of the society that shaped Sam Clemens's mind and feelings: that its post-pioneer, frontier stage stops short of the industrial revolution, and that the sectional conflict which produced the Civil War has not yet shown itself. The life which is always most desirable in Mark's thinking is the pre-industrial society of a little river town; it is a specific identification of Hannibal. Whereas the evils of life are the eternal cruelties, hypocrisies, and stupidities of mankind which have nothing to do with time or place but result from Our Heavenly Father's haste in experimenting when He grew dissatisfied with the monkey.

As the St. Petersburg of *Tom Sawyer*, Hannibal is one of the superb idyls of American literature, perhaps the supreme one. A town of sun, forest shade, drowsy peace, limpid emotions, simple humanity—and eternity going by on the majestic river. Even here, however, a mood of melancholy is seldom far away: a melancholy of the river itself, of our westering people who had always known solitude, and of a child's feeling, which was to grow through the years, that he was a stranger and a mysterious one under the stars. And below the melancholy there is a deeper stratum, a terror or disgust that may break through in a graveyard at midnight or at the sound of unidentified voices whispering above the water. This is in part fantasy, but in part also it is the weary knowledge of evil that paints Hannibal in far different colors in *Pudd'nhead Wilson* or *Huckleberry Finn*.

Almost as soon as he begins to write, Mark Twain is a citizen of the world, but he is always a citizen of Hannibal too....

A REAL-WORLD EDUCATION

While still a boy, Sam Clemens was apprenticed to a printer and so got the education that served more nineteenth-century American writers than any other. (It was a surprisingly extensive education. By twenty he knew the English classics thoroughly, was an inveterate reader of history, and had begun to cultivate his linguistic bent.) The trade eventually led him to newspaper reporting but first it took him on a series of *Wanderjahre* [aimless travels] toward which heredity may have impelled him. At eighteen he went to St. Louis and on to New York. Philadelphia followed, Muscatine, St. Louis again, Keokuk (where he began to write humorous newspaper sketches), and Cincinnati, always setting type on a newspaper or in a job shop. He was twenty-two years old (and, if his memory can be trusted, ripe with a characteristic fantasy of South American adventure) when the American spectacle caught him up. In 1857 he began his apprenticeship to a Mississippi pilot.... Those years vastly widened Mark's knowledge of America and fed his insatiable enjoyment of men, his absorbed observation of man's depravity, and his delight in spectacle.

The Civil War put an end to piloting. Mark has described his experience and that of many others in that war, in all wars, in a sketch which is one of the best things he ever wrote. "The Private History of a Campaign That Failed" could not be spared from the mosaic of our national catastrophe; it is one of the contexts in which Mark Twain has perfectly refracted a national experience through a personal one. When his military career petered out in absurdity, he joined the great national movement which even civil war could not halt. His older brother, the gentle zany Orion, was made Secretary of the Territory of Nevada and, paying the Secretary's passage west, Mark went along. In Nevada he found another national retort, another mixed and violent society, another speculative flush times. He became a drunkard of speculation, a prospector, a hunter of phantasmal mines, a silver miner, a laborer in a stamp mill, and at last a newspaperman. He went to work for that fabulous paper the *Territorial Enterprise* of Virginia City as an "editor," that is to say a reporter. And it was here that he took his immortal *nom de plume*, a phrase from the pilot's mystery. "Mark Twain" was signed to a species of humor in which Sam Clemens had been immersed ever since his apprenticeship, the newspaper humor of the Great Valley, which was in turn a development of the pungent oral humor he had heard from childhood on. Far from establishing a literary tradition, Mark Twain brought one to culmination.

After less than two years on the *Enterprise* he went to California, in 1864. He had met Artemus Ward in Nevada; now he joined the transient, bright Bohemia of the Golden Gate: Bret Harte, Prentice Mulford, Charles Warren Stoddard, Charles H. Webb, Ada Clare, Ina Coolbrith, still slighter and more forgotten names. He got a new kind of companionship and his first experience of literary sophistication. After a short time as a reporter he began to write humor for the Coast's literary papers, the *Californian* and the *Golden Era*. Promptly his work developed a strain of political and ethical satire which it never lost: the humorist was seldom separable from the satirist from this year on. That is to say, the individual humor of Mark Twain with its overtones of extravaganza and its undercurrent of misanthropy was, however crude and elliptical, fully formed by the end of 1864. He had not yet revealed the novelist's power to endow character with life, but it—together with a memorable talent for the vernacular—was made clear to anyone with eyes on [November 18,] 1865, when the New York *Saturday Press* published "Jim Smiley and His Jumping Frog."

The immortal story derived from still another Western experience, one which had made Mark, however lackadaisically, a pocket miner. He had sent it east at Artemus Ward's suggestion, but only an accident got it into type. It was a momentary smash hit, and so Mark was not altogether an unknown when he went to New York in 1867. Before he went there, however, he had reached the farthest limit of the expansionist dream, having gone to the Sandwich Islands as a newspaper correspondent. That voyage in turn had initiated his career as a lecturer. He had a marked histrionic talent; for years he barnstormed or made occasional appearances as a public "reader" and story-teller; all his life was making the after-dinner appearances of that vanished age, which pleased his vanity and gratified the longings of an actor *manqué*. But he went to New York as a correspondent: he had arranged to travel to Europe and the Holy Land with a conducted tour. In 1867 he published his first book, a collection of sketches called *The Celebrated Jumping Frog of Calaveras County* after the best of them, but the year is more notable for the travel letters he wrote for the *Alta California* and the New York *Tribune*. He made a book of them after his return, meanwhile writing freelance humor and Washington correspondence. The book, *Innocents Abroad*, was published in 1869.

All this has been detailed to show how deep and various an experience of American life Mark Twain had had when he began to write. The rest of his biography is also strikingly typical of nineteenth-century America, but the seed-time has now been accounted for. It is not too much to say that he had seen more of the United States, met more kinds and castes and conditions of Americans, observed the American in more occupations and moods and tempers—in a word had intimately shared a greater variety of the characteristic experiences of his countrymen—than any other major American writer.

Lessons in Extravagance at the Comstock Lode

Warren Hinckle and Fredric Hobbs

[Ed. note: The discovery in 1859 of the Comstock Lode—a veritable mountain of silver with gold in the leftovers—drew many fortune hunters to a desolate part of the Utah Territory on the slopes of the Washoe range, east of the forbidding peaks of the High Sierra in what is now known as Nevada. The town that grew nearby was Virginia City.] The fabulous amounts of money wrested from the earth created in Virginia City a fantastic setting of ostentation, extravagance, and exaggeration—which precisely suited the style of reporter Samuel Clemens. Dan De Quille, Clemens's colleague at the Virginia City *Territorial Enterprise*, had a strong effect on his developing style; and it was here that Clemens first used his most famous pseudonym, Mark Twain.

The world's most elegant dump grew up on the chalky yellow slopes below Virginia City [Nevada]. Each day, thousands of oyster shells were discarded with a woodpecker's indifference in piles that grew to the proportions of Indian burial mounds. The conspicuous consumption of oysters in a mountain city four thousand feet above the desert suggests all there is to say about the fabulous high life that came to Virginia City with the dawn of the 1860s. The extravagance began with the workers and spread upward. The miner, filthy from a long shift underground at the silver heart of the mountain, wanted to wrap his grimy hands around a glass of finest crystal and drink in surroundings consistent with the fabulous wealth within his grasp below. The saloons, which became the center of Virginia City social life, were the rivals in luxury of eastern gentlemen's clubs. As the wealth of kings poured out of the mines, money seemed an inexhaustible resource, water in the

---

Excerpted from *The Richest Place on Earth* by Warren Hinckle and Frederic Hobbs (Boston: Houghton Mifflin, 1978). Copyright 1978 by Warren Hinckle III and Fredric Hobbs. Reprinted by permission.

kingdom of Atlantis, something to splash around in style.

Optimism was a communicable disease in Virginia City and ostentation its competitive spirit.... Mine headquarters were studies in marble and polished brass. When directors and

WHAT *REALLY* HAPPENED ON THE WASHOE "FIELD OF HONOR"?

On May 24, 1864, the *Enterprise* published the entire Twain-Laird-Wilmington-Gillis correspondence, brimful of italics and indignation—no doubt to the amusement of its readers.

Anticlimax followed. On May 29 Twain and Gillis left for San Francisco by stage. There had been no meetings on the field of honor. In *Roughing It*, Twain would pass over his departure in a single paragraph, blaming it on his reluctance "to serve in the ranks after being General of the army." (He had been writing editorials during Goodman's absence.) Paine tells a different story, supplied by Steve Gillis. In this version, Laird accepted the challenge and at daybreak Gillis led his principal to the field. They arrived early, and Twain began target practice but could hit nothing; he closed his eyes when he pulled the trigger. Gillis seized the pistol to show him how to handle it, and shot off the head of a mud hen at thirty paces. At that Laird came in sight, attributed the marvelous shot to Twain, and retracted on the spot. The story is in the best tall-tale tradition, and completely false. Gillis had stolen his details from a humorous sketch by Twain himself, "How I Escaped Being Killed in a Duel," published in *Tom Hood's Comic Annual for 1873*.

A letter from Mark Twain to his brother on May 26 shows that no meeting took place. After asking for two hundred dollars, Twain tells his plans: "Steve & I are going to the states. We leave Sunday morning... Say nothing about it, of course. We are not afraid of the grand jury, but Washoe has long since grown irksome to us... We have thoroughly canvassed the Carson business, & concluded we dare not do anything either to Laird or Carson men without spoiling our chances of getting away."...

He would soon have left Nevada in any case. Mark Twain was nomadic by nature and he was ambitious.... In his brief stay he had found his vocation and had become "Mark Twain"; he had enjoyed a freedom to develop his abilities that he could have found nowhere else; and in the year and a half since taking his new name, he had become the best known, if not the best loved, humorist in the West.

John Lauber, *The Making of Mark Twain*, 1985.

stockholders came from "down there"—as the Comstock referred to San Francisco—they were treated as visiting royalty. They rode through the crowded streets in coaches-and-four rigged with silver harnesses, dined on oysters and frogs' legs served on silver platters, wiped their bearded mouths on the finest French linens, and washed down the feast with vintage Moselle with champagne and brandy for dessert. The six-story International Hotel opened in 1861 for the pleasure of visiting grandees and was known far and wide as the finest hostelry west of Chicago. It even had an elevator.

As Virginia City's terraced streets were cut into the mountainside, no one gave a thought to cross-traffic; the quickest way to get from one block to another was to go through someone's living room. The levels of the town developed along layers of caste and discrimination approximating those of our own day. C Street, the main business street, was lined with saloons, brick commercial establishments, and balconied houses with iron shutters. Most buildings had second-story balconies that left the wooden boardwalk below in shadows. Up the hill on A and B streets were the splendidly appointed homes of mining executives and well-to-do merchants, while the miners crowded into tent houses and makeshift clapboard apartment houses farther down the slope. Immediately below the main business district on D Street were the prostitutes' white cabins.... A full-blown Chinatown grew up on E Street, where ducks and salamanders dried on lines and opium dens and laundries abutted. Farther below the Chinese, near the oyster-encrusted dump, the exploited and vanquished Indians camped, living off the table scraps of white and yellow alike.

Everything but ice cubes had to be imported to Virginia City, and the High Sierra streamed with caravans hauling heavy machinery and luxuries into the mountain mining metropolis. Even the highwaymen had class. The most distinguished of their breed was Jack Davis, who spread a buffalo rug on the ground and treated his victims to champagne and cold chicken while his men picked their pockets and rifled the strongbox. The boys admired such style, as they admired any extravagance; one miner bragged of filling the water tower with imported champagne to quench the thirst of his wedding party. Virginia City thrived on what J. Ross Browne termed "an atmosphere of exaggeration."...

STYLE AND SUBSTANCE AT THE *TERRITORIAL ENTERPRISE*

Down C Street each day Italian fresco painters hired to decorate mansions mixed with the Celestials [Chinese] in their pigtails, real Indians mingled with cigar-store Indians, and booted German engineers with muleskinners wearing the traditional Sierra Stetson. Joe Goodman, the poet who was editor of the *Territorial Enterprise*, watched this surreal parade from the copy room behind the red brick façade of his newspaper building on C Street. The *Enterprise*, founded in the Carson Valley hamlet of Genoa in 1858, had relocated in Virginia City early in 1860. Its daily bill of fare included the highly literate output of Rollin Daggett, a walking whiskey barrel who was part Iroquois, and the bowie knife–carrying William Wright, better known as Dan De Quille. These frontier journalists were tough and aggressive to the extreme, writing in a spirited exaggerated style that was well-received by the *Enterprise*'s ribald, grim-humored readers, the miners of the Comstock Lode.

For the muckers [miners], their subterranean struggle with the earth was also a daily confrontation with death. The outrageous phantasmagoria of the *Enterprise* style befitted this fact of Washoe life. The *Enterprise* soon acquired a circulation beyond the confines of Nevada, both for its literary style, unsurpassed in the American West, and the hard, unquestioned knowledge of geology and mineralogy that made it the most informed mining periodical in the United States.

While reporting the blush of exuberance that was Virginia City in the early sixties, the editors of the *Enterprise* began receiving a series of frontier sketches postmarked from an anonymous prospector in Aurora, a mining camp 130 miles away. The copy was signed simply "Josh." The unknown correspondent described the Fourth of July oration by George Turner, the egotistical new territorial Chief Justice, thusly: "It was impossible to print his lecture in full, as the typecases had run out of capital I's." The writer nicknamed the Chief Justice "Mr. Personal Pronoun." Goodman offered "Josh" a job. Two months later, Samuel Clemens arrived in Virginia City by stage to take up apprenticeship in the sagebrush school of journalism.

"Mark Twain" and "Dandy Quille"

"Josh" Clemens quickly acclimated himself to the exotic demands of the Sun Mountain reading public. He was an authentic American Original, and his columns had a wild and powerful imagination. On Groundhog Day, 1863, he emerged into the demonic sunshine of his art with his first report signed with yet another alias, this one to last forever—"Mark Twain."

Mark Twain, the developing journalist, owed the most to Dan De Quille. Behind the dry mask of the expert mining reporter, behind his long cape and wide black hat, "Dandy Quille" (as his friends called him) nurtured an acerbic surreal wit. In stories he called "Quaints," he loosed a barrage of deadpan science fiction in the pages of the *Enterprise*. De Quille's "Travelling Stones of Pahrangat Valley," which fantasied the discovery of peripatetic pieces of magnetic iron ore in southeastern Nevada, motivated German physicists to experiment with electrolysis and electromagnetic currents; with singularly Teutonic stuffiness, they addressed scientific inquiries to the "Hochvolgeboren Herr Doktor Dan De Quille, physicist of Virginiastadt," and could never understand the hilarity involved. Even P. T. Barnum was fooled, offering De Quille $10,000 to exhibit his traveling stones under the big top.

The best part of the story to De Quille's Washoe [Nevada] readers was the laugh that the "primitive" Comstock was having on the sophisticated outside world. Another De Quille hoax, a report of a giant windmill atop Sun Mountain as a sump-pump energy source, was judged feasible by a respectable Boston engineering journal whose editor proceeded to calculate its exact horsepower. His greatest fictional "news story" remains his report of "Solar Armour"—an ice helmet invented for crossing the scorching Forty Mile desert east of Virginia City. Fitted with an ammonia tank, the helmet furnished a cold vapor that neutralized the 117-degree desert heat and guaranteed the wearer a safe voyage to the Utah Territory. De Quille filed an eyewitness dispatch of the inventor's last trek across Forty Mile, which, alas, resulted in the demise of the genius. When a rescue party found the overdue inventor, he was seated on a boulder in the middle of the desert, frozen to death, icicles hanging from his body. De Quille solemnly attributed his death to a mechanical defect that refrigerated the man before he could shut his helmet off.

The *Enterprise*'s story was repeated as fact by many other newspapers, and when it was exposed as fiction the pompous San Francisco press was furious. The *Times* of London, taking a more relaxed view, proposed that Queen Victoria equip her imperial legions with this new device for protection against the infernal noonday sun.

The *Enterprise*'s brand of humor filtered through the polluted upper atmosphere of Sun Mountain like a long, low belly laugh. The boys in the mines loved it. Toiling in a bleached-bone desert landscape, they rarely bothered to separate truth from fantasy, and it seemed to them perfectly natural that a newspaper wouldn't either.

THE HAZARDS OF JOKING IN PRINT

The defense of one's literary opinion in the late-night saloon world of Virginia City often became as hazardous as mining itself. Mark Twain learned this the hard way in the spring of 1864. While Virginia City was debating the misappropriation of $3000 of a "Sanitary Fund" raised for victims of the Civil War, Twain wrote in the *Enterprise* that the ladies who presided over the Sanitary Dress Ball in Carson City had sent the money to a miscegenation society [one that supposedly promoted racial mixing] back east. James Laird, editor of the opposition Virginia City *Daily Union*, defended the ladies' honor under the front-page headline: "ENTERPRISE LIBEL OF THE LADIES OF CARSON." Laird portrayed Twain as a man "who conveyed in every word, and in every purpose of all his words, such a grovelling disregard for truth, decency, and courtesy as to seem to court the distinction only of being understood as a vulgar liar."

This was dueling talk. The code was clear on the subject: public retraction by Laird, or Colt navies at fifteen paces.

The young Missourian, in principle opposed to violence, in practice scared to death of it, sought to retire, but the editorial staff of the *Enterprise* over sufficient whiskeys convinced the reluctant hero of the necessity for combat. On the front page of the next morning's *Enterprise*, Twain denounced Laird as "an unmitigated liar and abject coward." This rhetoric was a gloved slap across the face. Laird's acceptance was not long in coming. The duel was set for the next sunrise in Six Mile Cañon.

A feisty *Enterprise* pressman, Steve Gillis, was chosen as Twain's second. As Gillis attempted to instruct his neophyte charge in the care and use of firearms, additional lethal challenges poured into the newspaper's C Street office. The outraged husband of the president of the Sanitary Dress Ball Committee also demanded satisfaction, and the defamed lady's many friends promised horsewhippings in the unlikely event her tormentor turned out to be the survivor of the duel. The *Enterprise*'s star reporter spent a sleepless night. When Gillis rousted Twain from bed for some predawn target practice, his fingers shook like the leaves on a cottonwood.

The sunrise splayed jagged yellow rays around the silhouette of Sugarloaf Mountain down Six Mile Cañon and a spring breeze nipped at Twain's bony frame as he and his second approached the dueling ground. Gillis set up a barn door for target practice and balanced a squash on top to represent a human head. The two men were sighting down the ravine when the shock of the shots rang out in the still Washoe morning. Laird was already there before them, practicing *his* marksmanship. To say that both journalists were less than sharp with a revolver is to understate the facts. Twain could not hit the squash; he could not even hit the barn door. Then the desert walls were still and Laird's seconds could be heard advancing up the hill. As Twain sighted for one last futile practice shot, a mud hen flew across his vision to light in the sage thirty paces distant. In sheer frustration with his partner's ineptitude, Gillis whipped his navy Colt in line and blew off the bird's squawking head. The headless body flapped pathetically on the canyon floor.

Gillis could not have picked a more opportune time to kill a mud hen. For as Laird's seconds approached the dueling ground they saw Twain standing alone, gazing off over the cottonwood, with a smoking pistol in his hand and the mud hen flapping about on the ground. The spring air echoed with Gillis' gleeful shouts about his man's superiority at thirty paces; look what he had done to a hen in flight! Laird's men beat a hasty retreat from the rocky battleground and frantically informed the editor that his opponent was a better shot than Bad Sam Brown.

Laird canceled the duel and departed the Washoe in disgrace. Mark Twain was not far behind. He had no desire to face the line of avengers waiting to take Laird's place. And his old enemy, Judge "Personal Pronoun," had issued a warrant for Twain's arrest—for dueling. That night the curlyheaded bard sat slumped in the darkness of the racing stage that brought him over the Sierra to San Francisco and another kind of immortality.

An Interpreter of American Character

Charles Miner Thompson

Mark Twain's deprived childhood, stripped of the advantages of a good education and refined surroundings, prevents him from achieving greatness as a literary artist. He is not a skillful writer or a great humorist, nor has he created eternal characters in his work. His real gift is for expressing himself—his own thoughts, feelings, and experiences. Since he is himself the prototype of the typical American, and his characters reflect his own life, Twain has interpreted the national character in his writing.

Mark Twain, as we all prefer to call the writer whose real name of Samuel Langhorne Clemens has still a less familiar sound in our ears, was born in the town of Florida, in Missouri, on the 30th of November 1835. His father, who belonged to a Virginian family, had moved there only a little time before from Tennessee, where, like his prototype in *The Gilded Age*, he owned much land. But it was in Hannibal, then "a loafing, out-at-elbows, down-at-the-heels, slaveholding Mississippi River town," now "a flourishing little city," to which the family presently removed, that Mark Twain spent those boyhood days of which *Tom Sawyer* is the diverting chronicle. It was not a very attractive place. "The morality"—the quotation is from a gentle criticism by Mr. Howells—"was the morality of a slaveholding community, fierce, arrogant, one-sided; the religion was Calvinism in various phases, with its predestinate aristocracy of saints and its rabble of hopeless sinners. His [Twain's] people, like the rest, were slaveholders, but his father, like so many other slaveholders, abhorred slavery,—silently, as he must in such a time and place." The home of the Clemenses was—to quote from an ephemeral biography by Mr. Will Clemens—"a two-story brick, with a large tree

---

Excerpted from Charles Miner Thompson, "Mark Twain as an Interpreter of American Character," *Atlantic Monthly*, April 1897.

in front;" and in the village, in a "dingy" office, the furniture of which was "a dry-goods box, three or four rude stools, and a puncheon bench," the head of the family, "a stern, unbending man," held court as justice of the peace.

Amid these surroundings, which were curiously American, if not especially apt to nourish literary genius, Mark Twain, "a good-hearted boy," says his mother, but one who, although "a great boy for history," could never be persuaded to go to school, spent a boyhood which, it appears, was "a series of mischievous adventures." When he was twelve years old his father died, and the circumstances of his mother were such that he had to go to work as printer's apprentice in the office of the Hannibal *Weekly Courier*. . . .

There is no need to pursue his career further. Brief and incomplete as the sketch is, it is long enough to explain much in his writings. The horrid little town, with its poverty of intellectual life, its complete barrenness of all the means for æsthetic cultivation, is hardly the place in which to expect the birth of a refined literary genius. There is a deal of truth in Mr. J.M. Barrie's remark that "nothing that happens after we are twelve matters very much." And these early years, impressionable as a photographic plate, were those which supplied him with the vivid memories upon which he based his strongest works, *Tom Sawyer* and *Huckleberry Finn*. One piece of singular good fortune was indeed his: by his home flowed the mighty Mississippi. The river was the one thing which he knew in all his early days that could appeal to his imagination and uplift it. Its fascination was upon all the boys in the village. They had passing ambitions, he says,—such, for example, as that "if they lived and were good, God would permit them to become pirates;" but the one unchanging desire of their hearts was to be "steamboat men." Any one who can remember his boyhood can easily understand how their young thoughts were always of the river, which, huge and sombre, flowed out of the land of mystery, by their commonplace doors, into the land of promise, and how they envied the river-men to whom both lands were as familiar as the streets of Hannibal. Poor lads, they doubtless found out in after-life that the river touched neither of these enchanting countries, but simply flowed on, not bored only because it was an insensate thing, past thousands of doors little if any less tedious than their own! But fact is unimportant in the training of a sensitive imagination, and the influence of the river upon that of Mark Twain can hardly be exaggerated. Nor is it difficult to comprehend how it is that through whichever of his books the Mississippi flows, it fills them with a certain portion of its power and beauty. To it is owing all that in his work which is large and fine and eloquent. The river is what makes *Huckleberry Finn* his most vivid story and *Life on the Mississippi* his most impressive autobiographic narrative.

THE ADVANTAGES OF AN INQUIRING MIND OVER AN EDUCATED ONE

Of education Sam Clemens had but little. Till he was twelve years old he attended school in his native town. He learned to "read and write and cipher," as the phrase was, with a little elementary geography and history. Beyond that, nothing. High school he never saw; college he never knew. Nearly all that he acquired he picked up for himself. He seems to have carried in himself a native desire for information, in particular for facts and figures, which was perhaps increased and strengthened by the early cessation of his schooling. . . .

There seem, indeed, to be two distinct means by which a man of native genius may succeed in life. The one is by receiving a sound and complete education; the other by not getting any at all. It is likely that if Mark Twain had attended college and learned to rehearse the wisdom of other men and to repeat the standardized judgments of the past, he would have been badly damaged by the process. It is the crowning triumph of his life that Oxford in his old age should have awarded him its honorary degree, doctor of literature. But if he had ever earned and received its B.A., it would probably have knocked all the "Mark Twain" out of him.

Stephen Leacock, *Mark Twain*, 1974.

Unfortunately, there was nothing else in the boy's early surroundings which could help him to become a literary artist, for the river, however it might dominate and uplift his imagination, could not teach him the most delicate and beautiful art of writing well. For that the child must at least have books, good works of the imagination, from which he may unconsciously learn the modest secret of good taste, the value of the apt word, the mysteries of the rise and fall of the rhythm of lovely prose. When one recalls the lack of æsthetic advantages which was so plentiful in his boyhood, in that "loafing, out-at-elbows, down-at-the-heels, slaveholding" village, in his wandering, unprosperous youth in cis-Mississippi [this side of the Mississippi] printing-offices, and in his impecunious journalistic young manhood in the rough and lawless West, one cannot wonder that he is so imperfectly an artist. He has a rude native gift for firm and vigorous narration. He has, too, an inborn eloquence which sometimes rises superior to his faulty periods, and at its best carries the critical reader out of the mood of fastidious objection. But his style,—which he has improved steadily,—even when correct, is technically without distinction.

He fails no less in the handling of large masses of composition: he is singularly devoid of any aptitude for construction....

No, he is not a great or a skillful writer. The influences of his early years were not such as would make him one....

Neither is Mark Twain—bold as the assertion may seem—a great humorist or a great wit.... Mark Twain has shaken the sides of the round world with laughter; but after all, has he, in the mass of his writings, uttered any witticism which touches intimately, much less radiantly expresses, some eternal truth of life? Has he ever created any character bearing so plainly a lasting relationship to human nature that it will live on to be hailed brother by future men? Unless indeed some of the clever sayings of *Pudd'nhead Wilson* have greater depth and reach of meaning than they now seem to have, the answer to the first question is plainly "No." Not many of Mark Twain's witticisms will appear in the *Familiar Quotations* of the coming century. The answer to the second question is perhaps susceptible of a moment's debate. But probably not more than two characters will rise in the memory of any one who may wish to answer it otherwise than also by a "No." These will be Tom Sawyer and Huckleberry Finn. And surely Tom Sawyer is only one presentment more of the general idea—boy—added to the thousands which any one familiar with the commercial industry of writing books for boys can name only too readily. ... Huck is simply the usual vagabond boy, with his expected shrewdness and cunning, his rags, his sharp humor, his practical philosophy. The only difference between him and his type would be found in his essential honesty, his strong and struggling moral nature, so notably Anglo-Saxon....

Now, if Mark Twain has neither uttered memorable witticisms nor created any finely humorous character, it will not be as a great humorist that he will survive. Nor is the reason for his failure hard to find. His lack of mastery of form, his constant offense against taste, is, of course, a large part of it, but not all. The humor which finds in him its chief source of expression is that of a shifting and evanescent semi-civilization, the humor of new men in new circumstances in a suddenly developing country, wherein the ups and downs of life, immensely exaggerated both in speed and in span, made a grotesque appeal to the sense of incongruity of a naturally humorous people. The society of the West is not yet settled into its final form, as that of the East may be considered to be; but already it, and we who know it, have traveled far from the possibility of appreciating fully its special humor. A few years more, and most of its fun will seem to all, as it seems to many now, the merest extravagance, as hard to understand as the spirit which prompted the gargoyle on the mediæval church. A humor based upon the transient conditions of such a life can hardly be more permanent than the life itself.

A Strangely Conspicuous Position

Not in the technical sense a skillful writer, not a good novelist or story-teller, not a great wit or a great humorist, Mark Twain occupies a strangely conspicuous position in the world of contemporary letters. He has long been accepted of the people, never of the critics. Although his name is a household word in all places where the English language is spoken, and in many where it is not, he has never been accorded any serious critical notice. There have been, indeed, in various magazines, a few articles—mostly of no critical intention or pretension—about him, but almost the only fact which looks like a recognition of him as a real author, and not as an inconsequential buffoon, is the publication, now going forward, by Messrs. Harper and Brothers, of a uniform edition of his complete works. Yet a general sense of his importance may be found existing even among the critical who neglect him, and some natural, mild wonder why it has never found expression.... The circus clown were as likely to attract the attention of the dramatic critic as Mark Twain that of the serious reviewers. But his enormous vogue should have won the notice of some inquiring mind, and led its possessor to ask if his popularity had not some deeper cause than the love of the crowd for the antics of one who professionally wears the cap and bells. If deeper cause there be, it may well prove something which throws light upon American life and character. Perhaps it were as well to attribute the popularity of Abraham Lincoln to his jokes as to ascribe that of Mark Twain to his extravagant foolery. In the conventional sense, Mark Twain is no more a literary artist than, in the conventional sense, Lincoln was a gentleman. But in spite of lack of polish Lincoln was great: may not Mark Twain, the writer, in spite of his crude literary manners, be great, also? The mere possibility ought to be enough in itself to secure him sympathetic and thoughtful consideration.

    Criticism is always concerned with the man behind the book.... Mark Twain belongs to the race of literary egotists. The narrations which are his best work are almost entirely autobiographic. *Roughing It* relates his experiences in the West. *Innocents Abroad* sets forth his own peculiarly American view of Europe. *Life on the Mississippi* is very Twain, and naught else. *Tom Sawyer* is less real than *Huckleberry Finn*, because—one cannot doubt—he is less the young Clemens than is Huck. Indeed, the rule may be laid down that the interest of Mark Twain's books is in direct proportion to the amount of autobiographic matter in them. What he is gifted to express is plainly himself, his own thoughts, feelings, experiences....

THE WAY TO A NATION'S HEART

Perhaps it is possible to discover in what [his] charm consists. The comparison between Abraham Lincoln and Mark Twain which was suggested a little while ago doubtless appeared fantastical enough. But after all, is not the feeling of kinship which the people had with the statesman the same which they have with the writer? There is certainly no way to a nation's heart more nearly direct than to make it feel that you are of one flesh and blood with it. It loves to see itself literally personified in the executive chair; it likes best that writer who thoroughly expresses its own ideas, gives form to its own moral and mental nature. That is always the secret of success,—the one thing in common between popularly successful mediocrities and popularly successful great men....

    If one were to summon his vague recollections of the figure set forth as that of the typical American by such various authorities as the playwright, the caricaturist, the story-teller, and the novelist, there would gradually emerge from the haze a certain quite definite figure of a man.... [The] figures which chance to come to mind blend easily—do they not?—into a sort of composite personality, a shrewd, ready, practical, irreverent, humorous, uncultivated man, who is apt to jeer at art and the civilization of Europe, but for whom you have, nevertheless, a large affection and a high respect, partly because he has, to a striking degree, such excellent qualities as essential seriousness of character, self-reliance, courage, kindliness, honesty and simplicity of heart, the domestic virtues; and still more, perhaps, because you are a good American yourself, and know him to be the man you would like to be, were good manners and cultivation added to him. This is, after all, the type among the many that we recognize as American which is most generally found throughout the United States. It is a type with which, indeed, the American people are a little too well satisfied. Our public is too apt to be to his virtues very kind, and very blind to his faults,—a course of conduct admirable to adopt toward your friend, but not toward yourself if you aim to improve. And is it not this type which Mark Twain is continually drawing? Tom Sawyer and Huckleberry Finn are certainly the typical American in little [in a smaller version]. Is not the view of Europe expressed in *Innocents Abroad* that of the same humorous, irreverent, uncultivated man? The Connecticut Yankee who went to King Arthur's court would undoubtedly have preferred to any castle in England that house in America "with gas and water connections, and steam-heat through to the top." *Pudd'nhead Wilson* and the pilots in *Life on the Mississippi* conform perfectly to the type. They are all Americans,—raw, if you will, but real, native, typical. Essentially they and the others are one and the same man always. Now, let the reader recall that Mark Twain's work is almost wholly autobiographic, and he will at once perceive the obvious corollary: this man, this typical American, is Mark Twain himself.

His life has been typically American. There is something delightfully national in that "two-story brick with a large tree in front" in which it had its beginnings. To attain fame and fortune is supposed to be the special privilege of the poor, self-educated American boy. American versatility, which has been our doubtful boast, is strikingly exemplified in this man's variety of occupation,—printer, pilot, private secretary, miner, reporter, lecturer, inventor (that is especially American!), author, publisher. It all recalls the biographies—not likely, one may guess, to be written in the future as they have been in the past—of the *From the Towpath to the White House* sort. It is American through and through. Having lived this life, how could Mark Twain fail to go straight to the hearts of his countrymen, attracting them to himself at first through their sense of humor, holding them afterwards through their sense of kinship? If a man can thoroughly express the individuality of a nation, he may fairly be called great. We may lament the artist lost, but we may rejoice in the man. He has drawn the national type, interpreted the national character. For that service we may be grateful. And he has taught unobtrusively, but none the less powerfully, the virtues of common sense and honest manliness. If it comes to a choice, these are better than refinement.

Mark Twain as Prospective Classic

Theodore de Laguna

Despite his despising the prevailing canons of sound taste, Mark Twain has many admirers. Those who most enthusiastically applaud his work do not suspect him of greatness; he simply seems unpretentious, one of their own kind. Yet although his diction offends the educated taste, his humor is common clay, and his powers of sustained narrative are seriously questioned, his charm is irresistible. Mark Twain has given to the world one great character: his own—and the world should be grateful.

It is an anomaly unprecedented in the history of criticism, that Mark Twain should live to receive even a doubtful recognition from the schoolmen of his time. For he has consistently despised prevailing canons of sound taste, and yet has reached the hearts of men. In the eyes of the few, he has been that most contemptible of creatures, a popular scribbler. With talents that might have justified a more select ambition, he has been willing to be popular.

Too Good to Be Literature?

His most enthusiastic admirers have been farthest from suspecting in him the elements of greatness. They can so thoroughly enjoy him without the least sense of intellectual inferiority, that he seems one of their own kind, no better than themselves. His humor is the national humor,—so wild and free and lawless in its adventures, that it seems to the uncultured mind too good to be literature. He writes in the living language, in "modern English," as he calls it,—the unaffected speech of men in general, the medium of intelligent conversation, "the common drudge 'tween man and man."

Those who have enjoyed him most, I repeat, have been the

Theodore de Laguna, "Mark Twain as Prospective Classic," *Overland Monthly,* April 1898.

last to suspect him of greatness. The wonder is that within the century anyone should have awakened to the truth. How were we to respect a writer, who accumulates his "and's" like an enthusiastic child, who trails out tag-end prepositions with unconventional freedom; who with exasperating complacency inserts the adverbial modifier between the infinitive and its sign; who says "that much" and "feel badly"? Such practices may be pardonable when committed in the privacy of home; but in literature are they not unclean and repulsive? The educated taste answers in the affirmative. In a language as old as ours, it is inevitable that the diction and idiom of culture should be widely differentiated from common speech and serenely elevated above its coarseness and vulgarity. But Mark Twain has persisted in his attachment to his mother tongue. It is hard for a college-bred man to forgive him.

"I Knew That He Was My Friend"

I was fourteen years old when I first met Mr. Clemens.... The instant I clasped his hand in mine, I knew that he was my friend. He made me laugh and feel thoroughly happy by telling some good stories, which I read from his lips. I have forgotten a great deal more than I remember, but I shall never forget how tender he was.

He knew with keen and sure intuition many things about me and how it felt to be blind and not to keep up with the swift ones—things that others learned slowly or not at all. He never embarrassed me by saying how terrible it is not to see, or how dull life must be, lived always in the dark. He wove about my dark walls romance and adventure, which made me feel happy and important.

Once when Peter Dunne, the irrepressible Mr. Dooley, exclaimed: "God, how dull it must be for her, every day the same and every night the same as the day," he said, "You're damned wrong there; blindness is an exciting business, I tell you; if you don't believe it, get up some dark night on the wrong side of your bed when the house is on fire and try to find the door."

Helen Keller, *Midstream*, 1929.

When we consider that his treatment of language is of a piece with his conduct toward the traditional in general, we may not care to forgive him. For the irreverent Westerner has acted upon the principle, that the only memorial of the past worthy of respect is the inheritance of truth. The shams of the past and of the present are indiscriminately the subjects of his humor. Of all forms of falsehood, that which he has held up to most insulting ridicule is false sentimentality. In an age of effete romanticism, this is likely to hurt decent people's feelings.

His humor, like his language, is common clay. We have rightly called it the national humor; but to some minds, that is little to its credit. A constant feature is the adaptation of popular material. "She resurrected nothing but the cat," has been criticised as brutal violence perpetrated upon a word that is hallowed by a sacred connotation. We shall not deny the justice of the criticism; but Mark Twain is not to blame. He used the word as he found it. When the Western mother dives into an ancient clothes-chest and brings to the surface a faded relic of former years,—"resurrected" is the very word she uses and relishes. It is a piece of popular whimsicality like a thousand others that mold the vocabulary of a nation, and which are the national humorist's crude material.

Innocent Humor

It has for centuries been a commonplace of criticism, that laughter is equally degrading to the laughable object and to the man who laughs. That there could be innocent humor has been a childish superstition. But Mark Twain very evidently supposes that his humor degrades neither himself, nor his readers, nor, necessarily, the subject of his discourse. Chaucer, as we remember, assigned to himself the unappreciated Tale of Sir Thopas—satirized the romantic craft in his own person. There was an assumption of moral greatness in this, which later Englishmen have not attempted to imitate. But with Mark Twain, self-satire is so frequent an artifice as altogether to escape comment.

We have observed that "innocent humor" is a contradiction in terms. We might go farther and demonstrate upon infallible premises that the æsthetic worth of humor is strictly limited by its coarseness; not that the two are necessarily commensurate, but that the degree of coarseness measures the possibilities of humor. From this it would appear, that for the noblest humorous effects, sensual impurity is necessary. The science of rhetoric asserts no more certain principle; and no rhetorical law has been more carefully respected by genius of all times and nations. How then were we to recognize greatness in a humorist, whose writings contain not one unwholesome word or thought or suggestion?

It was a bitter commentary upon our narrow-mindedness,

that Mark Twain should have conceived it necessary or advisable to publish his *Personal Memoirs of Joan of Arc* anonymously. He had been marked, apparently forever, as the "prince of funny men," and from such a character we could not be expected to tolerate so noble a romance—until, indeed, it had won its own fair fame. Just so, in the careless judgments passed upon his earlier works, the general conception of the American humorist had swallowed up all due appreciation of his magnificent abilities in serious art.

"I Felt at Home"

Mark Twain is not all of Samuel Clemens. He was much more than humorous. He was a great fictionist and a rough-hewn stylist uttering himself in his own way, which was a large, direct and forceful way. No amount of Old World contact could destroy his quaint drawl, and not all his reading nor his acquired personal knowledge of other writers could conventionalize his method. He remained the mid-Western American and literary democrat to the last.

I shall never forget the impression he made upon me when I called upon him in London some twelve years ago. The hotel in which he was staying was one of those highly refined, almost complete femininized, institutions with which the west end of London is furnished, but when the shock-haired, keen-eyed man from Missouri took my hand and said "Howdy" I felt at home. I thought him then as I think him now: one of the greatest of American authors. Not of the cultured type, but of the creative type. A figure to put beside Walt Whitman as a representative of our literary democracy.

Hamlin Garland, *North American Review*, June 1910.

The charm of a few of his word pictures has at times been casually noticed. But he has never been celebrated for their worth. Yet scattered through his miscellaneous writings are not a few of the most sublime or beautiful natural descriptions in our literature. If we could name our favorite among them all, we might choose from *Tom Sawyer* an account of the wakening of nature, as the little runaway beheld it in the dawning of his first day of freedom,—a piece of exquisite simplicity and loveliness. Human scenes are pictured no less effectively. In *The Gilded Age*, the paragraphs upon the death of Laura Hawkins bear many signs of our author's technic; and they contain a description which is among the glories of American literature. Let us repeat the concluding sentences:—

When the spring morning dawned, the form still sat there, the elbows resting upon the table and the face upon the hands. All day long the figure sat there, the sunshine enriching its costly raiment and flashing from its jewels; twilight came, and presently the stars, but still the figure remained; the moon found it there still, and framed the picture with the shadow of the window sash, and flooded it with mellow light; by and by the darkness swallowed it up, and later the gray dawn revealed it again, and still the forlorn presence was undisturbed.

A Story-Teller, Not a Novelist

Mark Twain has not been generally acknowledged a narrative writer of the first ability. In the briefest form of narrative, the anecdote, he has, indeed, known few rivals; perhaps he may be said to have perfected the American variety as a literary type. But his powers of sustained narration have been seriously questioned. In the books of travel, nothing is sustained. And it has been unreservedly declared that in every one of his works where a plot is necessary, the plot is a failure. But the author of this criticism has evidently a narrow view of the possible merits of plot-construction. Mark Twain is assuredly not a novelist, and few would wish him one. He is a story-teller; let him be judged as such. Now it is commonly a high merit in a story to make the episode or incident an immediate object of pleasurable interest, not inferior to the narrative as a whole. For proof of this recall the story of Aladdin,—which must certainly take rank among the world's best half dozen,—or almost any one of Chaucer's tales, or *Robinson Crusoe*, or *Tom Sawyer*. In a pure story, the distinctly climacteric development of one dominant idea is a fault. As Mr. Thomas R. Lounsbury has pointed out in his *Studies in Chaucer*, the peculiar charm lies in the even distribution of interest. Story-telling is the simplest form of literary art, but not in the sense of being the least difficult. The curious history of *Pudd'nhead Wilson* and *Those Extraordinary Twins* well illustrates the difficulty of combining in one whole a host of equally interesting details. *Huckleberry Finn* certainly lacks artistic unity—not because almost any one of the episodes is in itself of equal æsthetic worth with the fortunes of the vagabond hero; but because it is a poor sequel and the connective tissue is flabby. *Tom Sawyer* is almost beyond criticism. In general, Mark Twain's plots appear to be excellent in their kind. The details are everywhere effectively presented, and they are not too diverse to be unified by the bonds of American humor.

Still less has he won distinction as a stylist, a master of the effects of tone and rhythm. In the might of his occasional eloquence, he shows a strength that cannot be denied, but his average style is said to have done more for the debasing of the English language than any other recent influence. It is the old story of the return to nature—or barbarism; it matters not which. It is a return to the living source of all inspiration and power,—the genius of the spoken language. Historically—as we believe—Mark Twain's style is of infinite import. Æsthetically, it has been seriously undervalued. Quite unpretentious, it is none the less admirably adapted to its peculiar content. "The strangling hero sprang up with a relieving snort," is no less a master-stroke than this (from a descriptive passage before mentioned): "It was the cool gray dawn, and there was a delicious sense of repose and peace in the deep pervading calm and silence of the woods." This quality of "harmony," as the rhetoricians call it, was once held to be the rare and distinguishing charm of the highest literary genius. Latterly it has fallen into less repute, as a Popish artificiality. With Mark Twain, the charm is unaffected, unostentatious, and irresistible.

One Great Character

Like several other writers of this century, he has given to the world one great character,—his own. How great the world has lately learned. It has been wisely said that no mere humorist can be great, even as a humorist; but it seems hard to believe that the intended victim of the aphorism was Mark Twain. Perhaps the critic's knowledge of our author was limited to a very few pages of *Innocents Abroad*. Surely he had never read *The Prince and the Pauper* or *Tom Sawyer*.

But perhaps he had read the latter; for it has met with some strange misappreciation. When that young scamp is brought face to face with darkness, loneliness, horror, agony, and death, with a timid, helpless child clinging to him alone for comfort in her utter despair,—his thoughtfulness, his patient kindness, his boyish soul's long-suffering endurance, must—it would seem—suffice to distinguish him from "the thousands which anyone familiar with the commercial industry of writing books for boys can name only too readily." We quote the words with a certain pleasure.

Huck is evidently the prose, as Tom is the poetry, of Mark Twain's younger self,—and no less a genuinely heroic spirit. "The widow's been good friends to me sometimes, and I want to tell," has long been to us the typical utterance of a stirring manliness.

"The world," said a distinguished professor of literature, "should be thankful for Mark Twain." Could words better suggest the way in which the man and his books have been taken for granted? He has not taken himself for granted, but has striven toward ideals of his own clear judgment. And it is far from a misfortune, that the people have always so received him. No better foundation could be laid for an edifice of enduring fame, than such a popularity.

A Call to Authorship

Joseph Twichell

When the Civil War shut down commerce on the Mississippi River, riverboat pilot Sam Clemens (Mark Twain) lost his livelihood. He tried his hand at a variety of occupations over the next few years, but succeeded best at newspaper work. Assorted inhibitions—among them the lack of a literary education—kept him from conceiving of himself as an "author" until well after he had become one. In the years since, he has read and studied widely to repair the deficiencies in his education.

The outbreak of the civil war in 1861 found Mark Twain, then twenty-six years old, in the calling of a Mississippi River pilot, which, including the term of his apprenticeship, he had followed since 1851, and in which he had no thought but to spend his life. By the ensuing suspension of commerce on the great river his occupation was suddenly gone. In his own view he had suffered a sore stroke of misfortune. The present writer has often heard him tell how entirely at a loss he was, in that emergency, where to look for the means of livelihood. Though between the end of his school days and the time he became a "cub" pilot he had learned and practised type-setting, that almost forgotten art did not seem to him an available resource.

How he managed for the next few years—to what different things he turned his hand—there is no need to recapitulate. He has himself told the story in *Roughing It*, and in the short twenty-first chapter of *Life on the Mississippi*. But he succeeded best in newspaper work.

Unaware of His Gift

The significant thing is that at so late a period as that at which he was by the war thrust aside from his fixed employment, and when he had reached an age at which most men have discovered their peculiar talent or capacity, if such they have, he

---

Excerpted from Joseph Twichell, "Mark Twain," *Harper's New Monthly Magazine*, May 1896.

was not in the least aware of his possession of that incomparable gift, the display of which was by-and-by to make him one of the famous men of his time. Nothing was further from his thoughts than that a literary career lay before him. His humorous turn had, indeed, always been recognized among his acquaintance. He remembers that even as a lad his way of saying and telling things would make his school-fellows laugh. The celebrated "Jumping Frog of Calaveras County," which was his original essay in its line, and first called public attention to him, was a story (it had some basis of fact) with which he had long been wont on occasion to entertain private circles. When at some one's urgency he at length wrote it out, it appeared to him so poor and flat that he pigeonholed it in contempt, and it required further urgency to persuade him to let it be printed. The favor with which it was received was a surprise and marvel to him, as, it may be added, was the tide of success that presently set in, and in a short time floated him into national and international popularity.

He will sometimes speak of his astonishment at that popularity as it developed,—for an item, of the sensation it caused him to see something from his pen copied in an English journal. Other writers have experienced a like sensation; but he was not yet, in his own esteem, a writer in the literary sense at all. As for being a candidate for admission to the Guild of Authors, it was quite undreamed-of. It was not, in fact, till the multitude of the readers of *The Innocents Abroad* were applauding far and wide in full chorus what one of them called "the dear, delightful genius of Mark Twain," as shining out in that book, that he began to apprehend his call to the profession of letters. And even then he was not fully convinced. For when, in 1868, he finally quit the Pacific coast and came East to live, where he had found a publisher, and soon found a wife, he still judged that journalism would be his permanent main pursuit, with perhaps lecturing, which he had tried successfully, for an adjunct. Accordingly he accepted a position as editor on the staff of the Buffalo *Express*, and took up his residence in that city. It was not long, however, before the demand for his literary product pointed him so unmistakably to his proper field that he relinquished his editorship, and in 1872, various considerations inclining him thither, removed to Hartford, which has been his home ever since.

SMALL QUALIFICATION FOR HIS NEW ROLE

But thus it was that authorship sought the man, and not the man authorship. Nor is it any wonder that he was somewhat difficult to persuade of his vocation. His qualification for it, in the ordinary reckoning, was small, as he perfectly well knew. He was not what is called an educated man. He had no formal literary culture. His acquaintance with books was limited. The extraordinary grip on the English language exhibited in his earliest writings must be chiefly accounted for by his extraordinary native talent. His only training in the use of the pen was such as had been acquired in five or six years of much-interrupted newspaper service, generally of the humbler sort. Up to the time he turned his face eastward the most serious attempts at composition he had made were the few pieces gathered into his first thin volume, *The Jumping Frog, and Other Sketches*, two or three lectures, and his letters of travel as press correspondent from the Sandwich [Hawaiian] Islands and on the noted *Quaker City* excursion. The last-named, to be

---

WITH A LITTLE HELP FROM HIS FRIENDS...

Although Clemens published hundreds of items in the San Francisco *Morning Call*, it is apparent that in July and August 1864 he was seriously questioning his career as a writer. John McComb recalled a conversation with him in 1864, when Clemens was "city editor of the *Morning Call*." According to McComb, they met at the corner of Clay and Montgomery streets and Clemens said, "Mac, I've done my last newspaper work; I'm going back East." He had secured an appointment to act as a government pilot on the Mississippi, for a salary of $300 a month, and he planned to take the job. McComb, who "conceived a high regard for his literary ability," urged against this radical step:

> Sam, you are making the mistake of your life. There is a better place for you than a Mississippi steamboat. You have a style of writing that is fresh and original and is bound to be popular. If you don't like the treadmill work of a newspaper man, strike up higher; write sketches, write a book; you'll find a market for your stuff, and in time you'll be appreciated and get more money than you can standing alongside the wheel of a steamboat.... No, Sam, don't you drop your pen now, stick to it, and it will make your fortune.

After listening carefully to this admonition, and thinking it through, Clemens is reported to have told McComb, "Now, Mac, I've taken your advice. I thought it all over last night, and finally I wrote to Washington declining the appointment, and so I'll stick to the newspaper work a while longer."

Edgar Marquess Branch and Robert H. Hirst, eds., *The Works of Mark Twain: Early Tales & Sketches.* vol. 1, (1851–1864), 1979.

sure, had disclosed his powers, and obtained recognition of them sufficient to satisfy a sagacious Yankee publisher—the late Mr. Elisha Bliss, of the American Publishing Company, of Hartford—of a probable market for them if made into a book. A fortunate conjecture to all concerned it proved. Within three years of its issue in 1869, *The Innocents Abroad* had a sale of 125,000 copies, and it continues saleable to this day.

AN AUTHOR BY CHANCE

Yet to Mark Twain it seemed, and quite naturally, that he was an author in the case, as it were, by chance, and that it was unlikely that his name would ever appear on another title-page. No more books, at any rate, were in sight to him.

But his genius was in him, and his big fertile brain; and copious material of which he was unconscious lay stored and ripening in his mind, waiting to be produced in the due season. Regarding that material, it was presumably due to the fact that in the years when, by his penetrating observation, and study of men in the active scenes of a life full of change, adventure, vicissitude, it was accumulating, he was, as has been said, distinctly unliterary in the habit of his thoughts, that he was slow to appreciate the literary value of it—to see that it *was* literary material at all. For example, in 1880, or thereabout, he said to a friend whom he met on the street, "I've had a letter from Osgood asking me to write a series of articles for *The Atlantic Monthly*, and I want to do it; I would like to very much indeed, but I can't think of anything in the world to write about; no faintest idea of a practicable subject has come to me. I believe I've got through." Now it had happened but two or three evenings before, that Mark, at this friend's fireside, had fallen into reminiscent talk of his old pilot days; and kindling with the theme as he proceeded, had gone on and on in his own unapproachable style, vivid, picturesque, eloquent, dramatic, till far into the night, the captivated listeners completely under his spell, and, like himself, oblivious of the flight of time. Never, they thought, had they heard anything so fascinating before. Recalling this, the friend said, "Why don't you write up the Mississippi River, and work in all those things you were telling us about the other evening?" At which Mark only stared. But of that hint came his book *Life on the Mississippi*, which for one feature contains a description of the Father of Waters that for beauty and splendor and deep feeling of Nature in some of her rarer aspects and most bewitching moods was doubtless never surpassed. It appeared, though, to have been to him the first suggestion that his pilot experience, so rich in elements of both comedy and tragedy, could be turned to literary use. It had never occurred to him in that light. . . .

REMEDYING HIS EDUCATIONAL DEFICIENCY

Reference has been made to his lack of educational furnishing at the outset of his literary career. That deficiency he has, during the thirty years that have since elapsed, applied himself with large diligence to repair. All that time he has been an eager, industrious reader and student. He has acquired French and German, and is able to read both languages with facility; also to speak them pretty well. He has widely acquainted himself with literature—modern literature especially—in various departments. His literary tastes are in instances surprising; *e.g.*, he does not relish Dickens, and he does not much enjoy Charles Lamb. In poetry he is an ardent admirer of Browning, whose works he has not only himself studied with enthusiasm, but has been a promoter of their study by others. For a considerable period in late years a company of ladies—his neighbors—met in his house a forenoon a week to listen to his readings from them. A great treat they had, for he is a wonderfully fine reader, with few superiors, if any. Whoever may have had the good fortune to hear his rendering of anything from Browning—for instance, "Up at a Villa—Down in the City," which is one of his favorites—will not be likely to forget the pleasure of it.

But the subject which, above all others, he has delighted to pursue is history—preeminently that of England and of France from the Middle Ages. In those fields he has been an indefatigable, it is not too much to say, exhaustive, reader, while, by grace of a rarely tenacious memory, his learning in them is remarkably at hand and accessible to him. Hardly ever will an event of any importance in their annals be mentioned in his presence that he cannot at once supply the date of it.

The aspect of remote times that chiefly fascinates his interest is the social. Books like Pepys's *Diary*, that afford the means of looking narrowly and with human sympathy into the life and manners of bygone generations, have a peculiar charm to him. Of the kindling of his historic imagination from such and other sources, *The Prince and the Pauper*, *A [Connecticut] Yankee in King Arthur's Court*, and *Personal Recollections of Joan of Arc*, none of which could he possibly have written twenty-five years ago, are evidence.

Great as, in the circumstances, is the merit of his attain-

Dear Old Joe

The Reverend Joseph Twichell—"Joe" to all who knew him—had performed Sam and Livy's wedding. Although Twain frequently railed against the church, he and Joe were intimate friends for many years. Their closeness is reflected in this letter, written to Joe a few months after the death of Susy Clemens; her father was still deeply mourning her.

Do I want you to write to me? Indeed I do. I do not want most people to write but I do want you to do it. The others break my heart but you will not. You have a something divine in you that is not in other men. You have the touch that heals, not lacerates. And you know the secret places of our hearts. You know our life—the outside of it—as the others do—and the inside of it—which they do not. You have seen our whole voyage. You have seen us go to sea, a cloud of sail, and the flag at the peak. And you see us now, chartless, adrift—derelicts, battered, water-logged, our sails a ruck of rags, our pride gone. For it is gone. And there is nothing in its place. The vanity of life was all we had, and there is no more vanity left in us. We are even ashamed of that we had, ashamed that we trusted the promises of life and builded high—to come to this!

I did not know that Susy was part of us. I did *not* know that she could go away. I did not know that she could go away and take our lives with her, yet leave our dull bodies behind. And I did not know what she was. To me she was but treasure in the bank, the amount known, the need to look at it daily, handle it, weigh it, count it, *realize* it, not necessary. And now that I would do it, it is too late. They tell me it is not there, has vanished away in a night, the bank is broken, my fortune is gone, I am a pauper. How am I to comprehend this? How am I to *have* it? Why am I robbed, and who is benefited? . . .

Some day you and I will walk again, Joe, and talk. I hope so. We could have *such* talks! We are all grateful to you and Harmony—*how* grateful it is not given to us to say in words. We pay as we can, in love, and in this coin practicing no economy. Goodbye, dear old Joe!

Mark Twain, letter to Joe Twichell, January 19, 1897.

ment, it is to his credit that his own estimate of it is even more than modest. He does not in the least share the slighting regard of the learning of the schools which so-called self-made men are prone to entertain. When, in 1888, Yale College conferred on him the honorary degree of Master of Arts, he expressed in the most positive terms, as he has done on many occasions, his sense of his disadvantage without remedy in having been denied the opportunity of a classical training in his youth.

Some of those who know him best have strongly felt that he was capable of literary production in other lines than those in which he has wrought, which, if less popular, would more amply have exhibited the higher range of his powers as a cultivated thinking man. Had he not, indeed, begun with "managing" (to quote the recent expression of a New Zealand journal) "to tickle the midriff of the English-speaking races," and so made it an inexorable and fated thing, as it were, by the compulsory force of public expectation, that his permanent principal *rôle* should be that of humorist, there is no telling what he might have done. The consideration, however, of what has thus been possibly missed will scarcely produce widespread grief.

Pure American English

Brander Matthews

Although Mark Twain is known for his characters' vernacular language, he was very precise in his use of words. He spoke and wrote American English—distinct from British English—yet he used language so pure that the English have no trouble understanding him. A self-taught linguist, he wrote as he talked, with a fine accuracy and a flowing freedom.

In an after-dinner speech which Mark Twain made in 1907 in London, at the Savage Club, he protested against an interviewer's having made him say that a certain address was *bully*, and he asserted that this distressed him, because "I never use slang to an interviewer or anybody else," adding that if he could not describe that address without using slang, he would not describe it at all. "I would close my mouth and keep it closed, much as it would discomfort me."

Possibly a few of those who heard Mark make this assertion, and probably more than a few of those who have read it in the volume in which his speeches are collected, may have been surprised and perhaps a little inclined to wonder whether Mark was not here indulging in his customary humorous unveracity. Some of them may have recalled the slang which fell unbroken from the lips of Scotty Briggs when he was enlisting the services of the preacher for Buck Fanshawe's funeral.

ENGLISH PURE, DIRECT, AND UNCOMPROMISING

But in saying that he never used slang to an interviewer or anybody else, Mark was only asserting what must be plain to every careful reader of his works and to every one who has had the delight of hearing him tell a story. In the person of Scotty Briggs, who knew no other way of expressing himself, Mark could disclose his knowledge of the energetic and boldly imaginative speech of the unlettered Westerners:

Excerpted from Brander Matthews, "Mark Twain and the Art of Writing," in *Essays on English*, edited by Brander Matthews (New York: Scribner's, 1921).

Phrases such as camps may teach,
Saber-cuts of Saxon speech.

In his own person, as Samuel L. Clemens, or in his assumed personality, as Mark Twain, he refrained from this well of English undefiled by pernicketty precision, tempting as many of its vigorous vocables must have been to him, with his relish for verbal picturesqueness. He knew better than to yield to the easy allurement; and his English is as pure as it is direct and uncompromising. As he eschewed slang so he did not disfigure his pages with localisms, current only sectionally. He avoided dialectic peculiarities however picturesque in themselves and however expressive. Of course he let his local characters express themselves in their local vernacular; and he took pride in the intimacy of his acquaintance with sectional vagaries of vocabulary. In an explanatory note prefixed to *Huckleberry Finn* he told his readers that he had therein used a number of dialects, "to wit: the Missouri negro dialect; the extremest form of the backwoods Southwestern dialect; and the ordinary Pike County dialect, and four modified varieties of this last. The shadings have not been done in a haphazard fashion, or by guesswork, but painstakingly, and with the trustworthy guidance and support of personal familiarity with all these several forms of speech." To a friend who had inquired as to his collaboration with Bret Harte in an unsuccessful and unpublished play, *Ah Sin*, he explained that they had talked out the plot and that he had played billiards while his collaborator wrote the play, adding, "Of course, I had to go over it and get the dialect right. Bret never did know anything about dialect."

While Mark never conformed to the British standard, often insular, and sometimes parochial, he disclosed no individual aberrations either in vocabulary or in usage. The Americanisms he employed on occasion are all legitimate, in that they are what may be called American contributions to the language; and he enlisted very few even of these.

With his sensitiveness to the form and color of words, he was acutely conscious of the many differences between our habitual speech and that of our kin across the sea. In a chapter, which was crowded out of *A Tramp Abroad* to find refuge later in a volume of his sketches, he tells us of an interview he had with an Englishman who complimented him on his English. "I said I was obliged to him for his compliment—since I knew he meant it for one—but that I was not fairly entitled to it, for I did not speak English at all—I only spoke

American." Then he pointed out that he judged that even the educated classes in England had once dropped their h's in *humble* and *heroic* and *historic*, "because your writers still keep up the fashion of putting *an* before those words, instead of *a*. This is what Mr. Darwin might call a rudimentary sign that an *an* was justifiable once and useful.... Correct writers of the American language do not put *an* before those words." And he concluded by assuring his chance companion that "if I wanted to, I could pile up differences here until I not only convinced you that English and American are separate languages, but that when I speak my native tongue in its utmost purity an Englishman can't understand it at all!"

A NEW WORLD TO AN ENGLISHMAN

Mark Twain did more than any other man to make plain people in England understand plain people in America. That alone was a big work, and he did it ... without setting out to do it.

I shall never forget my first reading as a boy of *Huck Finn*. It was an entirely new world to me as an Englishman. Yet wholly lovable and familiar and understandable though a trifle strange as well. It was all I knew of America then, and so it was to thousands of English boys.

George Macaulay Trevelyan, quoted in Cyril Clemens, *My Cousin Mark Twain*, 1910.

This final statement is the extravagant whimsy of a humorist. Yet it is a fact that Mark spoke his native tongue in its utmost purity, which is why every Englishman could understand him. He spoke pure English, as free from obtruded Americanisms as from obsolete Briticisms, the English current on both shores of "the salt, unplumbed estranging sea," the English of Defoe and Bunyan, of Franklin and Lincoln. He knew that English was his native tongue, a birthright and not a loan or a gift, and he was content with its ample resources, seeking always the exact noun and the inexorable adjective. As William Dean Howells put it with his delicate felicity, Mark "used English in all its alien derivations as if it were native to his own air, as if it had come up out of American, out of Missourian ground"; Howells also pointed out that Mark had a "single-minded use of words, which he employs as Grant did to express the plain, straight meaning their common acceptance has given them, with no regard to their structural significance or their philological implications. He writes English as if it were a primitive and not a derivative language, without Gothic or Latin or Greek behind it, or German or French beside it." And he added that the word Mark prefers is "the Abraham Lincolnian word, not the Charles Sumnerian; it is American, Western."

A Spoken Tongue—Even in Writing

There is a superstition among those who have been educated beyond their intelligence that no man can be a master of English who does not possess Latin, at least, and perhaps French also. But this absurdity is exploded by the vital vigor of Bunyan and Defoe, not less than by that of Franklin and Lincoln, Grant and Mark Twain. And the vitality of Mark's English was a gainer also by the fact that to him English was always a spoken tongue; he wrote as he talked; but then he was always as careful in his choice of words when he talked as when he wrote. He imparted to the printed page the vivacity of the spoken word, its swiftness and its apparently unpremeditated ease. His sentences never seem labored, no matter how deeply they may have been pondered. In reading them they appear spontaneous; and whatever the labor they may have cost him, they are not stained with the smoke of the casting or scratched with the mark of the file. Self-taught as he was, no apprentice to the craft of composition ever had a severer teacher. He so mastered the secrets of our stubborn tongue that he was able to write it as he spoke it, with precise accuracy and yet with flowing freedom.

They Understand All the Words . . .

Two Englishmen were discussing with Mark Twain the old topic of American humor as not appreciated by foreigners.

"But are the English really so obtuse?" asked one of them.

"Obtuse! You can't get an idea into an Englishman's head with a surgical operation," declared Mark Twain.

The questioner remained in solemn thought for a moment. Then he broke into a hearty laugh. "Quite a delicious joke!" he exclaimed. "Though, of course, if you were to open the Englishman's skull you would kill him, would you not!"

Mark Twain turned to the second Englishman. "What did I tell you? He wants to know whether it wouldn't kill him!"

The countenance of the second Englishman was like a blank wall. "Wouldn't it?" he queried.

Paul M. Zall, ed., *Mark Twain Laughing*, 1985.

In this Mark all unwittingly (for he was never interested in the history of critical theories) was only acting on the principle laid down two and a half centuries ago by Vaugelas, the linguistic law-giver of the French: "The rule is general and without exception, that what one does not say in speaking, one ought never to say in writing." And again: "The greatest of all errors in the matter of writing, is to think, as many do, that one must not write as one talks."

The same point had been made even earlier by the Italian Castiglione, in his own famous book on the *Courtier*:

> Writing is nothing but a form of speaking, which continues to exist after man has spoken, and is, as it were, an image of the words he utters. It is consequently reasonable to use greater diligence with a view to making what we write more polished and correct, yet not to do this so that the written words shall differ from the spoken, but only so that the best in spoken use shall be selected for our composition.

This is precisely what Mark trained himself to accomplish. He selected for his composition the best in spoken use. He profited by one of the advantages of writing as we speak, if only we are in the habit of speaking with due respect for the nobility of our tongue, that he did not cumber his pages with dead and gone words. Like every growing language, English has a host of words which have fallen into innocuous desuetude, and are no longer understanded of the people. They might run off the pen of the pedantic, but they never fell from the lips of Mark Twain. He was a man of his own time, with no hankering after the archaic. His language is the living speech of those who have English for their mother-tongue, however scattered they may be on all the shores of all the seven seas.

A Serious Humorist

Simeon Strunsky

Because Mark Twain was an incomparable humorist, people paradoxically insist on praising him as a philosopher. Twain did indeed have a serious side, but this was a result of his being a humorist: the aftermath of much laughter is a rebound toward grief.

Mark Twain's memory may suffer from a certain paradoxical habit we have fallen into when passing judgment on the illustrious dead. The habit consists in picking out for particular commendation in the man what one least expects. If the world thinks of him as a great humorist, the point to make is that at bottom he was really a philosopher. If his shafts struck at everybody and everything, the thing to say is that he liked best what he hit hardest. If one of his books sold five thousand copies, the attempt is made to base his future fame on the comparatively unknown book. The motive behind such reasoning is commendable enough. It is the desire not to judge superficially, the desire to get at the "real" man behind the mask which all of us, according to tradition, wear in life. It is a praiseworthy purpose, but, in the hands of the unskilled or the careless, a perilous one. And worse than either is the intellectual snob whose business it is constitutionally to disagree with the obvious. We make no attempt to classify the writer who has declared that Mark Twain, when he wrote *Innocents Abroad*, was terribly in earnest; that he set out to satirize and was funny only because he could not help it. This represents the extreme of a tendency that is made manifest on every side, to turn Mark Twain into everything but what he was—a great compeller of laughter.

One gets dreadfully weary of such topsy-turvy criticism. There are times when one would like to believe that Napoleon will be remembered because he won Austerlitz and Marengo, and not because he divided up France into a vast number of small peasant holdings; that Lincoln was a great man because

> **THE AUTHOR OF "THE JUMPING FROG": PRIMARILY A MORALIST**
>
> As early as 1867 the publisher of Twain's first book, Charles Henry Webb, insisted that the author was primarily a *moralist* and only secondarily a *humorist:* "By his story of the Frog, he scaled the heights of popularity at a single jump, and won for himself the *sobriquet* [nickname] of the Wild Humorist of the Pacific Slope. He is also known to fame as The Moralist of the Main: and it is not unlikely that as such he will go down to posterity."
>
> Philip S. Foner, *Mark Twain: Social Critic*, 1958.

he signed the Proclamation of Emancipation and wrote the Gettysburg address, and not because he kept his temper under criticism and in adversity. It is well to try to pierce behind the veil of Maya, but no amount of analysis can do away with the popularly accepted beliefs that mothers are primarily maternal, that actresses' talents lie in the direction of the stage, that joyful people laugh, and that people who make wry faces are either pessimists or dyspeptics. What use is there in trying to make a serious book out of the *Innocents Abroad*, when we know well that the Mark Twain who wrote it was primarily a fun-maker? For ourselves, we confess that we have been unable to find any grave purpose in the "Jumping Frog of Calaveras." We recall the Hawaiian stranger whom Mark Twain kissed for his mother's sake before robbing him of his small change. We recall the horse he rode in Honolulu; it had many fine points, and our traveller hung his hat upon one of them. We recall that other horse behind which he went driving one Sunday with the lady of his choice; it was a milk-dealer's horse on week-days, and it persisted in travelling diagonally across the street and stopping before every gate. These adventures are easy to recall, but the hidden serious purpose within them remains hidden from us.

TWAIN'S SERIOUS ELEMENT CANNOT BE DENIED

The serious element in Mark Twain the man and the writer, it would, of course, be futile to deny. His hatred of sham, his hatred of cruelty, his hatred of oppression, appear in the *Innocents Abroad*, as they do in his *Connecticut Yankee* and in his bitter assaults on the Christian Scientists and the American missionaries in China of the Boxer days. But to say that Mark Twain was a great humorist because he was an intensely serious man is not true, whatever truth there may be in the formula that humorists are humorists because they are men of sorrow. We would reverse the formula. We would say that humorists are often sad because they are humorists, and that from much laughing the rebound must necessarily be towards much grief. If it is commonly asserted that the humorist laughs because of the incongruities of life, it is, nevertheless, just as safe to maintain that the man born to laughter will be driven by his instincts to search for incongruities. There was no fundamental pessimism in Mark Twain. As Mr. William Dean Howells brings out in his chapter of reminiscences in the last *Harper's*, Mr. Clemens had the soul of untamed boyishness. He was boyish in his exuberance of manner, in his taste for extraordinary clothes, and in his glee at earning a great deal of money:

> The postals [announcing his share of the daily profits from the stage play of *The Gilded Age*] used to come about dinner-time, and Clemens would read them aloud to us in wild triumph. $150—$200—$300, were the gay figures which they bore, and which he flaunted in the air before he sat down at table, or rose from it to brandish, and then, flinging his napkin into his chair, walked up and down to exult in.

One thing there was in Mark Twain that was not apparently boyish or simple. Mr. Howells asserts positively that in his later years Twain believed neither in the Christian theology, in God, nor in immortality:

> All his expressions to me were of a courageous renunciation of any hope of living again, or elsewhere seeing those he had lost. He suffered terribly in their loss, and he was not fool enough to try ignoring his grief. He knew that for that there were but two medicines; that it would wear itself out with the years, and that meanwhile there was nothing for it but those respites in which the mourner forgets himself in slumber. I remember that in a black hour of my own when I was called down to see him, as he thought from sleep, he said, with an infinite, an exquisite compassion, "Oh, did I wake you, did I *wake* you?" Nothing more, but the look, the voice, were everything; and while I live they cannot pass from my sense.

Here at last we have the disillusion that is said to dwell in the innermost soul of the great humorist. But here, too, we seem to feel that the gray vision of the future was with him not a cause, but a result. When the buoyant soul sinks back upon itself it is apt to feel the riddle of life very keenly indeed.

An Unfulfilled Genius

Van Wyck Brooks

Mark Twain's pessimism and cynicism, made light of by his contemporaries, actually expressed a deep malady of his soul. Although he had the talent and ability to become a great creative force, Twain failed to realize his genius. His feeling of failure—regardless of the world's high regard for him—explains the sadness and bitterness of his old age.

For some time before his death Mark Twain had appeared before the public in the rôle less of a laughing philosopher than of a somewhat gloomy prophet of modern civilization. But he was old and he had suffered many misfortunes and the progress of society is not a matter for any one to be very jubilant about: to be gloomy about the world is a sort of prerogative of those who have lived long and thought much. The public that had grown old with him could hardly, therefore, accept at its face value a point of view that seemed to be contradicted by so many of the facts of Mark Twain's life and character. William Dean Howells, who knew him intimately for forty years, spoke only with an affectionate derision of his "pose" regarding "the damned human race," and we know the opinion of his loyal biographer, Mr. Albert Bigelow Paine, that he was "not a pessimist in his heart, but only by premeditation." These views were apparently borne out by his own testimony. "My temperament," he wrote, shortly after the death of his daughter Jean, "has never allowed my spirits to remain depressed long at a time." That he continued to be active and buoyant to the end was, in fact, for his associates, sufficient evidence that his philosophical despair was only an anomaly, which had no organic part in the structure of his life.

A CHARMED LIFE

Was it not natural that they should feel thus about him, those contemporaries of his, so few of whom had seen his later writ-

Excerpted from Van Wyck Brooks, *The Ordeal of Mark Twain* (New York: Dutton, 1920).

ings and all the tell-tale private memoranda which Mr. Paine has lately given to the world? What a charmed life was Mark Twain's, after all! To be able to hold an immense nation in the hollow of one's hand, to be able to pour out into millions of sympathetic ears, with calm confidence, as into the ears of a faithful friend, all the private griefs and intimate humours of a lifetime, to be called "the King" by those one loves, to be so much more than a king in reality that every attack of gout one has is "good for a column" in the newspapers and every phrase one utters girdles the world in twenty minutes, to be addressed as "the Messiah of a genuine gladness and joy to the millions of three continents"—what more could Tom Sawyer, at least, have wished than that? And Mark Twain's fame was not merely one of sentiment. If the public heart was moved by everything that concerned him,—an illness in his household, a new campaign against political corruption, a change of residence, and he was deluged with letters extolling him, whatever he did or said, if he won the world's pity when he got into debt and the world's praise when he got out of it, he was no sort of nine-days' wonder; his country had made him its "general spokesman" and he was quite within his rights in appointing himself, as he said, "ambassador-at-large of the United States of America." Since the day, half a century back, when all official Washington, from the Cabinet down, had laughed over *The Innocents Abroad* and offered him his choice of a dozen public offices to the day when the newspapers were freely proposing that he ought to have the thanks of the nation and even suggested his name for the Presidency, when, in his person, the Speaker of the House, for the first time in American history, gave up his private chamber to a lobbyist, and private [railroad] cars were placed at his disposal whenever he took a journey, and his baggage went round the world with consular dispensations, and his opinion was asked on every subject by everybody, he had been, indeed, a sort of incarnation of the character and quality of modern America. "Everywhere he moved," says Mr. Paine, "a world revolved about him." In London, in Vienna, his apartments were a court, and traffic rules were modified to let him pass in the street. A charmed life, surely, when we consider, in addition to this public acclaim, the tidal waves of wealth that flowed in upon him again and again, the intense happiness of his family relations, and the splendid recognition of those fellow-members of his craft whose word to him was final—Rudyard Kipling, who "loved to think of the great and godlike

Clemens," and Brander Matthews, who freely compared him with the greatest writers of history, and George Bernard Shaw, who announced that America had produced just two geniuses, Edgar Allan Poe and Mark Twain. Finally, there was Howells, "the recognized critical Court of Last Resort in this country," as he called him. Did not Howells, like posterity itself, whisper in his ear: "Your foundations are struck so deep that you will catch the sunshine of immortal years, and bask in the same light as Cervantes and Shakespeare"?

How Did He Betray His Destiny?

This is the "Ordeal" of Mark Twain: that, desiring to be an artist (a rebel against society), he surrendered to the ideals of materialistic America and so betrayed his deepest self. So he suffered throughout his life from a sense of profound guilt, the product of a conflict between art and conformity. What is the mechanism by which he systematically betrayed his destiny? Well, he wrote humor.

Mr. Brooks dislikes humor.

Bernard De Voto, *Mark Twain's America*, 1932.

The spectators of this drama could hardly have been expected to take the pessimism of Mark Twain seriously, and all the more because he totally refuted the old and popular notion that humorists are always melancholy. I have already quoted the remark he made about his temperament in one of the darkest moments of his life, four months before his own death. It is borne out by all the evidence of all his years. He was certainly not one of those radiant, sunny, sky-blue natures, those June-like natures that sing out their full joy, the day long, under a cloudless heaven. Far from that! He was an August nature, given to sudden storms and thunder; his atmosphere was charged with electricity. But the storm-clouds passed as swiftly as they gathered, and the warm, bright, mellow mood invariably returned. . . .

Now this was the Mark Twain his contemporaries, his intimates, had ever in their eyes,—this darling of all the gods. No wonder they were inclined to take his view of "the damned human race" as rather a whimsical pose; they would undoubtedly have continued to take it so even if they had known, generally known, that he had a way of referring in private to "God's most elegant invention" as not only "damned" but also "mangy." He was irritable, but literary men are always supposed to be that; he was old, and old people are often afflicted with doubts about the progress and welfare of mankind; he had a warm and tender heart, an abounding scorn of humbug: one did not have to go beyond these facts to explain his contempt for "the Blessings-of-Civilization Trust," with its stock-in-trade, "Glass Beads and Theology," and "Maxim Guns and Hymn-Books," and "Trade Gin and Torches of Progress and Enlightenment." All his closest friends were accustomed to little notes like this: "I have been reading the morning paper. I do it every morning, well knowing that I shall find in it the usual depravities and basenesses and hypocrisies and cruelties that make up civilization and cause me to put in the rest of the day pleading for the damnation of the human race." Might not any sensitive man, young or old, have written that? . . .

A DEEP MALADY OF THE SOUL

Can we accept any of the usual explanations of Mark Twain's pessimism? Can we attribute it, with Mr. Paine, to the burdens of debt under which he laboured now and again, to the recurring illnesses, the death of those he loved? No, for these things would have modified his temperament, not his point of view; they would have saddened him, checked his vitality, given birth perhaps to a certain habit of brooding, and this they did not do. We have, in addition to his own testimony, the word of Mr. Paine: "More than any one I ever knew, he lived in the present." Of the misfortunes of life he had neither more nor less than other men, and they affected him neither more nor less. To say anything else would be to contradict the whole record of his personality.

No, it was some deep malady of the soul that afflicted Mark Twain. . . .

In fact, the more one scans the later pages of Mark Twain's history the more one is forced to the conclusion that there was something gravely amiss with his inner life. There was that frequently noted fear of solitude, that dread of being alone with himself which made him, for example, beg for just one more game of billiards at 4 o'clock in the morning. There were those "daily self-chidings" that led him to slay his own conscience in one of the most ferocious of his humorous tales. That conscience of his—what was it? Why do so many of his jokes turn upon an affectation, let us say, of moral cowardice in himself? How does it happen that when he reads *Romola* the only thing that "hits" him "with force" is Tito's compromise with his conscience? Why those continual fits of remorse, those fantastic self-accusations in which he charged himself, we are told, with having filled Mrs. Clemens's life with privations, in which he made himself responsible first for the death of his younger brother and later for that of his daughter Susy, writing to his wife, according to Mr. Paine, that he was "wholly and solely responsible for the tragedy, detailing step by step with fearful reality his mistakes and weaknesses which had led to their downfall, the separation from Susy, and this final, incredible disaster"? Was there any reason why, humorously or otherwise, he should have spoken of himself as a liar, why he should have said, in reply to his own idea of writing a book about Tom Sawyer's after-life: "If I went on now and took him into manhood, he would just lie, like all the one-horse men in literature, and the reader would conceive a hearty contempt for him"? That morbid feeling of having lived in sin, which made him come to think of literature as primarily, perhaps, the confession of sins—was there anything in the moral point of view of his generation to justify it, in this greatly loved writer, this honourable man of business, this zealous reformer, this ever-loyal friend? "Be weak, be water, be characterless, be cheaply persuadable" was, he said, the first command the Deity ever issued to a human being on this planet, the only command Adam would never be able to disobey. And he noted on the margin of one of his books: "What a man sees in the human race is merely himself in the deep and honest privacy of his own heart. Byron despised the race because he despised himself. I feel as Byron did and for the same reason.". . .

A TALENT NEVER REALIZED

There was a reason for Mark Twain's pessimism, a reason for that chagrin, that fear of solitude, that tortured conscience, those fantastic self-accusations, that indubitable self-contempt. It is an established fact, if I am not mistaken, that these morbid feelings of sin, which have no evident cause, are the result of having transgressed some inalienable life-demand peculiar to one's nature. It is as old as Milton that there are talents which are "death to hide," and I suggest that Mark Twain's "talent" was just so hidden. That bitterness of his was the effect of a certain miscarriage in his creative life, a balked personality, an arrested development of which he was himself almost wholly unaware, but which for him destroyed the meaning of life. The spirit of the artist in him, like the genie at last released from the bottle, overspread in a gloomy vapour the mind it had never quite been able to possess. . . .

Wherever he walked among men he trailed with him the psychic atmosphere of a planet as it were all his own. Gigantic, titanic were the words that came to people's lips when they tried to convey their impression of him, and when he died it seemed for the moment as if one of the fixed stars had fallen in space.

This was the force, this the energy which, through Mark Twain's pen, found such a qualified expression. He was, as Arnold Bennett says, a "divine amateur"; his appeal is, on the whole, very largely, an appeal to rudimentary minds. But is not that simply another way of saying, in the latter case, that his was a mind that had not fully developed, and, in the former, that his was a splendid genius which had never fully found itself? . . .

A MECHANISTIC VIEW OF MAN

"You and I are but sewing-machines," he says in *What Is Man?* "We must turn out what we can; we must do our endeavour and care nothing at all when the unthinking reproach us for not turning out Gobelins [fine French tapestries].". . .

We are in possession now, it seems to me, of the secret of Mark Twain's mechanistic philosophy, the philosophy of that little book which he called his "Bible," *What Is Man?* He was extremely proud of the structure of logic he had built up on the thesis that man is a machine, "moved, directed, commanded by *exterior* influences, *solely*," that he is "a chameleon, who takes the colour of his place of resort," that he is "a mere coffee-mill," which is permitted neither "to supply the coffee nor turn the crank." He confessed to a sort of proprietary interest and pleasure in the validity of that notion. "Having found the Truth," he says, "perceiving that beyond question man has but one moving impulse—the contenting of his own spirit—and is merely a machine and entitled to no personal merit for what he does, it is not humanly possible for me to seek further. The rest of my days will be spent in patching and painting and puttying and calking my priceless possession and in looking the other way when an imploring argument or a damaging fact approaches." You see how it pleases him, how much it means to him, that final "Truth," how he clings to it with a sort of defiant insolence against the "imploring argument," the "damaging fact"? "Man originates nothing," he says, "not even a thought. . . . Shakespeare could not create. He was a machine, and machines do not create." Faith never gave the believer more comfort than this philosophy gave Mark Twain.

But is it possible for a creative mind to find "contentment" in denying the possibility of creation? And why should any one find pride and satisfaction in the belief that man is wholly irresponsible, in the denial of "free will"? One remembers the fable of the fox and the sour grapes, one remembers all those forlorn and tragic souls who find comfort in saying that love exists nowhere in the world because they themselves have missed it. Certainly it could not have afforded Mark Twain any pleasure to feel that he was "entitled to no personal merit" for what he had done, for what he had achieved in life; the pleasure he felt could have sprung only from the relief his theory afforded him, the relief of feeling that he was not responsible for what he had failed to achieve—namely, his proper development as an artist. He says aloud, "Shakespeare could not create," and his inner self adds, "How in the world, then, could I have done so?" He denies "free will" because the creative life is the very embodiment of it—the emergence, that is to say, the activity in a man of one central, dominant, integrating principle that turns the world he confronts into a mere instrument for the registration of his own preferences. There is but one interpretation, consequently, which we can put upon Mark Twain's delight in the conception of man as an irresponsible machine: it brought him comfort to feel that if he was, as he said, a "sewing-machine," it was the doing of destiny, and that nothing he could have done himself would have enabled him to "turn out Gobelins."

THE ARTIST WITHERED INTO THE CYNIC

From his philosophy alone, therefore, we can see that Mark Twain was a frustrated spirit, a victim of arrested development, and beyond this fact, as we know from innumerable instances the psychologists have placed before us, we need not look for an explanation of much of the chagrin of his old age. He had been balked, he had been divided, he had even been turned against himself; the poet, the artist in him, consequently, had withered into the cynic and the whole man had become a spiritual valetudinarian.

Who Owns the Uncrowned King?

Upton Sinclair

Although Mark Twain was treated like an uncrowned American king, he was bitterly unhappy because his genius was repressed. He allowed the repression both of his style—as his wife and later his daughters edited his work to maintain a provincial respectability—and of his ideas. In order to be successful, he wrote to appeal to the bourgeois dictates of the ruling classes, which were in conflict with his liberal sympathies.

This work is a study of the artist in his relation to the propertied classes. Its thesis is that from the dawn of human history, the path to honor and success in the arts has been through the service and glorification of the ruling classes; entertaining them, making them pleasant to themselves and teaching their subjects and slaves to stand in awe of them.

Throughout this work the word artist is used, not in the narrow sense popular in America, as a man who paints pictures and illustrates magazines; but in its broad sense, as one who represents life imaginatively by any device, whether picture or statue or poem or song or symphony or opera or drama or novel. It is my intention to study artists from a point of view so far as I know entirely new; to ask how they get their living, and what they do for it; to turn their pockets inside out, and see what is in them and where it came from; to put to them the question already put to priests and preachers, editors and journalists, college presidents and professors, school superintendents and teachers: WHO OWNS YOU, AND WHY? . . .

We come now to study America in the second half of the nineteenth century.

The dominating factor in this period was the Civil War, a conflict in which the physical and moral energy of the country was exhausted. There followed the inevitable reaction:

Excerpted from Upton Sinclair, *Mammonart* (Pasadena, CA: Upton Sinclair, 1925).

Abraham Lincoln was succeeded by the carpetbagger in the South and the tariff-boodler in the North. The very hero who had led the nation to victory, and had said, "Let us have peace," [Ulysses S. Grant] entered the White House to turn the government over to corruptionists. In the two generations following the Civil War America made enormous material and some intellectual progress, but no moral progress discernible. As I write this book, our political morals are embodied in a post-campaign jest: "The Republicans should have stolen the Washington monument, and then Coolidge would have carried Florida and South Carolina."

Provincial America in the decades following the Civil War based its religion upon the dogma that it was the most perfect nation upon God's footstool. The whisky-drinking, tobacco-chewing, obscenity-narrating, Grand Old Party–voting mob would tolerate no criticism, not even that kind implied by living differently. To it an artist was a freak, whom it punished with mockery and practical jokes. There were only two possible ways for him to survive; one was to flee to New York and be lost in the crowd; the other was to turn into a clown and join in laughing at himself, and at everything he knew to be serious and beautiful in life. This latter course was adopted by a man of truly great talent, who might have become one of the world's satiric masters if he had not been overpowered by the spirit of America. His tragic story has been told in a remarkable study, *The Ordeal of Mark Twain*, by Van Wyck Brooks.

THE UNCROWNED KING

For something like forty years Mark Twain lived as an uncrowned American king; his friends referred to him thus—"the King." His was a life which seemed to have come out of the Arabian Nights' enchantment. His slightest move was good for columns in the newspapers; when he traveled about the world he was his country's ambassador at large—his baggage traveled free under consular dispensation, and in London and Vienna the very traffic regulations were suspended. When he went to Washington to plead for copyright laws, the two houses adjourned to hear him, and the speaker of the House turned over his private office to the king of letters. He made three hundred thousand dollars out of a single book, he made a fortune out of anything he chose to write. The greatest millionaires of the country were his intimate friends; he had a happy family, a strong constitution, inexhaustible energy—what more could a human being ask?

And yet Mark Twain was not happy. He grew less and less happy as time passed. Bitterness and despair began to creep into his writings; sentences like this: "Pity is for the living, envy is for the dead." Stranger yet, it began to be whispered that America's uncrowned king was a radical! In times of stress some of us would go to him for help, for a word of sympathy or backing, and always this strange thing was noticed; he was full of understanding, and would agree with everything we said; yes, he was one of us. But when we asked for a public action, a declaration, he was not there.

The Jungle was published [1906], and he wrote me a letter. It was burned in the Helicon Hall fire, and I recall only one statement: he had had to put the book down in the middle, because he could not endure the anguish it caused him.

THE GORKY AFFAIR

On April 10, 1906, Maxim Gorky arrived in America on a mission to solicit money and support for the Russian revolutionary movement. He was accompanied, according to the newspapers, by his "young charming wife.". . . Wearing boots and a blue peasant blouse, he was feted the day after at a dinner at which plans were announced for a great gala fund-raising banquet; its sponsors were, among others, Clemens, William Dean Howells, Finley Peter Dunne, and Jane Addams. "If we can build a Russian republic to give its persecuted peoples the same freedom which we enjoy," Clemens said that evening, with the guest of honor seated at his right, "let us by all means go on and do it." "Let there be light!" said a cartoon in the New York *World* on April 12; it showed the Statue of Liberty bending down to light Gorky's torch. The *World*'s cartoon the next day showed Mark Twain, a "Yankee in Czar Nicholas' Court," toppling the Romanov throne with a mighty push of his pen. ("The Czar's Soliloquy," Clemens' most extended statement on the subject, had appeared in March 1905 in the *North American Review*.) But by Saturday, April 14, just four days after Gorky's arrival, the honeymoon was over. In reprisal against Gorky, who, after all these nice gestures, had just signed an exclusive contract with a rival paper, Hearst's *American*, the *World* broke a story apparently based on information supplied by the Russian Embassy. "Gorky Brings Actress Here as 'Mme. Gorky'" the headline ran. Gorky's "young charming wife," as his inner circle of supporters had known and worried about from the start, was his mistress, Maria Andreyeva, an actress (he had been separated from his legal wife for years). . . . That Saturday

Naturally, I had my thoughts about such a remark. What right has a man to refuse to endure the anguish of knowing what other human beings are suffering? If these sufferings cannot be helped, why then perhaps we may flee from them; but think what the uncrowned king of America could have done, in the way of backing a young author who had aimed at the public's heart and by accident had hit it in the stomach! [Sinclair's book *The Jungle*, about the Chicago meat-packing industry, was intended to expose the evils of capitalism; instead it provoked horror at meat-packing practices and led to the enactment of the Pure Food and Drug Act.]

Then came the Gorki case. The great Russian writer came to America to plead for freedom for his country, and to raise money for the cause. The intriguers of the tsar set out to ruin

---

afternoon Albert Paine ran into Howells coming out of Clemens' house at 21 Fifth Avenue. Howells was wearing "an unhappy, hunted look"; upstairs was Clemens, agitated and brusque. Paine wondered if the two had quarreled; they had only been trying to solve the problem of what to do with the reporters downstairs. "I am a revolutionist—by birth, breeding, principle, and everything else," Clemens finally told them, but he explained that Gorky's "efficiency as a persuader" was now seriously "impaired"—"I was about to say destroyed"—by his violation of certain "laws of conduct." Soon after this he and Howells resigned as sponsors, and the fundraising banquet was abandoned.

It had been a remarkable week, the sociologist Franklin Giddings wrote in an article which Clemens found uncomfortably, remorselessly severe: In Missouri three innocent Negroes had just been physically lynched, in New York two visiting Russians had just been socially and morally lynched, and no one protested. There was no doubt that as advance man for the revolution Gorky had botched his job. He should have had a guardian to keep him out of trouble, Clemens said—"The man might just as well have appeared in public in his shirt-tail." Soon, in an attempt to justify his own uncomfortable retreat, he was saying that Gorky had violated custom and that this was worse than violating the law, because law is only sand, while "custom is custom; it is built of brass, boiler iron, granite; facts, reasonings, arguments have no more effect upon it than the idle winds have upon Gibraltar." Still, it was humiliating to have to postpone the liberation of 150,000,000 Russians just because one of them had left his pants at home.

Justin Kaplan, *Mr. Clemens and Mark Twain*, 1966.

him, and turned the bloodhounds of the capitalist press upon him. A dinner in Gorki's honor had been planned, and Mark Twain and William Dean Howells were among the sponsors. The storm of scandal broke, and these two great ones of American letters turned tail and fled to cover.

THE KING LIVED A DOUBLE LIFE

A year or two later Mark Twain was visiting Bermuda, and came to see me. He had taken to wearing a conspicuous white costume, and with his snow-white hair and mustache he was a picturesque figure. He chatted about past times, as old men like to do. I saw that he was kind, warm-hearted, and also full of rebellion against capitalist greed and knavery; but he was an old man, and a sick man, and I did not try to probe the mystery of his life. The worm which was gnawing at his heart was not revealed, until in the course of time his letters were given to the public. Now we know the amazing story—that Mark Twain lived a double life; he, the uncrowned king of America, was the most repressed personality, the most completely cowed, shamed, and tormented great man in the history of letters.

He was born in a Missouri River town in 1835. His father was a futile dreamer with a perpetual motion machine. His mother was a victim of patent medicines, who had seen better days, and reared a family of ragged brats in a foul and shabby environment, where a boy saw four separate murders with his own eyes. "Little Sam" was a shy, sensitive child, his mother's darling, and she raised him in a fierce determination to have him grow up respectable and rich. He became a printer, then a pilot on the Mississippi River. This latter was a great career; the river pilot was the uncrowned king of this western country. He saw all the world in glorious fashion, he was a real artist, and at the same time carried a solemn responsibility.

The Civil War destroyed this career, and Mark Twain went out to Nevada to become a gold miner, promising his mother that he would never return until he had made a fortune. He failed as a miner, and was forced to live by journalism. So he drifted into becoming the world's buffoon. He always despised it—so much so that he put a pistol to his head. But he lacked the courage to pull the trigger, and had to go on and be a writer. His "Jumping Frog" story went around the world; after which he came East, and wrote *Innocents Abroad*, and made his three hundred thousand dollars.

Shortly after that he exchanged the domination of his mother for that of a wife. He fell in love with the daughter of a wealthy coal-dealer in Elmira, New York. There was a terrible "to do" about it in respectable "up-State" circles, for Samuel Clemens was a wild and woolly westerner, who didn't know how to handle a knife and fork, while the daughter of the coal-dealer had been brought up on an income of forty thousand dollars a year. However, this strange lover was a "lion," so they decided to accept him and teach him parlor tricks. They gave the young couple a carriage and coachman, and a house which had cost twenty-five thousand dollars; it wasn't long before he was completely justifying their faith, by living at the rate of a hundred thousand a year.

The wife was a frail woman, a semi-invalid, and Mark Twain adored her; also, he was awe-stricken before her, because of her extremely high social position. She was ignorant, provincial, rigidly fixed in a narrow church-going respectability; by these standards she brought him up, and raised a couple of daughters to help him. As Clemens phrased it, his wife "edited" him; as his daughters phrased it, they "dusted papa off."

SUPPRESSING THE ARTIST'S VITALITY

What these women did to America's greatest humorist makes one of the most amazing stories in the history of culture. They went over everything he wrote and revised it according to the standards of the Elmira bourgeoisie. They suppressed the greater part of his most vital ideas, and kept him from finishing his most important works. When he wrote something commonplace and conventional they fell on his neck with delight, and helped to spend the fortune which it brought in. When he told the truth about America, or voiced his own conclusions about life, they forced him to burn it, or hide it in the bottom of a trunk. His one masterpiece, *Huckleberry Finn*, he wrote secretly at odd moments, taking many years at the task, and finally publishing it with anxiety. Mrs. Clemens came home from church one day, horrified by a rumor that her husband had put some swear words into a story; she made him produce the manuscript, in which poor Huck, telling how he can't live in the respectable world, exclaims: "They comb me all to hell." Now when you read *Huckleberry Finn*, you read: "They comb me all to thunder!"

Mark Twain had in him the making of one of the world's great satirists. He might have made over American civilization, by laughing it out of its shams and pretensions. But he was not permitted to express himself as an artist; he must emulate his father-in-law, the Elmira coal-dealer. The unhappy wretch turned his attention to business ventures, and started a huge publishing business, to publish his own and other books. He sold three hundred thousand copies of General Grant's Memoirs, and sold hundreds of thousands of copies of other books, utterly worthless from the literary point of view.

He was always at the mercy of inventors with some new scheme to make millions. For example, there was a typesetting machine; he sunk a huge fortune into that, and would spend his time figuring what he was going to make—so many millions that it almost made a billion. He was a wretched business man, and failed ignominiously and went into bankruptcy, losing his wife's money as well as his own. H.H. Rogers, master pirate of Standard Oil, came forward and took charge of his affairs, incidentally playing billiards with him until four o'clock every morning. And then some young radical brought him an exposure of the Standard Oil Company, expecting him to publish this book as a public service!

Going back to Mark Twain's books, we can read these facts between the lines, and see that he put his balked and cheated self, or some aspect of this self, into his characters. We understand how he poured his soul into Huck Finn; this poor henpecked genius, dressed up and made to go through the paces of a literary lion, yearns back to the days when he was a ragged urchin and was happy; Huck Finn and Tom Sawyer represent all that daring, that escape from the bourgeois world, which Sam Clemens dreamed but never achieved. He put another side of himself into Colonel Sellers, who imagined fortunes; and yet another side into Pudd'nhead Wilson, the village atheist who mocked at the shams of religion. Secretly Mark Twain himself loathed Christianity, and wrote a letter of cordial praise to [agnostic lecturer] Robert Ingersoll; but publicly he went to church every Sunday, escorting his saintly wife, according to the customs of Elmira!

A Double Personality

The more you read this story the more appalling you find it. This uncrowned king of America built up literally a double personality; he took to writing two sets of letters, one containing what he really wanted to say, and the other what his official public self was obliged to say. He accumulated a volume of "unmailed letters," one of the weirdest phenomena in literary history. He was indignant at the ending of the Russian-Japanese war, because he believed that if it had continued for a couple of months more the tsar would have been overthrown. When Colonel George Harvey invited him to dine with the Russian emissaries to the Portsmouth Conference he wrote a blistering telegram, in which he declared himself inferior as a humorist to those statesmen who had "turned the tragedy of a tremendous war into a gay and blithesome comedy." But he did not send that telegram; he sent another, full of such enraptured praise of the Russian diplomats that Count Witte sent it to the tsar!

That is only one sample out of many. He wrote a War Prayer, a grim satire upon the Christian custom of praying for victory. "I have told the whole truth in that," he said to a friend; and then added the lamentable conclusion: "Only dead men can tell the truth in this world. It can be published after I am dead." He explained the reason—this financier who had fortunes to blow in upon mechanical inventions: "I have a family to support, and I can't afford this kind of dissipation." And again: "The silent, colossal National Lie that is the support and confederate of all the tyrannies and shams and inequalities and unfairnesses that afflict the peoples—that is the one to throw bricks and sermons at. But let us be judicious and let somebody else begin."

A Humiliating Tragedy

Of course a man who wrote like this despised himself. It was the tragedy of Leo Tolstoi, but in a far more humiliating form; Tolstoi at least wrote what he pleased, and did in the end break with his family. But Mark Twain stayed in the chains of love and respectability—his bitterness boiling and steaming in him like a volcano, and breaking out here and there with glare and sulphurous fumes. "The damned and mangy human race," was one of his phrases; and again he wrote: "My idea of our civilization is that it is a shabby poor thing and full of cruelties, vanities, arrogances, meannesses and hypocrisies. As for the word, I hate the sound of it, for it conveys a lie; and as for the thing itself, I wish it was in hell, where it belongs."

In the effort to excuse himself, this repressed personality evolved a philosophy of fatalism. Man was merely a machine, and could not help doing what he did. This was put into a book, *What Is Man?* But then he dared not publish the book! "Am I honest?" he wrote, to a friend. "I give you my word of honor (privately) I am not. For seven years I have suppressed a book, which my conscience tells me I ought to publish. I hold it my duty to publish it. There are other difficult tasks I am equal to, but I am not equal to that one." He did publish the book at last, but anonymously, and with a preface explaining that he dared not sign his name.

He, America's greatest humorist, had a duty laid upon him; he saw that duty clearly—how clearly we learn from a story, "The Mysterious Stranger," a ferocious satire upon the human race, published after his death. In this book Satan asks:

> Will a day come when the race will detect the funniness of these juvenilities and laugh at them—and by laughing at them destroy them? For your race, in its poverty, has unquestionably one really effective weapon—laughter. Power, money, persuasion, supplication, persecution—these can lift at a colossal humbug—push it a little—weaken it a little, century by century; but only laughter can blow it to rags and atoms at a blast.... As a race, do you ever use it at all? No; you lack sense and the courage.

Such was the spiritual tragedy going on in the soul of a man who was going about New York, clad in a fancy white costume, smiled upon and applauded by all beholders, crowned by all critics, wined and dined by Standard Oil millionaires, dancing inexhaustibly until three or four o'clock in the morning, and nicknamed in higher social circles "the belle of New York."

The Great Critical Controversy

Philip S. Foner

When Van Wyck Brooks published *The Ordeal of Mark Twain* in 1920, he set off a major controversy among Twain analysts. Using the relatively new psychoanalytical tools of Freudianism, Brooks charged that several psychological and social factors had derailed Twain from realizing his full potential as a social satirist. His analysis was met head-on by Bernard De Voto, whose *Mark Twain's America* attacked Brooks's thesis, assumptions, and conclusions. Most Twain criticism written since 1920 has been affected by this controversy. Fortunately, the public has ignored the critics and continued to read Twain, rather than just reading about him.

In *America's Coming of Age*, published in 1915, Van Wyck Brooks had advanced the thesis that America's great democratic experiment had taken a false turn just after the Civil War when an acquisitive and corrupt business civilization had destroyed all that was worthwhile in the American tradition. This vulgar, money-grabbing, oppressive environment had proved fatal to creative talent, especially to writers who, except for Walt Whitman, had either compromised with the stultifying environment, conforming to its tastes and sharing its material rewards, or had sought escape in Europe.

The first critic to apply Brooks' general theory to specific cases was Waldo Frank who, in *Our America*, published in 1919, used Twain as one of two significant examples. First he dealt with Jack London, "corporeally mature, innerly a child," then more important, with Mark Twain, whose life he considered a failure. Though Twain was a greater writer capable of producing works of genius, he had capitulated to the mores of his time, and with one exception, *Huckleberry Finn*, published

Excerpted from Philip S. Foner, *Mark Twain: Social Critic*; ©1958 by International Publishers Co., Inc. Reprinted by permission of the publisher.

nothing of value. "His one great work was the result of a burst of spirit over the dikes of social inhibition and intellectual fears." Frank split Twain into two parts—a tendency of much modern criticism. There was the real, deeper Twain, the potentially great writer, and the clownish Twain who truckled to the standards of his time, produced worthless writings, and lost his soul in the process.

VAN WYCK BROOKS' *THE ORDEAL OF MARK TWAIN*

Waldo Frank devoted only a few pages to this thesis, but Van Wyck Brooks gave it a whole book: *The Ordeal of Mark Twain*, published in 1920. As the title itself indicates, Brooks rejected Albert Bigelow Paine's presentation of Twain's life as an unbroken success story, and contended, instead, that it had been a prolonged agony which had turned him into an embittered cynic: "That bitterness of his was the effect of a certain miscarriage in his creative life, a balked personality, an arrested development of which he was himself wholly unaware, but which for him destroyed the meaning of life."

Brooks' analysis of the reasons for Twain's "arrested development" was fundamentally simple. He claimed that there was in Twain the making of a great satirist—"the great purifying force with which nature had endowed him, but of the use of which his life deprived him." He could have been a Voltaire, a Swift, a Cervantes; indeed, "If anything is certain . . . it is that Mark Twain was intended to be a sort of American Rabelais who would have done, as regards the puritanical commercialism of the Gilded Age, very much what the author of *Pantagruel* did as regards the obsolescent medievalism of sixteenth-century France." But Twain's genius had been diverted from its true path into the production of humor by several factors—psychological and social: (1) his Calvinistic upbringing (mainly exemplified by his mother), which tended to inhibit all artistic creation; (2) his life on the frontier, beginning at Hannibal, a "desert of human sand," and continuing through his Nevada and California years, which forced him into the common mold of the pioneer, compelled him to repress all standards of individuality, and further stifled his creative impulses; (3) the softening influence of [his wife] Olivia Langdon Clemens, a product of the narrow, provincial Elmira horizon, and of William Dean Howells, and the other representatives of the genteel tradition. These three forces produced Mark Twain's bitter duality—the artist unsuccessfully striving to emerge through the clown, the resulting frustration manifesting itself in his pessimism.

> From his philosophy alone ... we can see that Mark Twain was a frustrated spirit, a victim of arrested development, and beyond this fact, as we know from innumerable instances the psychologists have placed before us, we need not look for an explanation of the chagrin of his old age. He had been balked, he had been divided, he had even been turned, as we shall see, against himself; the poet, the artist in him, consequently, had withered into the cynic and the whole man had become a spiritual valetudinarian.

"As we know from innumerable instances the psychologists have placed before us." In these words on page 2 of his book, Brooks announced his intention of applying psychoanalysis to literary criticism. The rest of the book is replete with Freudian interpretations of the details of Twain's life. For example, take the famous death-bed incident related by Paine—there is no other evidence that the incident ever took place. When Twain's father died, writes Paine, his mother led him to the coffin and there extracted the promise that he would be a good boy. The fact that the twelve-year-old boy walked in his sleep for several nights after the event leads Brooks to conclude that Twain was from then on a dual personality. In Brooks' opinion, the incident set the pattern for Twain's subsequent career:

> His "wish" to be an artist, which had been so frowned upon and had encountered such an insurmountable obstacle in the disapproval of his mother, was now repressed, more or less definitely, and another wish, that of winning approval, which inclines him to conform with public opinion, has supplanted it. The individual, in short, has given way to the type. The struggle between these two selves, these two tendencies, these two wishes or groups of wishes, was to continue throughout Mark Twain's life, and the poet, the artist, the individual, was to make a brave effort to survive. From the death of his father onward, however, his will was definitely enlisted on the side opposed to his essential instinct.

Twain's reluctance to become a reporter for the [Virginia City, Nevada] *Territorial Enterprise*, his choice of a pen-name, his dreams, even his drawl, are also interpreted in psychoanalytic terms, to prove the disintegration of the artist. So complete was that disintegration, in Brooks' eyes, that he regards nothing that Twain wrote as in any way approaching his potentialities—not even *Huckleberry Finn* and *Tom Sawyer*, about which he shared Arnold Bennett's opinion that they are "episodically magnificent," but "as complete works ... of quite inferior quality."

In his conclusion, Brooks cited the tragic fate of Mark Twain as an example of what happens to a writer who betrays his vocation and his country—for "if any country ever needed satire it is, and was, America"—and he pleaded with the writing fraternity to avoid the path of compromise Twain had followed: "Read, writers of America, the driven, disenchanted, anxious faces of your sensitive countrymen; remember the splendid parts your confères have played in the human drama of other times and other peoples, and ask yourselves whether the hour has not come to put away childish things and walk the stage as poets do."

THE ESSENCE OF HIS TEMPERAMENT

There seems a flat contradiction between the work and the public image, and the private personality. Yet we should avoid the stereotype of the tragic clown, and we need not assume that either Twain's despair or his humor must have been false. His view of the world—a continuous, amused perception of incongruity, of the discrepancies between convention, or ideal, or pretense, or supposition, and reality—was essentially humorous. To use his own term, that way of looking at life, combined with his verbal gifts, constituted his "call.". . . His depressions, as he well knew, were genuine and deep, but also brief. The essence of Mark Twain's temperament was its extraordinary mobility; he could no more be continuously despairing than he could be continuously laughing.

John Lauber, *The Making of Mark Twain*, 1985.

The Ordeal of Mark Twain has had a tremendous effect on Mark Twain criticism. Every book or article written about Twain since 1920 has had, as a matter of course, to weigh Brooks' thesis. As Edward Wagenknecht put it: "One may agree with Mr. Brooks or one may disagree with him. One may even disagree with him acrimoniously. The only thing that one cannot do with Mr. Brooks is to ignore him."

Brooks' interpretation created a literary sensation, and started a controversy which raged for almost a decade, and was revived in 1933, with the second "revised" edition of his work. (While there are some changes in details, there are few in viewpoint, the most significant being the toning down of derogatory references to Mrs. Clemens and the admission that Twain "accomplished a great deal.") Every literary magazine in the 'twenties carried articles and reviews (sometimes entire issues) which praised or condemned Brooks' thesis.

To the now familiar charges against Twain, the followers of Brooks added new ones such as that he was a man of "immeasurable conceit," a Philistine, and an exponent of Victorian sentimentality. (Brooks' followers included such critics as Lewis Mumford, Alfred Kreymborg, Vernon L. Parrington, Carl Van Doren, Fred Lewis Pattee, Granville Hicks, V.F. Calverton, Upton Sinclair, Edgar Lee Masters, Frank Harris.) But their central thesis was a restatement of Brooks': namely, that Mark Twain had failed to fulfill his promise, or to grow to his full stature, because he had sold out to the idols of the gilded age. Some of them carried Brooks' psychoanalytic method to further extremes. Thus Alfred Kreymborg, writing in the London *Spectator*, said:

> Mark Twain remained throughout his career a "fumbling, frantic child," with Howells as "his father confessor in literature," and with his family, led by that arch-Puritan, Mrs. Clemens, and his multitudes of friends and millions of readers serving as the unconscious ranks upon ranks of enemies who secretly crippled and killed the creator of at least one masterpiece: *Huck Finn*. Puritanism hemmed him in; he had to conform to innumerable taboos, religious, moral and social.

Not all of Brooks' followers, however, accepted his thesis uncritically. Some, like Carl Van Doren, agreeing that "the picture ... drawn of our great humorist is substantially accurate as well as brilliant," disagreed with Brooks' method, and regarded suspiciously "a good many of the details of his psychoanalyzing." Others felt that Brooks did not go far enough in analyzing the extent to which the social and economic changes in Twain's lifetime and his inability to understand them was responsible for his failure and his pessimism.

If several of Brooks' followers criticized some of his conclusions and methods, those who rejected his thesis were often violent in their reaction. They questioned both his "pseudo-Freudian method" and his derogatory evaluations of Twain's works; accused him of lacking a sense of humor and thus being temperamentally unfit to appraise Twain's achievements; charged that he devoted more space to what Twain might have been than to what he actually was; and claimed that his real target was not Twain but America and its institutions, and that these were never as hopelessly corrupt as Brooks assumed. Some critics insisted that, contrary to Brooks' opinion, Twain had never been repressed by his mother, his wife or Howells, and that the proof was that he expressed the boldest social views. Writing in the *Saturday Review of Literature in* 1924, an anonymous critic exclaimed:

Mark Twain was a radical.... His attack upon vested injustice, intolerance, and obscurantism in *A [Connecticut] Yankee at King Arthur's Court* and *The Prince and the Pauper* is quite as indignant as Samuel Butler's *The Way of All Flesh*. Critics forget the social courage of his anti-imperialism and the commercial courage of his onslaught upon Christian Science.

BERNARD DE VOTO'S *MARK TWAIN'S AMERICA*

By far the most significant answer to Brooks was Bernard De Voto's *Mark Twain's America*, published in 1932.

De Voto attacked Brooks' thesis mercilessly, and rejected all his conclusions. He charged Brooks with choosing only that evidence which bore out the "frustration" theory, and he proved that some of Brooks' most impressive psychoanalytical conclusions, like the famous oath which Twain is supposed to have taken in front of his father's coffin and which Brooks held to be the key to his subsequent ordeal, were based on the most fragile evidence. Going further, he pointed out factual errors in Brooks' book, and took Brooks to task for knowing nothing about Twain's background. He insisted that it was nonsense to assume, as Brooks did, that Twain's humor involved some surrender of his real desires. He denied Brooks' thesis that Twain really wanted to be a satirist, asserting that his "earliest impulses led to the production of humor and nothing whatever suggests any literary impulse or desire of any other kind." At the same time, De Voto denied that the production of humor was for Twain a safe retreat from social satire. In a scorching paragraph, he wrote:

> Criticism has said that he directed no humor against the abuses of his time: the fact is that research can find few elements of the age that Mark Twain did not burlesque, satirize, or deride. The whole obscene spectacle of government is passed in review—the presidency, the disintegration of power, the corruption of the electorate—bribery, depravity, subornation, the farce of the people's justice. Criticism has said that he assented in the social monstrosities of his period: yet the epithet with which criticism batters corrupt America, The Gilded Age, is his creation, and in the wide expanse of his books, there are few social ulcers that he does not probe. Criticism has said that he was incapable of ideas and all but anaesthetized against the intellectual ferment of the age: yet an idea is no less an idea because it is utilized for comedy, and whether you explore the descent of man, the rejection of progress, or the advances of feminism or the development of the insanity plea or the coalescence of labor, you will find it in that wide expanse.

De Voto flatly rejected a major contention of Brooks—that Olivia Clemens and William Dean Howells were guilty of suppressing Twain's real genius. Their revisions of Twain's manuscripts consisted of the deletion of a few slang words and the softening of statements likely to offend. Basically, the change in his writings wrought by these censors was purely verbal and in no way affected the content.

Many of the points De Voto raised to demolish the Brooks thesis had already been advanced by previous critics, though none had done the job so thoroughly and offered so much evidence to refute Brooks. What De Voto presented that was entirely new was an illuminating analysis of American frontier life, a contribution which he was singularly equipped to make, having experienced life in a frontier society himself.

Whereas Brooks and most of his followers argued that the frontier had thwarted Twain's creative impulses, De Voto demonstrated that it had actually shaped his genius. Indeed, he insisted that Twain was born at the right time and place to inherit and fulfill the tradition of back-country humor—especially since his appearance before the public had been well prepared by a generation of lesser Southwestern comic writers. Nor was this inheritance a barren one, as the Brooks' school contended. The frontier had a life of its own that was freer and more joyful than that on the [Atlantic] sea-board, with a culture whose ballads, stories, tall-tales, and folk-tales combined Negro, white, and Indian elements. All of this Twain absorbed and later embodied in his novels and stories. In short, Mark Twain's America—nineteenth century frontier life—laid the foundations for the fullest expression of his genius.

The reviews by Brooks' champions of De Voto's *Mark Twain's America* were bitter counter-counter-attacks. The De Voto thesis was ridiculed as "a shallow and romantic theory," his conception of Western society as "infantile," and his assertion that Twain had never "sold out" to the upper classes as mere wishful thinking. Most critics, however, treated *Mark Twain's America* as a significant contribution to American literary criticism, though many felt that De Voto, carried away by his desire to demolish the Brooks' thesis, had unreasonably painted everything white that Brooks had described as black. Furthermore, his book, in its overbalanced emphasis on Twain's Western surroundings, did not do full justice to the complete man and his career.

FOUR CRITICAL CAMPS

By 1935, the centenary of Mark Twain's birth, the critics were divided into four camps. There were the Brooks forces, who reiterated or extended the Brooks thesis that Twain had not fulfilled his potentialities as a great social satirist, but became a mere buffoon, and that if he saw the evils corrupting American life, he lacked the courage effectively to combat them. The opposed, followers of De Voto, among whom were John Macy, Max Eastman, C. Hartley Grattan, Minnie M. Brashear, and Cyril Clemens, while not accepting certain of De Voto's interpretations, agreed that there was no basis for the charge that Twain had allowed himself to be twisted out of the proper path of his genius. A third group, represented best by Edward Wagenknecht, whose *Mark Twain—The Man and His Work* was published in 1935, held aloof from the Brooks–De Voto controversy, and sought the truth somewhere between these two camps. The fourth group condemned both the Brooks and De Voto schools for devoting so much energy to analysing and psychoanalysing Mark Twain that they had none left for reading and studying his works. Fortunately, the people, who had never paid much attention to the critics, did what the analysts failed to do—they continued to read and to enjoy Mark Twain. "Mark Twain," wrote Charles H. Crompton in the *American Mercury*, after announcing that Brooks' and De Voto's books had bored him, "is today the most widely read American author, living or dead.... Do we need to feel concerned about what the critics say about Mark Twain? He has the same place that he always had in the hearts of the people, and in that place, he is secure."

Twain's Inescapable Disillusionment

Owen Wister

Although Mark Twain was not a man of arts and letters, he was deeply involved with life. His tempestuous nature as a boy helped him escape the dread of the Calvinist creed he grew up with. But the seeds of that creed, along with a new understanding of history, his disillusioning experience of America in the half-century following the Civil War, personal grief, and perhaps illness—all combined to nurture the bitterness of his later years.

That laughter was expected, and for a long while laughter only, from whatever Mark Twain wrote, is quite natural when you remember that he made his first appearance with *The Jumping Frog*. There ran a very different thread beneath, destined to be uppermost in after years. Plenty of seriousness can be found in *The Innocents Abroad*; but it was such passages as his finding the tomb of Adam at Jerusalem which caught the appreciation of his readers. "The tomb of Adam! How touching it was, here in a land of strangers, far away from home, and friends, and all who cared for me, thus to discover the grave of a blood relation. . . . I leaned upon a pillar and burst into tears. . . . Noble old man—he did not live to see me. . . ."

Habit dies hard. *Roughing It* and *Tom Sawyer* were not at first perceived to be better portraits of their period than any history has been. I remember (and this was during the 1890s) telling a dear old clergyman who had taught me Greek, Latin, and English twenty years before, that Mark Twain was a great writer and a master of style. He was utterly astonished. I sent him *Life on the Mississippi*. It converted him. He was precisely the cultivated, delicate, civilized American of college tradition and gentle background whom the spirit of *Innocents Abroad* shocked. That class of Americans bowed down too

Excerpted from Owen Wister, "In Homage to Mark Twain," in *The Family Mark Twain* (New York: Harper & Bros., 1935).

low to Europe and all her works; with them whatever was European was right.

Innocents Abroad was a sort of Declaration of Independence in matters æsthetic, and in several other matters too; the comment of a strong, original, raw, voraciously inquiring mind suddenly confronted with the civilized, complicated Past. Now and then it got his back up. In consequence he was too sweeping, and remained so. Do you remember his furious outburst against *Lohengrin*? A remark about the composer of that opera, made by Bill Nye, delighted him. "I am told that Wagner's music is better than it sounds." Well, that is certainly delightful: Nye and Clemens were chips of the same American block. Do you remember what Mark Twain says about St. Mark's of Venice? Or his wholesale scorn and rejection of the Old Masters? Do you remember his remarks about the "divine Hair Trunk of Bassano"? He will take no man's valuation but his own for Titian, Tintoretto, Giotto—anybody. Indeed he seldom takes it for anything, till in middle life he adopts W.D. Howells as his literary mentor. Beneath his genius, realistic and humorous, lies changeless independence of judgment. I think it is the foundation of his nature, the root of his upstanding moral and intellectual integrity. But it doesn't seem to have struck him that other people may have been occasionally right. Very American, this, of its epoch! We flourished ourselves and our institutions in the Old World's face, and defied it to show us anything there as good as everything here.

NOT ON CLOSE TERMS WITH ARTS AND LETTERS

Mark Twain never lived on close terms with either art or letters. At sixty-eight, Walter Scott becomes known to him, and he is amazed that such artificial trash should be admired until he reads and likes *Quentin Durward*. He speaks of paintings by their area and the number of figures in them. Of that folk melody, the "Lorelei," he says: "I could not endure it at first, but by and by it began to take hold of me, and now there is no tune that I like so well." No wonder that Wagner had small chance with him. What would he have had to say about the B-minor Mass [of Johann Sebastian Bach]? . . .

But if art and letters counted little with Mark Twain, no author ever lived on closer terms with life. It must have begun in the cradle. I wish I knew what the neighbors in Florida and Hannibal thought of that boy. Probably that he would come to a bad end. He gives us a glimpse of himself at ten, sent to bed early on board a Mississippi steamboat, haunted with visions

THE WAR-PRAYER

In Twain's 1905 short story "The War-Prayer," a patriotic congregation fills the church to celebrate the imminent departure of their young heroes-to-be and to pray for their victory. A mysterious stranger appears and asks the gathering to consider the full meaning of their prayer—"Grant us the victory, O Lord our God!"—and to be sure that this is what they wish for. The stranger's elaboration is reprinted here. The story ends: "It was believed afterwards, that the man was a lunatic, because there was no sense in what he said."

"When you have prayed for victory you have prayed for many unmentioned results which follow victory—*must* follow it, cannot help but follow it. Upon the listening spirit of God the Father fell also the unspoken part of the prayer. He commandeth me to put it into words. Listen!"

> O Lord, our Father, our young patriots, idols of our hearts, go forth to battle—be Thou near them! With them—in spirit—we also go forth from the sweet peace of our beloved firesides to smite the foe. O Lord, our God, help us to tear their soldiers to bloody shreds with our shells; help us to cover their smiling fields with the pale forms of their patriot dead; help us to drown the thunder of the guns with the shrieks of their wounded, writhing in pain; help us to lay waste their humble homes with a hurricane of fire; help us to wring the hearts of their unoffending widows with unavailing grief; help us to turn them out roofless with their little children to wander unfriended the wastes of their desolated land in rags and hunger and thirst, sport of the sun-flames of summer and the icy winds of winter, broken in spirit, worn with travail, imploring Thee for the refuge of the grave and denied it—for our sakes who adore Thee, Lord, blast their hopes, blight their lives, protract their bitter pilgrimage, make heavy their steps, water their way with their tears, stain the white snow with the blood of their wounded feet! We ask it, in the spirit of love, of Him Who is the Source of Love, and Who is the ever-faithful refuge and friend of all that are sore beset and seek His aid with humble and contrite hearts. Amen.

Mark Twain, *Europe and Elsewhere*, 1923.

---

of wreck, snags, and bursting boilers, and later rushing in a scanty shirt to the ladies' saloon with wild cries of fire, when a kind old lady stops her knitting and advises him to go and put on his breastpin. He gives us another at thirteen, when by a string of taunts he induces morbidly shy Jim Wolf, aged seventeen, to get out of bed, climb out on a steep roof covered with snow, and stop the noise of a couple of cats. He watches, hopeful and safe, from a window until Jim Wolf creeps near enough to make a grab at a cat, loses his balance, slides and pitches headlong into a vine-thatched shelter below, where a party of girls and youths are having a candy-pull. He describes some horrible, violent deaths that he witnessed in the street—and adds that his teaching and training enabled him to see that they were inventions of Providence to beguile him to a better life. It's not in joke that he records his early notion of God.

Think of this. This boy, this triple essence of boyhood, this tempestuous nature, boiling with curiosity, mischief, humor, imagination, desire for adventure, all in collision inside him with the Calvinistic dread of hell. His splendid animal vigor shakes him loose from that black creed. Presently he wanders far from Hannibal and hell; he shifts for himself, he goes east, he goes west, he sails the Pacific, he edits, he reports, he invents, is challenged to a duel, is recommended to leave Nevada; he meets with Ambrose Bierce, Bret Harte, with all those lesser birds of his own feather; he sails to the Old World, returns, matures, lectures, writes book upon book, article upon article; sees straight, speaks out; a master of horse sense and nonsense, in money matters a flighty child, protected from his plunges by H.H. Rogers. He helps to overthrow Croker and Tammany. He brings a brutal and extortionate cab-driver to justice, spends time and trouble, doesn't drop it, sees the case through. Never from his San Francisco attack upon a corrupt politics in the sixties to his defense of Harriet Shelley [as presented in Edward Dowden's *Life of Shelley*] and later, is he long without some public or private cause to champion, some victim to right or to defend. The torture of a soldier in the Philippines by a commissioned officer so enrages him that he can write nothing possible to print, and can only walk the floor and "curse out his fury at the race that had produced such a specimen." Disaster meets him, he meets it; travels, lectures, pays his debts, is received and honored by the world as no other American, save three presidents—Grant, Theodore Roosevelt, and Woodrow Wilson—has ever been; Kipling calls him "the great and god-like Clemens," and says Cervantes was a relation of his—why, what writer in any age has so lived to the hilt, has tasted such triumph? Yet, when all lies behind him, he can write in his notebook: "The offspring of riches: Pride, vanity, ostentation, arrogance, tyranny. The offspring of poverty: Greed, sordidness, envy, hate, malice, cruelty, meanness, lying, shirking, cheating, stealing, murder. We may not doubt that society in heaven consists mainly of undesirable persons."

That is not all. Not nearly all. That he had such friends as Joseph Twichell, H.H. Rogers, W.D. Howells counts nothing. In the indictment he lays against mankind he surpasses Voltaire and equals Swift. But why? What underlies this pilgrim's progress from the sunshine dawn of *The Jumping Frog*, through the noon splendor of *Huckleberry Finn*, to the sinister dusk of *The Man Who Corrupted Hadleyburg*, with its grim, disillusioned lesson? Most of us die saddened, but not embittered....

CHILDHOOD SEEDS AND CIVIL WAR

Doubtless one can shake loose from a creed; but the seed planted in us during childhood lurks and bides its hour. Soon or late, it will sprout in some fashion. Shall we suppose that monstrous, inhuman Calvinism has something to do with what happened to Mark Twain's gay, electric, adventurous spirit; that his New England blood and the vengeful God he had said his childish prayers to, fermented? We know that in the article in which his conscience takes shape outside him and he chases and vainly tries to catch it, he tells it that if he could he would give it to a yellow dog. Is that an indication? We know that he saw straight, thought straight, spoke out; that when an ugly truth stared him in the face he didn't shut his eyes—a rare thing with Americans. How could he witness the death of the rough, heroic Lincoln era, the birth of our many-headed greed, the quality of our congressmen of whom he never speaks without contempt, and not feel that at this point in our growth we were like certain apples which rot while they are still green? Moreover, he came late to his knowledge *and realization* of history—empire after empire fallen, faith after faith turned to mythology. This realization can tear a man's illusions up by the roots; not every nature is able to withstand the shock; Mark Twain's *The Mysterious Stranger* is a tale by one in the bottomless pit of pessimism. We know also that he had been mortally wounded by grief; and perhaps illness played a part. I think these several reasons combined are more likely to have evoked in him his hostile gloom than the single explanation advanced by Mr. Van Wyck Brooks. Well, Mark Twain and his literary kin were the direct product of a buoyant epoch, just as the rout of the Persians at Salamis produced the age of Pericles. I believe that what set in after our Civil War accounts for the change in this glowing spirit....

Read again, if you will, as I have, that chapter in Mr. Albert Bigelow Paine's admirable biography, where Clemens at sixty-seven returns to Hannibal and goes over all the old playgrounds and swimming places with the old men, the playmates who in the days of the Lincoln era had been Tom Sawyer and Huckleberry Finn. You will be deeply moved, I think; and you will see how alive were warmth and affection in that emotional spirit; and you will wish that no cup of bitterness had ever touched his lips. For among all our writers he is not only the most interesting figure, but also the best beloved.

Using the Vernacular for Humor

Henry Nash Smith

Mark Twain's work was shaped by two opposing forces, but they were not the frontier/West versus established tradition, as other critics have argued. Rather, Twain used native humor to emphasize the contrast between rural simplicity (often masking homely wisdom and rugged honesty) and empty elegance and refinement (reflecting values that seemed dominant in American culture). Since the characters' speech is the main method used to distinguish between "straight" and "low" characters, it is appropriate to use the term "vernacular" not only for the language of rustic characters but also for the values and ethical assumptions they represent.

We must make a special effort to avoid seeing Mark Twain merely as a spokesman for the emergent energies of the frontier, the West, in opposition to established tradition. Although Van Wyck Brooks's *The Ordeal of Mark Twain* (1920) and Bernard De Voto's *Mark Twain's America* (1932) are necessary starting points for the study of his work, both books are flawed by such a distortion. Brooks is correct in his perception that Mark Twain was hampered by the necessity for accommodating himself to conventional attitudes at variance with his deepest impulses; De Voto is also correct in emphasizing Mark Twain's debt to native American humor and the subversive character of his best work. But both critics draw too sharp a contrast between West and East, between the supposedly primitive frontier environment of Mark Twain's youth and the New England where he lived when he was writing his principal books. Hannibal and the Far West were not so primitive as Brooks imagined; the inhibitions with which Mark Twain struggled were not peculiar to the East, as De Voto implied,

Excerpted from Henry Nash Smith, *Mark Twain: The Development of a Writer*. Copyright ©1962 by the President and Fellows of Harvard College. Copyright © renewed 1990 by Elinor Lucas Smith. Reprinted by permission of Harvard University Press.

but were implanted in him by his boyhood environment more deeply than by any later experience. Nor was his audience predominantly Western. Some Western critics denounced him violently and some of the most enthusiastic praise of his work came from the East. His work was shaped by two opposed forces, but they cannot be neatly identified with different regions. The conflict was rather between the conventional assumptions he shared with most of his countrymen and an impulse to reject these assumptions, also widely shared, that found expression in humor.

THE BASE OF HIS LITERARY EXPRESSION

"The difference between the *almost right* word and the *right* word," Mark Twain affirmed, "is really a large matter—'tis the difference between the lightning-bug and the lightning." Throughout his writing life he respected the search for the exact word whole-heartedly. . . . In fact, he learned so many right words from his reading and his listening to the talk of thousands of men and women, of every sort and condition, and he mastered so thoroughly the art of "sentencing" them (the word is Robert Frost's), that he became the prime mover and shaker in a revolution in the language of fiction, a "renewal of language," as Frost was to put it. Just as Emerson had called for an American poet who spoke the language of the street, phrases strong as the oaths in a New England farmer's mouth, sentences that if cut "they bleed," and Whitman consciously answering the appeal created a new lingo for poetry, so Mark Twain responding to other appeals such as Southwestern humor created a new language for prose. Words in the mouth translated to the page with a skill that no one yet has properly measured—this is the base of his literary expression.

William M. Gibson, *The Art of Mark Twain*, 1976.

If geography has any meaning in this connection, it lies in the fact that spokesmen for the conventional American culture attempted to maintain a connection with Europe. On the other hand, the tradition of humor that shaped Mark Twain's apprenticeship was indigenous insofar as anything in our culture can properly be so called. The cult of oral storytelling in the United States dated from colonial times, and had long given prominence to humorous anecdotes. It had undergone a rapid subliterary development during the two or three decades preceding the Civil War when amateur and later semiprofessional writers both in New England and in the South began to commit oral humor to print on a large scale in newspapers, magazines, and eventually books. In all its varied forms—tales, dialogues, essays, sketches, dramatic skits—the most usual subject matter of this humor was the language and the attitudes ascribed to uneducated characters of inferior social status. Although the humorists often pretended to be illiterate, they were exploiting a contrast between rural simplicity and urban sophistication that has affinities with the tradition of literary pastoral. Uncouth manners and speech could easily become a mask for homely wisdom and rugged honesty that were an implicit indictment of empty elegance and refinement. Thus native humor provided Mark Twain with themes, situations, a style, and above all a point of view hostile to the values ostensibly dominant in American culture.

"Vernacular": A Broad Definition

The most obvious distinction between "straight" and "low" characters in writing of this sort lay in their speech; the exploitation of local dialects was one of the most common sources of comedy. It is therefore appropriate to use the term "vernacular" to designate not only the language of rustic or backwoods characters but also the values, the ethical and aesthetic assumptions, they represent. Here is the focus about which cluster the native instincts and discoveries George Santayana discerned in the work of the American humorists.

Mark Twain, H.L. Mencken, and "The Higher Goofyism"

C. Merton Babcock

Comparing Twain to American humorist H.L. (Henry Louis) Mencken (1880–1956) highlights both their similarities and their differences. Although they shot humor at many of the same targets, Twain's warm style helped people laugh at themselves while Mencken's acerbic wit poked a harsher brand of fun. Mencken, who shared with Twain the belief that human life is basically a comedy, was one of the few critics of his time who understood that Twain was "America's greatest humorist."

Beneath the velvet paw of Mark Twain's amiable humor lurks a cruel fang which on occasion turns heart-warming hilarity into rage. H.L. Mencken's raillery, too, is like the cracking of a whip. Both writers belong to the cantankerous school of American humor, or what Max Eastman has called "the higher goofyism." While there are wide differences in their manner, their aims and purposes were much the same: to strip man of his pretentious robes, his fig leaves, his good conduct medals; to prick his iridescent bubbles of arrogance and pomposity; to puncture his cherished illusions; to hold a loony mirror up to his miserable nature so he can see himself in all his ungainliness.

Judging from the public images created by the two men, one would suppose they belong in quite different leagues. Twain, the "wild humorist of the Pacific Slope," on the one hand, radiated warmth and cordiality, despite his rancor and deep-seated bitterness. He possessed a rare knack for making people laugh at themselves: their ridiculous shortcomings and preposterous inconsistencies. When the famous American stepped forward

---

Excerpted from C. Merton Babcock, "Mark Twain, Mencken, and 'the Higher Goofyism,'" *American Quarterly*, vol. 16, no. 4, Winter 1964, pp. 587-94. Copyright 1964, University of Pennsylvania. Reprinted by permission of the John Hopkins University Press.

to receive his degree at Oxford University, the Chancellor paid him reverential tribute. "Most amiable and charming sir," he said, "you shake the sides of the whole world with merriment."

Mencken, the "Sage of Baltimore," on the other hand, posed as "a gay fellow who heaves dead cats into sanctuaries and then goes roistering down the highways of the world." He gained notoriety as a peddler of blasphemy and special agent for the powers of darkness, and his volcanic eruption, during the boisterous years, created a popular image of the man whom Malcomb Moos has described as "a dragon slayer poised with a cutlass in one hand and a three-ton blockbuster in the other." Whereas most of Mark Twain's subscribers might willingly have traveled many miles to meet him, Mencken's readers coveted an opportunity to wash his filthy mouth with laundry soap, and they prayed fervently for his demise and damnation.

Tactics and Timing

The differences in the humor of the two men were largely matters of tactics and of timing. Mark Twain usually fooled along, measuring his pauses, slurring his points, stringing incongruities and absurdities together in seemingly purposeless fashion, deriving pleasure from sheer elaboration of detail, camouflaging his deviltry under heaps of tangled verbiage and rhetorical debris. In his piece on "Corn-pone Opinions," for example, he chatted along casually on the subject of American conformity and then dropped this innocent remark armed with a double stinger: "If Eve should come again in her ripe renown and re-introduce her quaint styles, well, we know what would happen." At the end of chapter 39 of *Huckleberry Finn*, in the note signed "Unknown Friend," Mark Twain planted a semantic trap of uncanny ingenuity and covered it up with a misplaced modifier. "I am one of the gang," the note reads, "but have got religgion, and wish to quit it and lead a honest life again, and will betray the helish design."

Such verbal prestidigitation was not in the Mencken manner. Mencken was brief, vivid, villainous. He derived a kind of sadistic delight in burning the witch-burners. Twain used a hangman's rope, in true frontier fashion, and spent a good deal of time preparing the fatal noose. Mencken preferred a switchblade. "This is the United States, God's favorite country," he once wrote to Theodore Dreiser. "The fun of living here does not lie in playing chopping block to the sanctified, but in outraging them and getting away with it." Mencken adapted his weapon to the enemy and to the fight. Up to a point it is all laughter, but after that "there is the flash of the knife, a show of the teeth." "Sometimes I try to spoof them," he said, "and sometimes I use a club." His characteristic method was to stir up a witch's brew of high-potency prose with equal parts of incongruity and hyperbole and then use it to toast the simpletons. "No more democrat than a turkey buzzard is an archangel," he said of one politician. He could describe democracy with such outlandish figures as "the loading of a pair of palpably tin cannon with blank cartridges charged with talcum powder" or as "the science and art of running the circus from the monkey cage.". . .

Despite these and other recognizable differences, the two scribblers had much in common. Both were born with a high percentage of sawdust in their blood. Both were practical jokers. Both recognized the "thundering paradoxes" of American life and addressed themselves to the task of turning the sanctified idols into absurdities. In setting forth the essences of Mark Twain's humor, Mencken actually defined his own brand of mirth: "a capacity to discover hidden and surprising relations between apparently disparate things, to penetrate to the hollowness of common assumptions, and to invent novel and arresting turns of speech." The kind of expression that clearly meets these requirements occurs in Mencken's *Smart Set* and the *Prejudices* as well as in Twain's *Roughing It* and *Huckleberry Finn*. . . .

HYMNS OF DISPRAISE

Both Twain and Mencken were adept at composing hymns of dispraise in what the latter called "the key of E flat minor." The Sage spoke of Vachel Lindsay's resounding meters as "Buddha chanting ragtime through a megaphone," "the Twentieth Century Express in a flower garden," "the doxology performed on a steam calliope," and "Billy Sunday and Bert Williams reciting the Beatitudes." Mark Twain berated James Fenimore Cooper's *Deerslayer* as "literary delirium tremens" and John Ruskin's highly-praised Victorian prose as "a cat having a fit in a platter of tomatoes."

Another trick in the repertoire of both humorists is that of taking incidental side-shots at religion and its promoters while aiming directly at other targets. Speaking of a novel by Henry James, Mark Twain said, "I would rather be damned to John Bunyan's heaven than read that." And Mencken, criticizing a Broadway comedian, said, "His work bears the same relation to acting properly so-called as that of a hangman, a midwife or a divorce lawyer bears to poetry, or that of a bishop to religion."...

MENCKEN ON TWAIN

Like Brander Matthews, Charles Miner Thompson predicted that it would not be long before *Huckleberry Finn* was acknowledged in America, as it had already been in England, as "the great American novel." And both were correct! In 1901, Professor Berrett Wendell of Harvard University described Twain's novel as "the most admirable work of literary art as yet produced in this continent." Eight years later, H.L. Mencken wrote that *Huckleberry Finn* was "worth, I believe, the complete works of Poe, Hawthorne, Cooper, Holmes, Howells and James, with the entire literary output to date of Indiana, Pennsylvania, and all the States south of the Potomac thrown in."...

What Is Man? and Other Essays, published in 1917, stimulated another outburst of enthusiasm for the keenness of Twain's social criticism. "The truth about Mark Twain," wrote H.L. Mencken in the *Smart Set*, "is that he was a colossus, that he stood head and shoulders above his country and his time, that even the combined pull of Puritanism without and philistinism within could not bring him down to the national level."

Philip S. Foner, *Mark Twain: Social Critic*, 1958.

While Mark Twain could crash a Boston tea party dressed as a cowpuncher, swinging a lariat and contaminating the poshy atmosphere with the crude lingo of the West, Mencken, posing as a city slicker, with the profane and lascivious accents of one slightly "spifflicated" on his tongue, could send prohibitionists, pedagogues and tinhorn politicians into what one writer has called "semi-incoherent fits of rage." Mark Twain made good use of every opportunity to insult "royalty." Mencken lavished his attention on the "boobs."

Perhaps this was the most remarkable difference between Twain and Mencken: that, whereas the former felt at home with the verbal patterns of unsophisticated people, the latter consistently depreciated the unintellectuality of homely idioms. Here are examples of their respective uses of the vernacular as a humorous device. In the first passage, Mark Twain is explaining how the Unabridged Dictionary made the popular reading list at Angel's Camp on the mining frontier. Books were scarce, and the cumbersome lexicon went "sashaying around from shanty to shanty and from camp to camp":

> Dyer can hunt quail or play seven-up as well as any man, understand, but he can't pronounce worth a cuss; he used to worry along well enough, though, till he'd flush one of them rattlers with a clatter of syllables as long as a string of sluice-boxes, and then he'd lose his grip and throw up his hand; and so finally Dick Stoker harnessed her, up there at his cabin, and sweated over her and cussed over her and rastled with her for as much as three weeks, night and day, till he got as far as R, and then passed her over to 'Lige Pickerell, and said she was the all-firedest dryest reading that ever *he* struck.

The second passage, from Mencken's translation of the Declaration of Independence into the patois of yokeldom, exhibits no such linguistic playfulness. On the contrary, it is an exercise in innuendo and carefully controlled mockery:

> When things get so balled up that the people of a country got to cut loose from some other country, and go it on their own hook, without asking no permission from nobody, excepting maybe God Almighty, then they ought to let everybody know why they done it, so that everybody can see they are not trying to put nothing over on nobody.

INGENIOUS WORDSPINNERS

... Twain and Mencken were both wordspinners of unusual ingenuity. While the former's verbal creations are examples of tall talk in the best Western tradition, the latter's contributions to the American language, like his witticisms, contain a snarl. The frontier screamer [Twain] could throw the lexicographers into a mental tailspin with words like *hogglebumgullop* or *preforeordestination*. Babylon's ring-tailed roarer [Mencken] could incite a riot among strip-tease artists by calling them *ecdysiasts*, or upset the emotional equilibrium of schoolma'ams with words like *dithrambophobia* or *grammatomaniac*. Perhaps his best contribution to a lexicon of wit is *booboisie*, which contains the essence of his social criticism, that "the lunatic fringe has begun to wag the underdog." Both writers could compose definitions of existing words that would make a lively supplement to Ambrose Bierce's *The Devil's Dictionary*. Mark Twain, for example, defined *puritanism* as "that kind of so-called housekeeping where they have six Bibles and no corkscrew." Mencken called it "the haunting fear that someone somewhere may be happy."

Mark Twain and Mencken fired their pieces at almost exactly the same targets: the "chiropractors" of prohibition, the "philistines" of art, the "undertakers" of religion and all manner of phony intellectuals. Both were deeply concerned with the moral depravity evident among those who posed as arbiters of American thought: scoundrels sobbing for prohibition while carrying a flask in their pockets, politicians trying to outlaw cigarettes while puffing away at their cigars, legislators attempting to repeal the law of natural selection by an Act of Congress. "The uplift has damn near ruined the country," Mencken wrote to one of his cronies. Mark Twain said, "When I reflect upon the number of disagreeable people who I know have gone to a better world, I am moved to lead a different life." After reading the morning paper, full of the usual "depravities and baseness and hypocrisies and cruelties that make up civilization," he put in the remainder of the day, Twain said, "pleading for the damnation of the human race." In one of his attacks on the national mentality, Mencken accused the uplifters of reducing the unknowable to the not worth knowing. Mark Twain concluded that God, having made man at the end of the work week, was obviously tired.

Mencken was well aware that public opinion denounced him, as it had denounced Mark Twain (in some circles at least), as hopelessly uncultured, disgustingly immoral and repulsively immature. He knew that the majority of his readers could find no wisdom in his political criticism, no real sense in his editorials and no genuine humor in his witticisms. He, of course, had helped provoke such opinion and had supplied overwhelming "evidence" in its support. Furthermore, he made no attempt to reverse the popular decision. Upon receipt of the most scathing note of retaliation from one he had insulted with his poisonous pen, he retorted with disconcerting courtesy: "Dear Sir–Perhaps you are right." This was his way of cutting off discussion and of reserving for himself the last and most exquisite laugh.

NOT JUST A CLOWN

Mencken was also fully aware, as Mark Twain was probably not, of the low esteem in which even the greatest of our comedians is held–of the truth, so strikingly expressed by E.B. White, that the world "decorates its serious writers with laurel and its wags with Brussels sprouts." In the case of Mark Twain, who strongly influenced the Sage's style, Mencken discovered, after careful inspection of the record, that the "learned authors" (between 1870 and 1900), without exception, had dismissed Mark as a clown "belonging to the lodge of Petroleum V. Nasby and Bill Nye." The thing that bothered Mencken was that Twain, who didn't realize that *Huckleberry*

Finn eclipsed all attempts at serious American humor, actually yielded to the apologetic appraisals himself. Mark Twain's humor surpassed that of men like Josh Billings and Artemus Ward, who belonged to the same comic tradition, in its mastery of the homely patterns of an indigenous folk literature compounded of the diverse elements that make up the cultural heritage of the American people. Mencken was one of the few critics of his day who understood what is now almost universally accepted: that Mark Twain was "America's greatest humorist." While the Sage possessed little if any of Twain's intuitive appreciation of the folk mentality, he shared with his literary kinsman a sincere belief that human life is basically a comedy and that happiness, as he himself put it, is "the capacity to detect and relish the comic touches in human tragedy."

Mark Twain and Mencken shared a disdain for the puerilities and pretenses of American life, and both men were severely "moral" in a way that average Americans cannot comprehend. Both men believed that the people Americans admire most extravagantly are the most daring liars, and the ones they detest most violently are those who try to tell them the truth. But Mark Twain had a streak of compassion in his makeup that Mencken did not possess. After heaping "blame after blame" and "censure after censure" upon one of his selected whipping boys, Mark Twain indulged in a moment of penitence for his caustic remarks. When his temper had cooled, he said, "It is my conviction that the human race is no proper target for harsh words and bitter criticisms." "It did not invent itself," he added, "and it had nothing to do with the planning of its weak and foolish character."

Mencken was equipped with a "petrified diaphragm" that was impervious to emotional appeals. He could laugh himself to sleep every night at what he called "the greatest show since Rome caved in." Speaking of a prank he once played on an unsuspecting victim, he said, "I shall recall it upon the scaffold, and so shock the sheriff with a macabre smile."

Twain's Twinning

Susan Gillman

A recurring theme in Twain's work is that of duality, of identities borrowed and exchanged. This fascination with the double personality appears in many works, including *Tom Sawyer*, *Huckleberry Finn*, *The Prince and the Pauper*, and *Pudd'nhead Wilson*—as well as in the author's own dual persona as Samuel L. Clemens and Mark Twain.

> *A book is the writer's secret life, the dark twin of a man.*
> —William Faulkner, *Mosquitoes*

Ever since William Dean Howells insisted in his 1910 memoir *My Mark Twain* on defying his own title and calling his friend "Clemens ... instead of Mark Twain, which seemed always somehow to mask him," the peculiarly double personality Samuel Clemens/Mark Twain has continued both to elude and to fascinate. A critical language of twinning, doubling, and impersonation has subsequently developed around this writer, in part fostered by what James Cox calls "the primal creative act of inventing Mark Twain." There is also all the fascination with alternate selves in his writing: the paired and disguised characters, the mistaken, switched, and assumed identities, the confidence men and frauds that everyone remembers as part of Twain's fictional world, even if they have read only *Tom Sawyer* and *Huckleberry Finn*. Gender and genetic twins seem especially to proliferate: lookalikes (*The Prince and the Pauper*), putative half-brothers (*Pudd'nhead Wilson*), Siamese twins (*Those Extraordinary Twins*), and characters such as Huck and Tom Driscoll who through imposture become twin selves of both genders. The writer also doubles himself through autobiographical projections within the fictions and by his pseudonym. As Howells recognized, though, the problem with these writerly doubles (as with the treatment of doubles/twins) is that they tend not only

Excerpted from *Dark Twins* by Susan Gillman (Chicago: University of Chicago Press, 1989). Copyright © 1989 by The University of Chicago. All rights reserved. Reprinted with permission from the author and the publisher.

to multiply confusingly but to entangle one another in complex ways.... Samuel Clemens himself invents a persona that not only becomes a second self but after a time enslaves the first, so that the twin Twain eclipses Clemens. "Mark the Double Twain," Theodore Dreiser once entitled a short critical piece on Samuel Clemens.

The proliferating doubles therefore seem frustratingly as much to mask as to reveal the self they also project. No wonder that the language of doubling used by Howells and others since has sought to identify the overlapping series of masks that constitute the writer's invented personae—funny man, satirist, public performer/reformer—and to situate these roles in the context of his life and times. The primacy of his biography was of course encouraged by Mark Twain himself as a writer of autobiographical fiction. Certain biographical explanations are repeatedly, almost ritualistically cited as evidence that Twain felt himself to be a man divided: he was a southerner living in the North; a frontier bohemian transplanted to urban life in genteel Hartford; an American who lived in Europe for at least ten years of his life; a rebel who criticized, inhabited, and even named the world of the Gilded Age.

The most insightful of Mark Twain's biographers, Justin Kaplan, recognizes that these biographical versions of dividedness were inflated by Mark Twain himself into the kind of legend that hides its subject by flaunting only a spectacular composite of his personality. In the suggestively titled *Mr. Clemens and Mark Twain*, Kaplan argues that even before the pseudonym Mark Twain had become an identity in itself and "swallowed up" Samuel Clemens, he was "already a double creature. He wanted to belong, but he also wanted to laugh from the outside. The Hartford literary gentleman lived inside the sagebrush bohemian."...

A FUNDAMENTAL SOCIAL ISSUE

Although Mark Twain writes obsessively about twinness, doubling for him was always less a literary than a social issue. Whether these lookalikes are random and contingent (such accused innocents as Muff Potter; the prince mistaken for a pauper; Huck Finn "born again" as Tom Sawyer) or willful and exploitative (the unexposed criminal Injun Joe; all Twain's confidence men), they raise a fundamental question: whether one can tell people apart, differentiate among them. Without such differentiation, social order, predicated as it is on division—of class, race, gender—is threatened. Thus Mark

Twain, champion of the subversive, also championed the law as one agent of control that resolves confusions about identity, restoring and enforcing the fundamental distinctions of society. A number of legal premises particularly fascinated him: that innocence and guilt are two distinct categories; that proofs in the form of legal evidence exist to back up that distinction; and that legal evidence is so rigorously defined as to constitute nearly "absolute" knowledge.

THE EMOTIONAL SOURCE OF HIS SOCIAL COMMENTARY

Twins again; two sets of twins in this enigmatic fable [*Pudd'nhead Wilson*] that provides a key insight into Mark Twain's life and art: his Twinish nature. The irrelevant Italian twins (who suggest how swiftly frontier society turned upon "foreign" royalty or European culture) lead us back to the original set of "white" and "black" twins who are interchanged—and hence interchangeable, despite all rigid racial taboos—and who constitute one of Mark Twain's most profound intuitions about not merely "the race problem" and the nature of slavery—but the nature of man himself. This shifting, enigmatic relationship of master and slave where the black child becomes the white child, and the white the black; where the seed of the "master race" becomes a perfect serf—and the scion of the submerged black race becomes a noxious, evil and degraded white "master": what a brilliantly disturbing central concept was *Pudd'nhead Wilson* based on! What contradictions, incongruities, contrarieties, hidden affinities, and polar oppositions does this mysterious fable suggest. . . .

The black slave who educates the white "master" in *Huck Finn*; the vagabond king and the king turned vagabond in *The Prince and the Pauper*; the central relationship of master-pilot and impudent cub in *Life on the Mississippi*—these are three obvious variations on this theme. It is quite true that these early meditations on black and white, master and slave, royalty and serfdom—and Twain's natural affinity with the black slave—were at the base of his later thinking, his mature role as America's conscience before the face of the world. This was the true emotional source of that whole later period of penetrating and prophetic social commentary; of that remarkable repudiation of a white Anglo-Saxon culture which was based on colonial conquest and oppression; and of that final identification with the dark-skinned races of the world which has made Mark Twain such a revered figure, not merely in revolutionary Russia, but in India, China, Asia, and South America today.

Maxwell Geismar, *Mark Twain: An American Prophet*, 1970.

In Mark Twain's fiction throughout the seventies and eighties, the law solves problems of identity by sorting out the captor/captive confusions in "Personal Habits of the Siamese Twins" (1869); by exonerating the falsely accused Muff Potter in *Tom Sawyer* (1876); and by rectifying the exchange of social identities in *The Prince and the Pauper* (1882). The problem, at once literary, social, economic, and legal, might better be called imposture than twinning or doubling, for by 1890 Twain is replacing the more legitimately confused, switched, or mistaken identities, which spill over in his fiction of the seventies and eighties, with the impostor, a figure of potentially illegitimate, indeterminate identity.

Yet imposture is a slippery term. Whereas twinning or doubling suggests merely mathematical division, imposture leads to a kind of logical vicious circle. Since "posture" already implies posing or faking, "imposture" is the pose of a pose, the fake of a fake: the word implies no possible return to any point of origin. Synonyms for imposture complicate this ambiguity by distinguishing degrees of intentionality on the part of the impostor. "Deceit," for example, is "strongly condemnatory" because it refers to "purposeful" deceiving or misleading, whereas "counterfeit" and "fake" may or may not condemn "depending on culpable intent to deceive." Thus imposture raises but does not resolve complex connections between morality and intentionality. Its multiple confusions leave room for lawyers, confidence men, and, ultimately, the writer himself to erase boundaries and circumvent the law, making suspect the premise that knowledge is possible—by legal or any other means.

An Ironic Capacity for Deception

P.T. Barnum, an artist at turning humbug into big business, recognized the difficulties in confining imposture to clear-cut boundaries. "Many persons have such a horror of being taken in," he noted shrewdly, "that they believe themselves to be a sham, and in this way are continually humbugging themselves." Mark Twain began his career by trading humorously on that horror, representing for entertainment the fictional impostors, including the deadpan narrators of frontier humor, that he observed in the world around him; he ended by getting entangled in the process of representation and convicting himself and his writing of imposture. In short, Twain initially assumed that imposture is a social problem that he could expose through the neutral lens of the writer's eye, but ended by turning that eye inward on himself and his own art. In the art of humor he discovered the same capacity for deception that he sought to expose in life. For imposture is intimately related to his art: the early journalistic hoaxes, the humor of the tall tale, even the humor of irony that works by making language itself duplicitous.

Clemens's extraordinarily successful self-creation as the humorist "Mark Twain" testifies both to his grasp of showmanship and to his exposure of all the attendant "anxieties of entertainment." In nineteenth-century America humor was perceived as a "popular" rather than a "serious" mode, and fame as a humorist was not easy to transcend. Still worse, the role of humorist, which Mark Twain alternately exploited and railed against, put him in the ambiguous position of being lionized by his own targets of derision. Telling tales about people being duped, Mark Twain reflects his own ambivalent relationship to his audience, those he entertained quite literally at their own expense. Kenneth Burke's comment on irony helps to discriminate the tangled boundaries among Twain, his art, and his audience: "True irony is based upon a sense of fundamental kinship with the enemy, as one *needs* him, is *indebted* to him, is not merely outside him as an observer but contains him *within*, being consubstantial with him." Mark Twain, wearing the mask of the ironic stranger observing the human race of "cowards," ultimately unmasks himself and discovers that he is "not only marching in that procession but carrying the banner."...

Twain was bitterly aware of the double bind of his success as an artist. "Playing professional humorist before the public" gave him a voice and an audience, he reflected late in life in his autobiography, but it was to the exclusion of other, more serious voices and at the cost of other, more serious audiences. Even as early as 1874, he wrote to William Dean Howells that his preferred audience was that of the highbrow *Atlantic Monthly*, "for the simple reason that it don't require a 'humorist' to paint himself striped & stand on his head every fifteen minutes." It was in part the ambiguities of his status as an artist—humorist or serious writer? master of audiences or their slave?—that led Twain to ... what he called in a January 1898 notebook entry the "haunting mystery" of "our duality."

A Short Summary of Some of Twain's Sources

Edward Wagenknecht

Mark Twain drew from many sources, both fictional and real, for his characters and settings. He made the material taken from his sources part of himself and through this assimilation transformed it into his own creations.

Mark Twain's use of literary materials in his travel writings ... began early; even his Philadelphia letters in the Muscatine *Journal* use material from R.A. Smith's *Philadelphia as It Is in 1852*. But the tendency is not confined to travel writings or to nonfiction either. It may be doubted that any modern writer has used "sources" more freely than Mark Twain.

NO AUTHOR EVER CREATED A CHARACTER

It was, of course, quite in accord with the philosophy of life to which he was committed in later years that he should do so. Just before he started out on his world tour, he told a newspaper interviewer in Portland, Oregon: "I don't believe an author, good, bad, or indifferent, ever lived, who created a character. It was always drawn from his recollection of someone he had known. ... We mortals can't create, we can only copy. Some copies are good and some are bad." And what applied to characterization applied as well to other aspects of literary work.

The matter may be studied in terms of general literary influences and also in terms of specific sources.

Mark Twain never wrote an essay on "Books That Have Influenced Me"; if he had, he must surely have begun with the Bible. Professor Henry A. Pochmann counted 124 Biblical allusions in his writing—eighty-nine of them, to be sure, in

Excerpted from Edward Wagenknecht, *Mark Twain: The Man and His Work*. Copyright © 1935 by Edward Wagenknecht; rights assigned for revised edition in 1961 to the University of Oklahoma Press; revised rights renewed in 1989 by Edward Wagenknecht. Reprinted by the permission of Russell & Volkening, as agents for the author.

the *Innocents*—far more than to any other book or writer. But not only does Mark Twain quote the Bible; he burlesques it; he takes the reader's knowledge of it absolutely for granted; he derives from it in every conceivable way. Charles W. Stoddard has described the thrilling beauty of his reading, one night in London, from the Book of Ruth. It is not difficult to agree with Paine that the limpid beauty and simplicity of Mark Twain's style at its best owe much to that well of English undefiled.

THE ORIGINAL HUCKLEBERRY FINN

"Huckleberry Finn" was Tom Blankenship.... [In] the Hannibal of the 'forties, ... Tom's father was at one time Town Drunkard, an exceedingly well-defined and unofficial office of those days. He succeeded General—(I forget the General's name) [Games] and for a time he was sole and only incumbent of the office; but afterward Jimmy Finn proved competency and disputed the place with him, so we had two town drunkards at one time—and it made as much trouble in that village as Christendom experienced in the fourteenth century, when there were two Popes at the same time.

In *Huckleberry Finn* I have drawn Tom Blankenship exactly as he was. He was ignorant, unwashed, insufficiently fed; but he had as good a heart as ever any boy had. His liberties were totally unrestricted. He was the only really independent person—boy or man—in the community, and by consequence he was tranquilly and continuously happy and was envied by all the rest of us. We liked him; we enjoyed his society. And as his society was forbidden us by our parents, the prohibition trebled and quadrupled its value, and therefore we sought and got more of his society than of any other boy's. I heard, four years ago, that he was justice of the peace in a remote village in Montana and was a good citizen and greatly respected.

Mark Twain, *The Autobiography of Mark Twain*, Charles Neider, ed., 1959.

Next to the Bible, the most important influence was that of Cervantes. This was pointed out in detail by Olin H. Moore as far back as 1922. This was the first literary influence to be studied in detail, and authorities on Mark Twain kicked hard against the pricks in their reluctance to accept it, but their struggles were in vain, for Mark had made his acknowledgment in *Huckleberry Finn* itself. Tom Sawyer is the Don Quixote to Huck Finn's Sancho Panza. Tom, like the Don, is an omnivorous reader who seeks to act out romantic adventures in his own experience, and some of the dialogue between the two boys follows the conversations between Don Quixote and Sancho Panza very closely. The picnic scene in *Tom Sawyer* is clearly indebted to the Don's attack upon the sheep, as well as to his adventures when he tries to halt the funeral procession. But *Tom Sawyer* did not represent Mark Twain's first use of this material; neither was it the last. Sancho and the Don had already appeared in the *Alta California* letters of 1866-67, which have now been reprinted as *Mark Twain's Travels with Mr. Brown*; in *A Connecticut Yankee*, Alisande was to enact Don Quixote and the Yankee himself his squire.

Minnie M. Brashear feels strongly that Mark Twain was importantly influenced by eighteenth-century writers. His strong social interest expresses itself in his passion for biography, diaries, and letters—all popular forms in the age of Queen Anne. This period was also greatly interested in the "character." Brashear found "Sir Roger at the Play" in the early Snodgrass letter on *Julius Caesar*, and pointed out that *The Spectator* was well known in the Middle West. The eighteenth century was also interested in fables, moralized legends, and maxims. She was able to do little with the fables, but there are plenty of maxims. Moralized legends appear in "The Man That Corrupted Hadleyburg," "The $30,000 Bequest," "Was It Heaven or Hell?," "A Dog's Tale," and "A Horse's Tale," the last two being "almost sentimental documents to illustrate the XVIII Century doctrine of nature's social union."

Brashear may have overstated the case for eighteenth-century influence upon Mark Twain; certainly his thinking was more influenced by nineteenth-century scientific writing than she believed. Jonathan Swift is the eighteenth-century writer with whom it is most interesting to compare him, but little or no direct influence can here be traced. There is one vague reference to Swift in *Roughing It*, and H.W. Fisher reports that Mark Twain once denounced Swift as a sadist and masochist whom it would be a waste of time to try to explain, but Mark seems to have only the vaguest information concerning Swift: he is not even certain when he lived. Friederich Schönemann compares Swift and Mark Twain interestingly, without actually asserting influence, and finds many parallels. Swift's attitude toward animals, as providing a refuge from the contemptible character of mankind, is interesting in this connection also.

Oliver Goldsmith was another matter. The Goldsmith of *The Vicar of Wakefield* was anathema, but the essayist was another story. Mark Twain knew him well at an early stage, and

Schönemann's suggestion that he may have influenced not only the "colloquial ease" of the American's style but even his philosophy of history is not altogether unreasonable. His most direct imitation of Goldsmith was in the essay "Goldsmith's Friend Abroad Again," that noble protest against the inhumanity shown by Americans to the Chinese on the Pacific Coast (this may now be read in *The Curious Republic of Gondour and Other Whimsical Sketches*), but Paul Fatout has most interestingly shown reason to suppose that Mark Twain's account of some of the circumstances of his first lecture, as related in *Roughing It*, may be fiction, suggested by Goldsmith's experiences on the first night of *She Stoops to Conquer*, as reported by Washington Irving.

Some points about Mark Twain's use of specific sources are too obvious to require discussion. The use of Thomas Malory in *A Connecticut Yankee* has always been clear, and everybody knows that "A Double-Barrelled Detective Story" took its point of departure from Sherlock Holmes, and *Captain Stormfield's Visit to Heaven* from *The Gates Ajar*, by Elizabeth Stuart Phelps, as everybody knows also that *Tom Sawyer, Detective* Americanizes a Danish novel, *The Parson of Vejlby*, by Steen Steensen Blicher, which Mark Twain heard about through Lillie de Hegermann-Lindencrone. Nobody would expect Mark Twain to be able to write *The Prince and the Pauper* or *Personal Recollections of Joan of Arc* without studying historical sources, though he did a more thorough job for the *Joan of Arc* at least than he is often given credit for, and it is surprising—and also illuminating for the understanding of his methods—that he should have used a Sut Lovingood story [by George W. Harris]—American as corn on the cob—along with all his French and British materials. Some of the sources that have been suggested are, of course, conjectural—like Miss Gladys Carmen Bellamy's suggestion that the death of Laura Hawkins in *The Gilded Age* is indebted to Hawthorne's description of Judge Pyncheon's end in *The House of the Seven Gables*, or Kenneth Lynn's idea that Roxy in *Pudd'nhead Wilson* may have been derived from Cassy in *Uncle Tom's Cabin*. There is no reasonable room for doubt, however, that *Tom Sawyer Abroad* uses material from Jules Verne's *Five Weeks in a Balloon*, and we know that Mark Twain prepared for sending Tom and Huck out among the Indians by ordering some "personal narratives" of life on the Plains.

It may seem surprising that a work like *The Mysterious Stranger* should have had so many literary connections, but the great surprise is *Huckleberry Finn*, which has now been shown to have had almost as many sources (one is tempted to say) as Reade's *The Cloister and the Hearth*, including *The Arabian Nights*, *The Lady of the Lake*, Carlyle's *The French Revolution*, Dickens's *A Tale of Two Cities*, Bird's *Nick of the Woods*, Mark's own *The Prince and the Pauper*, and (for that matter!) *The Cloister and the Hearth* itself. This is much too complicated to summarize here; the reader must go to Walter Blair's amazing adventure in scholarship, *Mark Twain and "Huck Finn,"* a necessity not to be lamented since this is a reading adventure second in enlightenment and pleasure only to *Huckleberry Finn* itself and one of which no sensible admirer of Mark Twain would willingly deprive himself.

DRAWING FROM LIFE

If this be true, why, then, do *Huckleberry Finn* and the rest of Mark Twain's best writings make such a strong impression of freshness and originality upon us that he has actually been called a folk artist? The answer is simple. Mark Twain drew a great deal from his reading, but he also drew a great deal from life. Moreover, he used what he read like an artist, not like a reporter; he assimilated it, as Chaucer did, and made it a part of himself. By the time he got through, he himself could not have told where he had got it; neither did it matter; for when a man reads as creatively as Mark Twain read, reading and experience and imagination become one. I have already noted Paul Fatout's suggestion that his description of the circumstances surrounding his first lecture may have been borrowed from Goldsmith. But Professor Walter Blair throws out an even more startling idea when he suggests that when Mark reported that his mother drowned kittens when she had to but always warmed the water first, he may have been thinking not about his mother, Jane Clemens, but about B.P. Shillaber's Mrs. Partington! Certainly Mrs. Partington resembled Aunt Polly (who was Jane Clemens), and her picture was used for Aunt Polly in the first edition of *Tom Sawyer*.

If Tom's Aunt Polly was indebted to Mark Twain's mother, then Judge Thatcher was his father, Sid was drawn from his brother Henry, and his sister Pamela furnished the original of Cousin Mary. Huck Finn is Tom Blankenship, the village vagabond; Nigger Jim was derived from Uncle Dan'l, a slave on the plantation owned by Uncle John Quarles. Tom Blankenship's father was town drunkard in Hannibal, as Huck's father is in the book, and Injun Joe was another local character, though the reality was much less vicious than the fiction. The "Duke" was a journeyman printer, whom Mark Twain met, at a later date, in Virginia City. Or at least all these identifications have been made. According to the preface, Tom Sawyer, too, was drawn from life, "but not from an individual—he is a combination of the characteristics of three boys whom I knew." It is no secret that the most important of these was named Sam Clemens.

Mark Twain used actual places as well as persons in his stories. John Quarles's farm was moved down to Arkansas both in *Huckleberry Finn* and in *Tom Sawyer, Detective*. "It was all of six hundred miles," said Mark Twain, "but it was no trouble; it was not a very large farm—five hundred acres, perhaps—but I could have done it if it had been twice as large."

I must not leave the impression that Professor Blair confines himself, in *Mark Twain and "Huck Finn,"* to describing the sources of the book in Mark Twain's reading; the sources indicated in his living are quite as impressive. Nor were the Mississippi books unique in this regard. *The Gilded Age* is full of contemporary references. Contemporary readers must have been immediately aware of the use made of the scandals involving the notorious Senator Pomeroy of Kansas, as well as the Fair-Crittenden murder case in San Francisco, and James Harvey Young has reasonably suggested that Ruth Bolton may have been taken in part from Anna Dickinson, whom Mark Twain seems to have admired. More interestingly, Fred W. Lorch has shown that many of the basic feudal concepts and practices which Mark Twain portrays and attacks in *A Connecticut Yankee* were actually observed by him in operation in the Sandwich [Hawaiian] Islands, when he visited there, and that up to a point the Yankee plays the same role in sixth-century England that the missionaries were enacting in Hawaii.

Whether Mark Twain got more material from literature or from life, there would seem to be no question that the material he got from life was the more vital. What he got from books was equally useful, but he could not use it until after it had been vitalized by his experience; his experience provided him with the means of making it seem real. Life vitalized literature; literature did not simply provide a means of escape from life, as is the case with later writers. As he grew older, his memory relinquished its hold on facts, but it retained impressions tenaciously. He may have stretched it a little when he described Tom Sawyer as belonging "to the composite order of architecture," but there are many things in his books which do belong to that order. So the last word belonged neither to reading nor to experience but to imagination. If he made himself Goldsmith and his mother Mrs. Partington, he altered what he saw and experienced no less freely than what he had read. The St. Petersburg of *Tom Sawyer* and *Huckleberry Finn* is not Hannibal, Missouri; it is a created town that has grown out of Hannibal, and the alterations made by Mark Twain have been determined by his artistic purposes. In his pages Mississippi steamboating moves away from cutthroat competition and becomes an idyll. The original of Widow Douglas was a woman of Hannibal, but the Widow Douglas is a much lovelier person than her prototype had been. In life, Injun Joe did not die in the cave, though he was lost there on one occasion, and Huck Finn's refusal to surrender Jim was based upon a very different set of circumstances in the life of Tom Blankenship.

"The ancients stole our best thoughts," and Mark Twain's originality was the only kind that is possible for a modern writer. His art was the art that conceals art. As he himself once observed, "Shakespeare took other people's quartz and extracted the gold from it—it was a nearly valueless commodity before."

A Turning Point in American Literature

Gerald Parshall

Although *The Adventures of Huckleberry Finn* has been found objectionable by some ever since it was published in 1885, others call it not only "the great American novel" but also "one of the world's best books." It is considered a seminal work by many major American authors.

> *All modern American literature comes from one book by Mark Twain called* Huckleberry Finn.
>
> —Ernest Hemingway

You don't know about me, without you have read a book by the name of *Adventures of Huckleberry Finn*, or read about it. The book was made by me and Mr. Mark Twain, and we told the truth, mainly. Professors today say it's a "masterpiece," which is the way they talk when they like a thing considerable. But back in 1885, the book no sooner come out than the quality was pecking at it. The *New York World* claimed it was "hackwork" and "rubbish." The *Boston Transcript* called it "coarse," the Concord Public Library throwed it out as "more suited to the slums than to . . . respectable people" and Louisa May Alcott, a lady author who made a book named *Little Women*, laid into Mr. Twain for pointing "our pure-minded lads and lasses" toward perdition.

I felt so dreadful blue I most wished I was dead. Mr. Mark Twain was getting bullyragged just for writing up what I said I done and what others done. You see, there was two schools of storytelling then. One was called Romantic, though it didn't have nothing to do with spooning. Romantic authors, they dressed up life in Sunday School clothes. But Mr. Mark Twain, a pioneer of what they called Realism, he showed life naked.

Gerald Parshall, "Huck Finn Adds a Postscript," *U.S. News & World Report*, April 22, 1991. Copyright 1991, U.S. News & World Report. Reprinted with permission.

Ruther than making mudcats like me sound highfalutin and respectable, which we warn't, he let on how we really talked.

Even so, there was sivilized people on our side, too, and plenty of common folk. And come 1891, a big critic they had over in England, Andrew Lang, called *Huckleberry Finn* "the great American novel." The professors has been praising us ever since, like to bust. Prof. William Lyon Phelps wrote in 1924 that "*Huckleberry Finn* is not only the great American novel. It is America." Prof. Lionel Trilling he didn't stop there. He said in 1950 that we was "one of the world's great books."

Mr. Twain decided to make the book pretty much just to keep bacon and cornpone on the table. But now his "simple, direct and fluent" sentences and his raising of "the vernacular to a great style" is credited with cutting a channel for most of the big-bug authors who come through later like Mr. Jack London, Mr. O. Henry, Mr. Theodore Dreiser, Mr. F. Scott Fitzgerald, Mr. Sinclair Lewis, Mr. Ring Lardner, Mr. John Dos Passos and Mr. Ernest Hemingway. The professors has cooked up more than 500 articles and more than a dozen whole books on the goings-on on that ol' 12-by-16-foot raft—more than they has inflicted on any other American novel. They call the book a Seminole work, though I'm blest if can see why, Injuns warn't no help at all on it.

Well, if I'm to tell the whole truth, I reckon I should put in here that we is still banned from some classrooms. Mostly it's 'cause I called Jim, Miss Watson's runaway slave, a "nigger." I called Jim a "nigger" 'cause that's the way I was brung up. You'll notice that I also helped him escape even though I'd been learned this was a bad sin—and I promised myself to "go to hell" ruther than turn him in. What I done, the professors like to explain, was spit on "conventional morality" to follow my heart, which is what true morality's all about, they says.

A galoot named T.S. Eliot once wrote that I am "one of the permanent symbolic figures of fiction," fit to take my place beside Ulysses and Hamlet. If they can stand the company I expect I can.

Three Coherent Elements in *Huckleberry Finn*

Henry Nash Smith

The Adventures of Huckleberry Finn follows three interweaving threads: adventure, social satire, and the developing character of Huck. The basic coherence of these interrelated parts indicates that Twain had all three in mind as he began writing, although they become deeper and richer in the later sections of the book. The exploration of Huck's psyche is the book's ultimate achievement.

Huckleberry Finn contains three main elements. The most conspicuous is the story of Huck's and Jim's adventures in their flight toward freedom. Jim is running away from actual slavery, Huck from the cruelty of his father, from the well-intentioned "sivilizing" efforts of Miss Watson and the Widow Douglas, from respectability and routine in general. The second element in the novel is social satire of the towns along the river. The satire is often transcendently funny, especially in episodes involving the rascally Duke and King, but it can also deal in appalling violence, as in the Grangerford-Shepherdson feud or Colonel Sherburn's murder of the helpless Boggs. The third major element in the book is the developing characterization of Huck.

All three elements must have been present to Mark Twain's mind in some sense from the beginning, for much of the book's greatness lies in its basic coherence, the complex interrelation of its parts. Nevertheless, the intensive study devoted to it in recent years, particularly Walter Blair's establishment of the chronology of its composition, has demonstrated that Mark Twain's search for a structure capable of doing justice to his conceptions of theme and character passed through sever-

Excerpted from Henry Nash Smith, *Mark Twain: The Development of a Writer*. Copyright ©1962 by the President and Fellows of Harvard College. Copyright © renewed 1990 by Elinor Lucas Smith. Reprinted by permission of Harvard University Press.

al stages. He did not see clearly where he was going when he began to write, and we can observe him in the act of making discoveries both in meaning and in method as he goes along.

The narrative tends to increase in depth as it moves from the adventure story of the early chapters into the social satire of the long middle section, and thence to the ultimate psychological penetration of Huck's character in the moral crisis of Chapter 31. Since the crisis is brought on by the shock of the definitive failure of Huck's effort to help Jim, it marks the real end of the quest for freedom. The perplexing final sequence on the Phelps plantation is best regarded as a maneuver by which Mark Twain beats his way back from incipient tragedy to the comic resolution called for by the original conception of the story. . . .

The difficulty of imagining a successful outcome for Huck's and Jim's quest had troubled Mark Twain almost from the beginning of his work on the book. After writing the first section in 1876 he laid aside his manuscript near the end of Chapter 16. The narrative plan with which he had impulsively begun had run into difficulties. When Huck and Jim shove off from Jackson's Island on their section of a lumber raft (at the end of Chapter 11) they do so in haste, to escape the immediate danger of the slave hunters Huck has learned about from Mrs. Loftus. No long-range plan is mentioned until the beginning of Chapter 15, when Huck says that at Cairo they intended to "sell the raft and get on a steamboat and go way up the Ohio amongst the free states, and then be out of trouble." But they drift past Cairo in the fog, and a substitute plan of making their way back up to the mouth of the Ohio in their canoe is frustrated when the canoe disappears while they are sleeping: "we talked about what we better do, and found there warn't no way but just to go along down with the raft till we got a chance to buy a canoe to go back in." Drifting downstream with the current, however, could not be reconciled with the plan to free Jim by transporting him up the Ohio; hence the temporary abandonment of the story.

A CHANGE OF PLAN

When Mark Twain took up his manuscript again in 1879, after an interval of three years, he had decided upon a different plan for the narrative. Instead of concentrating on the story of Huck's and Jim's escape, he now launched into a satiric description of the society of the prewar South. Huck was essential to this purpose, for Mark Twain meant to view his subject ironically through Huck's eyes. But Jim was more or less superfluous. During Chapters 17 and 18, devoted to the Grangerford household and the feud, Jim has disappeared from the story. Mark Twain had apparently not yet found a way to combine social satire with the narrative scheme of Huck's and Jim's journey on the raft.

While he was writing his chapter about the feud, however, he thought of a plausible device to keep Huck and Jim floating southward while he continued his panoramic survey of the towns along the river. The device was the introduction of the Duke and the King. In Chapter 19 they come aboard the raft, take charge at once, and hold Huck and Jim in virtual captivity. In this fashion the narrative can preserve the overall form of a journey down the river while providing ample opportunity for satire when Huck accompanies the two rascals on their forays ashore. But only the outward form of the journey is retained. Its meaning has changed, for Huck's and Jim's quest for freedom has in effect come to an end. Jim is physically present but he assumes an entirely passive role, and is hidden with the raft for considerable periods. Huck is also essentially passive; his function now is that of an observer....

HUCK'S DIALOGUES WITH HIS CONSCIENCE

The introduction of the Duke and the King not only took care of the awkwardness in the plot but also allowed Mark Twain to postpone the exploration of Huck's moral dilemma. If Huck is not a free agent he is not responsible for what happens and is spared the agonies of choice. Throughout the long middle section, while he is primarily an observer, he is free of inner conflict because he is endowed by implication with Mark Twain's own unambiguous attitude toward the fraud and folly he witnesses.

In Chapter 31, however, Huck escapes from his captors and faces once again the responsibility for deciding on a course of action. His situation is much more desperate than it had been at the time of his first struggle with his conscience. The raft has borne Jim hundreds of miles downstream from the pathway of escape and the King has turned him over to Silas Phelps as a runaway slave. The quest for freedom has "all come to nothing, everything all busted up and ruined." Huck thinks of notifying Miss Watson where Jim is, since if he must be a slave he would be better off "at home where his family was." But then Huck realizes that Miss Watson would probably sell Jim down the river as a punishment for running away. Furthermore, Huck himself would be denounced by everyone for his part in the affair. In this fashion his mind comes back once again to the unparalleled wickedness of acting as accomplice in a slave's escape.

The account of Huck's mental struggle in the next two or three pages is the emotional climax of the story. It draws together the theme of flight from bondage and the social satire of the middle section, for Huck is trying to work himself clear of the perverted value system of St. Petersburg. Both adventure story and satire, however, are now subordinate to an exploration of Huck's psyche which is the ultimate achievement of the book. The issue is identical with that of the first moral crisis, but the later passage is much more intense and richer in implication. The differences appear clearly if the two crises are compared in detail.

In Chapter 16 Huck is startled into a realization of his predicament when he hears Jim, on the lookout for Cairo at the mouth of the Ohio, declare that "he'd be a free man the minute he seen it, but if he missed it he'd be in a slave country again and no more show for freedom." Huck says: "I begun to get it through my head that he *was* most free—and who was to blame for it? Why, *me*. I couldn't get that out of my conscience, no how nor no way." He dramatizes his inner debate by quoting the words in which his conscience denounces him: "What had poor Miss Watson done to you that you could see her nigger go off right under your eyes and never say one single word? What did that poor old woman do to you that you could treat her so mean? Why, she tried to learn you your book, she tried to learn you your manners, she tried to be good to you every way she knowed how. *That's* what she done." The counterargument is provided by Jim, who seems to guess what is passing through Huck's mind and does what he can to invoke the force of friendship and gratitude: "Pooty soon I'll be a-shout'n' for joy, en I'll say, it's all on accounts o' Huck; I's a free man, en I couldn't ever ben free ef it hadn' ben for Huck; Huck done it. Jim won't ever forget you, Huck; you's de bes' fren' Jim's ever had; en you's de *only* fren' ole Jim's got now." Huck nevertheless sets out for the shore in the canoe "all in a sweat to tell on" Jim, but when he is intercepted by the two slave hunters in a skiff he suddenly contrives a cunning device to ward them off. We are given no details about how his inner conflict was resolved.

In the later crisis Huck provides a much more circumstantial account of what passes through his mind. He is now quite alone; the outcome of the debate is not affected by any stimulus from the outside. It is the memory of Jim's kindness and goodness rather than Jim's actual voice that impels Huck to defy his conscience: "I see Jim before me all the time: in the day and in the night-time, sometimes moonlight, sometimes storms, and we a-floating along, talking and singing and laughing." The most striking feature of this later crisis is the fact that Huck's conscience, which formerly had employed only secular arguments, now deals heavily in religious cant:

> At last, when it hit me all of a sudden that here was the plain hand of Providence slapping me in the face and letting me know my wickedness was being watched all the time from up there in heaven, whilst I was stealing a poor old woman's nigger that hadn't ever done me no harm, and now was showing me there's One that's always on the lookout, and ain't a-going to allow no such miserable doings to go only just so fur and no further, I most dropped in my tracks I was so scared.

In the earlier debate the voice of Huck's conscience is quoted directly, but the bulk of the later exhortation is reported in indirect discourse. This apparently simple change in method has remarkable consequences. According to the conventions of first-person narrative, the narrator functions as a neutral medium in reporting dialogue. He remembers the speeches of other characters but they pass through his mind without affecting him. When Huck's conscience speaks within quotation marks it is in effect a character in the story, and he is not responsible for what it says. But when he paraphrases the admonitions of his conscience they are incorporated into his own discourse. Thus although Huck is obviously remembering the bits of theological jargon from sermons justifying slavery, they have become a part of his vocabulary....

The greater subtlety of the later passage illustrates the difference between the necessarily shallow characterization of Huck while he was being used merely as a narrative persona, and the profound insight which Mark Twain eventually brought to bear on his protagonist.

EXPRESSING THE CONFLICT WITHIN A SINGLE CHARACTER

The recognition of complexity in Huck's character enabled Mark Twain to do full justice to the conflict between vernacular values and the dominant culture. By situating in a single consciousness both the perverted moral code of a society built on slavery and the vernacular commitment to freedom and spontaneity, he was able to represent the opposed perspectives as alternative modes of experience for the same character. In this way he gets rid of the confusions surrounding the pronoun "I" in the earlier books, where it sometimes designates the author speaking in his own person, sometimes an entirely distinct fictional character. Furthermore, the insight that enabled him to recognize the conflict between accepted values and vernacular protest as a struggle within a single mind does justice to its moral depth, whereas the device he had used earlier—in *The Innocents Abroad*, for example—of identifying the two perspectives with separate characters had flattened the issue out into melodrama. The satire of a decadent slaveholding society gains immensely in force when Mark Twain demonstrates that even the outcast Huck has been in part perverted by it. Huck's conscience is simply the attitudes he has taken over from his environment. What is still sound in him is an impulse from the deepest level of his personality that struggles against the overlay of prejudice and false valuation imposed on all members of the society in the name of religion, morality, law, and refinement.

The River Controls *Huckleberry Finn*

T.S. Eliot

Only one natural force can completely control the course of a human journey: a river. In *The Adventures of Huckleberry Finn*, the River gives the entire novel its form; it also controls the voyage of Huck and Jim. Yet Huck is also the spirit of the River. The end of the novel reflects the connection between Huck and the River: Huck, like the River, has neither beginning nor ending.

It is Huck who gives the book style. The River gives the book its form. But for the River, the book might be only a sequence of adventures with a happy ending. A river, a very big and powerful river, is the only natural force that can wholly determine the course of human peregrination. At sea, the wanderer may sail or be carried by winds and currents in one direction or another; a change of wind or tide may determine fortune. In the prairie, the direction of movement is more or less at the choice of the caravan; among mountains there will often be an alternative, a guess at the most likely pass. But the river with its strong, swift current is the dictator to the raft or to the steamboat. It is a treacherous and capricious dictator. At one season, it may move sluggishly in a channel so narrow that, encountering it for the first time at that point, one can hardly believe that it has travelled already for hundreds of miles, and has yet many hundreds of miles to go; at another season, it may obliterate the low Illinois shore to a horizon of water, while in its bed it runs with a speed such that no man or beast can survive in it. At such times, it carries down human bodies, cattle and houses. At least twice, at St. Louis, the western and the eastern shores have been separated by the fall of bridges, until the designer of the great Eads Bridge devised a structure which could resist the floods. In my own childhood, it was not unusual for the spring freshet to inter-

---

Excerpted from T. S. Eliot's Introduction to the 1950 Chanticleer edition of Mark Twain's *Huckleberry Finn*. Reprinted by permission of Faber and Faber Ltd., on behalf of the Estate of T. S. Eliot.

rupt railway travel; and then the traveller to the East had to take steamboat from the levee up to Alton, at a higher level on the Illinois shore, before he could begin his rail journey. The river is never wholly chartable; it changes its pace, it shifts its channel, unaccountably; it may suddenly efface a sandbar, and throw up another bar where before was navigable water.

It is the River that controls the voyage of Huck and Jim; that will not let them land at Cairo, where Jim could have reached freedom; it is the River that separates them and deposits Huck for a time in the Grangerford houschold; the River that reunites them, and then compels upon them the unwelcome company of the King and the Duke. Recurrently we are reminded of its presence and its power. . . .

THE SPIRIT OF THE RIVER

We come to understand the River by seeing it through the eyes of the Boy; but the Boy is also the spirit of the River. *Huckleberry Finn*, like other great works of imagination, can give to every reader whatever he is capable of taking from it. On the most superficial level of observation, Huck is convincing as a boy. On the same level, the picture of social life on the shores of the Mississippi a hundred years ago is, I feel sure, accurate. On any level, Mark Twain makes you see the River, as it is and was and always will be, more clearly than the author of any other description of a river known to me. But you do not merely see the River, you do not merely become acquainted with it through the senses: you experience the River. Mark Twain, in his later years of success and fame, referred to his early life as a steamboat pilot as the happiest he had known. With all allowance for the illusions of age, we can agree that those years were the years in which he was most fully alive. Certainly, but for his having practised that calling, earned his living by that profession, he would never have gained the understanding which his genius for expression communicates in this book. In the pilot's daily struggle with the River, in the satisfaction of activity, in the constant attention to the River's unpredictable vagaries, his consciousness was fully occupied, and he absorbed knowledge of which, as an artist, he later made use. There are, perhaps, only two ways in which a writer can acquire the understanding of environment which he can later turn to account: by having spent his childhood in that environment—that is, living in it at a period of life in which one experiences much more than one is aware of; and by having had to struggle for a livelihood in that environment—a livelihood bearing no direct relation to any intention of writing about it, of *using* it as literary material. Most of Joseph Conrad's understanding came to him in the latter way. Mark Twain knew the Mississippi in both ways: he had spent his childhood on its banks, and he had earned his living matching his wits against its currents.

Thus the River makes the book a great book. As with Conrad, we are continually reminded of the power and terror of Nature, and the isolation and feebleness of Man. Conrad remains always the European observer of the tropics, the white man's eye contemplating the Congo and its black gods. But Mark Twain is a native, and the River God is his God. It is as a native that he accepts the River God, and it is the subjection of Man that gives to Man his dignity. For without some kind of God, Man is not even very interesting.

Readers sometimes deplore the fact that the story descends to the level of *Tom Sawyer* from the moment that Tom himself re-appears. Such readers protest that the escapades invented by Tom, in the attempted "rescue" of Jim, are only a tedious development of themes with which we were already too familiar—even while admitting that the escapades themselves are very amusing, and some of the incidental observations memorable. But it is right that the mood of the end of the book should bring us back to that of the beginning. Or, if this was not the right ending for the book, what ending would have been right?

Unconscious Art

In *Huckleberry Finn* Mark Twain wrote a much greater book than he could have known he was writing. Perhaps all great works of art mean much more than the author could have been aware of meaning: certainly, *Huckleberry Finn* is the one book of Mark Twain's which, as a whole, has this unconsciousness. So what seems to be the rightness, of reverting at the end of the book to the mood of *Tom Sawyer*, was perhaps unconscious art. For Huckleberry Finn, neither a tragic nor a happy ending would be suitable. No worldly success or social satisfaction, no domestic consummation would be worthy of him; a tragic end also would reduce him to the level of those whom we pity. Huck Finn must come from nowhere and be bound for nowhere. His is not the independence of the typical or symbolic American Pioneer, but the independence of the vagabond. His existence questions the values of America as much as the values of Europe; he is as much an affront to the "pioneer spirit" as he is to "business enterprise"; he is in a state of nature as detached as the state of the saint. In a busy world, he represents the loafer; in an acquisitive and competitive world, he insists on living from hand to mouth. He could not be exhibited in any amorous encounters or engagements, in any of the juvenile affections which are appropriate to Tom Sawyer. He belongs neither to the Sunday School nor to the Reformatory. He has no beginning and no end. Hence, he can only disappear; and his disappearance can only be accomplished by bringing forward another performer to obscure the disappearance in a cloud of whimsicalities.

Like Huckleberry Finn, the River itself has no beginning or end. In its beginning, it is not yet the River; in its end, it is no longer the River. What we call its headwaters is only a selection from among the innumerable sources which flow together to compose it. At what point in its course does the Mississippi become what the Mississippi *means*? It is both one and many; it is the Mississippi of this book only after its union with the Big Muddy—the Missouri; it derives some of its character from the Ohio, the Tennessee and other confluents. And at the end it merely disappears among its deltas: it is no longer there, but it is still where it was, hundreds of miles to the North. The River cannot tolerate any design, to a story which is its story, that might interfere with its dominance. Things must merely happen, here and there, to the people who live along its shores or who commit themselves to its current. And it is as impossible for Huck as for the River to have a beginning or end—a *career*. So the book has the right, the only possible concluding sentence. I do not think that any book ever written ends more certainly with the right words:

> But I reckon I got to light out for the Territory ahead of the rest, because Aunt Sally she's going to adopt me and sivilize me, and I can't stand it. I been there before.

Huckleberry Finn and Censorship

Lance Morrow

Attempts have been made to deprive children of the right to read *The Adventures of Huckleberry Finn* on the grounds that it is a racist tract. The book is a rich, deep text on many important issues: not only race and slavery, but violence, child abuse, alcoholism, and many other problems still relevant to American society. At the same time, it is an inventory of essential values, such as kindness, courage, and the need to think through moral choices. Rather than being banned, the book should be thoroughly studied, and read in conjunction with works on the reality of slavery and the similarities between Huck and Mark Twain's many black friends.

Appendix: The Ruckus over Huckleberry Finn: A variety of critical objections to the novel have been made over the century since it was published, but some of the arguments have changed over time.

Reading these lists of the proscribed is a little like walking into a police station and seeing an unexpected lineup of suspects under glaring lights: The authors, who had seemed to be familiar, even admirable citizens, now look shifty and disheveled, their respectability torn aside to disclose their secret lives—corrupters of the young.

Isn't that John Steinbeck, guiltily clutching a copy of *Of Mice and Men*? J.D. Salinger—who would have thought it?—cringing there with *The Catcher in the Rye*? Roald Dahl, the filthy beast, holding *The Witches*? Shifty-eyed Maya Angelou trying to conceal *I Know Why the Caged Bird Sings*?

These authors and books are at the top of the list of those most frequently challenged or removed from course lists and

Excerpted from Lance Morrow, "In Praise of *Huckleberry Finn*," *Civilization*, January/February 1995. Reprinted by permission of the author. William Styron, Commentary, *New Yorker*, June 26 and July 3, 1995. Copyright ©1995 by William Styron. Reprinted by permission of Don Congdon Associates, Inc.

shelves, or otherwise anathematized in public schools and libraries across America. When I see the lists I am amazed and half-amused. *Of Mice and Men*? Really!? (Ah: The notorious glove.)

When I find Mark Twain in the lineup (and he is always there, around No. 5 in the rank of suspects), holding a copy of *The Adventures of Huckleberry Finn*, I am appalled and saddened. To sweep Salinger or Angelou from the shelves is bush-league intellectual folly, mere vigilante provincialism. But it is an act of real moral stupidity, and a desecration, to try to deprive the young of the voice of Huck Finn. . . .

The objections to *Huck Finn* arise mostly from African-American parents, who are also trying to draw some lines. With *Huck*, the argument focuses not upon sex or profanity but rather upon race, and the deepest, most painful American memory, slavery. The institution of slavery ended, of course, during the Civil War. The institution of racism still flourishes. And it is in the context of enduring racism that black parents naturally enough may wish to protect their children from *Huck Finn*.

I hope, however, that it is possible to honor the wishes of some black parents while at the same time keeping *Huck* on shelves and reading lists. To do so, it may be necessary to stipulate that children of 12 or so are a little too young to absorb the book's complexities. Better to wait until they are 14 or 15.

If *Huck Finn* were merely a 19th-century minstrel show—the n-word slurring around in an atmosphere of casual hatred above a subtext of white supremacy—then no one could object to African-American parents removing the book as a precaution to keep gratuitous germs away from their children. Taking books out of the hands of children, after all, does not raise the same absolute censorship issues posed when an adult audience is involved.

But American life, hardly a sanitary environment, harbors millions of germs that may be dangerous to the young. Black children should be judged quite capable, I think, of making certain moral and artistic distinctions. To focus upon *Huck Finn* as some kind of racist tract, and to suppress the book with all its countervailing glories, seems to me, in the end, both unimaginative and wrong. . . .

THE GLORIES OF *HUCK FINN*

In the story of Huck and Jim and the river, Twain confronts *the* American problems. *Huck Finn* is one of the earliest and deepest texts on race and slavery, on violence, on child abuse, alcoholism, class distinctions in America, hatred, hypocrisy, fraud, gaudily manifold stupidity, backwoods brainlessness, and lying in all its forms—creative, vicious and otherwise. *Huck Finn* is about American civilization and about what it means to be civilized in a vast, experimental, provisional and morally unsettled territory. Huck, who spells it "sivilized," is one of the most truly civilized characters in American letters. For a work often paired with *Tom Sawyer* as the *Iliad* and *Odyssey* of idealized American boyhood, *Huck Finn* carries an almost magic cargo of deeper grownup meanings. How racially condescending to assume that such meanings of American civilization—even as they are relayed by Huck through his white genius/ventriloquist, Mark Twain—cannot concern blacks. A number of black writers in the past, uncontaminated by the ideologies of correctness, have agreed.

Huck Finn is also, as Hemingway understood, the source from which modern American literature has flowed. Twain turned the American vernacular into literature, and an enormous number of later American writers, black and white, have been in his debt. Huck's voice echoes in Langston Hughes and Ralph Ellison and Alice Walker as well as in William Faulkner. In an interview with Shelley Fisher Fishkin, professor of American studies at the University of Texas, Ellison said that Twain's use of comedy and vernacular "allow us to deal with the unspeakable," meaning "the moral situation of the United States and the contrast between our ideals and our activities."

Is *Huck Finn* about kids' adventures on the Mississippi? In the same sense that *Moby-Dick* is about commercial fishing. Everyone should understand what is lost in shelving *Huck Finn*.... Twain (to make the sort of grand claim that he would have had fun with) created in *Huck* an origin myth of the nation's moral struggles.

Huck Finn is also one of the funniest books to be written in America. Sometimes the humor is gentle enough, and spoofy at the *Tom Sawyer* level of prankery. Much of the wit is deliciously literate, as in the duke's magnificent compression of the Shakespeare soliloquy....

But more often the humor has a philosophical savagery about it—as in this exchange toward the end of the book, when Huck shows up at Aunt Sally's, impersonating Tom and lying about a mythical steamboat trip downriver:

Huck: "We blowed out a cylinder head."

Aunt Sally: "Good gracious! anybody hurt?"
Huck: "No'm. Killed a nigger."
Aunt Sally: "Well, it's lucky; because sometimes people do get hurt."

Twain comes down to the moral core of *Huck Finn* in a chapter called "You Can't Play a Lie," wherein Huck wrestles with his conscience about whether to turn Jim in as a runaway slave. Huck's most attractive quality—is that for an inveterate and accomplished liar, he has a powerful need to find the truth, and to act on it.

Huck's two-page struggle over whether to betray Jim is a masterpiece of metaphysically comic inversion, a sardonic, hilarious examination of conscience. Huck accuses himself of low-down, ornery wickedness "in stealing a poor old woman's nigger." The law—righteousness, the society's definition of good—says Huck is doing an awful thing in harboring Jim. Huck tries to pray, but "my heart warn't right." At last, Huck decides he cannot turn in his friend Jim. In one of the great moments of American literature, a cousin to Melville's "No! In thunder!", Huck says, "All right, then, I'll go to hell." He tears up the note to Miss Watson in which he meant to betray his friend. He has done the loneliest, bravest work there is—making a life-or-death decision against the law and custom of his own tribe.

For all its deep indignation, *Huck Finn* is the tenderest and most decent of stories. When the king and the duke are finally caught, tarred and feathered, and run out of town, Huck, who has every reason to cheer the spectacle, instead reacts this way: "Well, it made me sick to see it; and I was sorry for them poor pitiful rascals, it seemed like I couldn't ever feel any hardness against them any more in the world. It was a dreadful thing to see. Human beings *can* be awful cruel to one another."

The book is an inventory of essential values: kindness, courage, loyalty to friends, abhorrence of cruelty, independence of conscience, the need to think through moral choices, and, of course, the inexhaustible power of creative lying—which is to say (putting a more edifying light on it) the inexhaustible power of imagination. . . .

APPRECIATING A COMPLEX NOVEL

The key to appreciating *Huck Finn*'s moral dimensions (and, for a black pupil, the key to tolerating the disturbing universe of white supremacy in which the story is told) is to understand that here, nothing is what it seems. At the beginning of

Huckleberry Finn, Mark Twain placed his famous "Notice":
"Persons attempting to find a motive in this narrative will be prosecuted; persons attempting to find a moral in it will be banished; persons attempting to find a plot in it will be shot."

Meaning: Watch out for all three of those items, for they will surely turn up—motive and moral unfolding just as plot unfolds. The "Notice" was the trickster declaring himself. Twain was saying one thing and meaning the opposite, lying and yarning his way along, spinning the moral landscape into a sort of trompe l'oeil tapestry wherein lies and the real thing play hide-and-seek with one another.

Twain's pseudo-stern, eyebrow-wagging opener (*I'm just here to tell some colorful provincial stories, so don't you dare go deep and moralistic on me*) goes to the secret of his game: the narrative sleight of hand, with the reversal that sets up one expectation in the reader's mind and then (*poof!*) replaces it with another. A theater of dancing contraries.

The minstrelsy is the surface stuff, just as the boys' adventure story is the shallowest dimension of the book. The first lesson to teach is that here, in some immense metaphysics of democracy's beatitudes, virtually everything and everyone swaps places and meanings: The first shall be last; the civilized shall be uncivilized; the king and the duke shall be white trash (these two white con men are, in fact, the Amos 'n' Andy of the plot—another racial switcheroo); the slave shall be free, betimes, on the river, and the free whites shall be enchained in various ways (by hereditary blood feud, by their own casually institutionalized hate, by alcoholism, by sheer bucolic idiocy); the child shall be wise and the grownup irresponsible; the boy shall be a philosopher and the father, Pap, a monster of the American id; the sub-adolescents' lark shall be profound in its consequence (Jim's life is at stake), and the allegedly profound (the Shakespeare soliloquy, for example) shall be a travesty.

In other words, *Huckleberry Finn* is, among other things, a complex, serious book. . . . The supposedly racially insensitive tale, with its repeated use of the word "nigger," is the most devastating portrait of American white trash and white-trash racism that has ever been written. *Huck Finn* savages racism as thoroughly as any document in American history.

But all of this is a lot to take in. I would suggest that in order to stabilize *The Adventures of Huckleberry Finn* in readers' minds, and to neutralize the surface hurts of apparent minstrelsy and race epithets, *Huck* should be accompanied by two texts that will serve, so to speak, as moral outriggers: (1) *Narrative of the Life of Frederick Douglass* and (2) *Was Huck Black?: Mark Twain and African-American Voices,* by Shelley Fisher Fishkin.

Twain and Douglass were friends. I would use Douglass's autobiography, a noble document by a noble man, as a kind of stringent reality enforcer. The narrative is, after all, a loftily pitiless record of what it was like to be a slave on Maryland's Eastern Shore in the first half of the 19th century. *Huck Finn* is slavery and the rest of the rural America of that time seen fictionally through the eyes of a kind of wild child. Frederick Douglass's narrative is an adult former slave's recollection of what it was like to be a slave child in that world.

At one point an eerie intersection occurs between Twain's novel and the ex-slave's story. Douglass records that on the plantation where he lived, property of a Colonel Lloyd, there was an overseer named Austin Gore. One day, Gore was whipping a slave named Demby, who "to get rid of the scourging, ... ran and plunged himself into the creek, and stood there at the depth of his shoulders, refusing to come out. Mr. Gore told him that he would give him three calls, and that, if he did not come out at the third call, he would shoot him." Gore gave the three calls, then "raised his musket to his face, taking deadly aim at his standing victim, and in an instant, poor Demby was no more. His mangled body sank out of sight, and blood and brains marked the water where he had stood."

This incident is strangely similar to the Colonel Sherburn story in *Huck Finn:* In the street of a river town, a drunk named Boggs starts railing and hurling boozy abuse against a local merchant named Colonel Sherburn. Sherburn finally comes out of his store and warns Boggs that he has until one o'clock to shut up. One o'clock comes. Boggs rants on. Sherburn coolly shoots him dead in the street and walks away.

In both stories, there is a note of absolute authenticity, a kind of savage Americana that is perfectly recognizable today.

Frederick Douglass's eyesight is clear and merciless on the subject of slavery. His story of painstakingly and surreptitiously learning how to read and write—activities that were forbidden to slaves—casts a complicated light on efforts in the late 20th century to keep other children from reading a book, *Huck Finn,* on grounds that it might offend them. Any kind of censorship, of course, implies a condescension toward the audience being "protected," but the ironies here are especially poignant.

The second book, Fishkin's *Was Huck Black?*, explores a fascinating thesis. The author's tabloid-headline title does not mean that Fishkin thinks Huck had African blood but rather that Huck's speech, the splendid, never-before-heard American voice that was Twain's great contribution to the stream of American letters, was based, in very large part, upon the vernacular and speech rhythms of blacks. *Le style, c'est l'homme* [the style is the man]. Dr. Fishkin argues that *l'homme* in this case, meaning Mark Twain/Huck Finn, owed a huge debt, in vocabulary, syntax, verbal strategy and style, to the blacks who were young Samuel Clemens's preferred playmates in Hannibal, Missouri, and to other blacks whom Mark Twain knew and listened to attentively in later life. The result, argues Fishkin, is that Huck, in his speech and his point of view, was black to a significant degree. And if that is true—Fishkin makes a scholarly and fascinatingly plausible case—then the most original voice in American literature, the source from which so much else has flowed, is black, or half-black, or anyway immensely tinted by precisely the African consciousness so long excluded from the official cultural life of the country....

Fishkin's thesis is not another dreary exercise in political correctness. When you have read her book, you say, Of course. The black component of *Huck*—and of the immense literature that derives from it—becomes as self-evident as the influence of African voices in American music.

After *Huckleberry Finn* was published in 1885, the Public Library in Concord, Massachusetts, banned the book. As the *Boston Transcript* reported: "One member of the committee says that, while he does not wish to call it immoral, he thinks it contains but little humor, and that of a very coarse type. He regards it as the veriest trash. The librarian and the other members of the committee entertain similar views, characterizing it as rough, coarse and inelegant."

The ambient light in Concord at the time was the Transcendental Emersonian moonbeam. The prevailing light in American education at the moment, unfortunately, is that pitiless, accusatory glare—flat and harsh as a zealot's mind—that pours down upon the lineup of suspect authors at the police station. That light is blinding. It is time to turn it off, at least where *Huck Finn* is concerned, in order to appreciate the novel's amazing play of intelligence and morality and shadow.

APPENDIX: THE RUCKUS OVER *HUCKLEBERRY FINN*

[Editor's note: *The Adventures of Huckleberry Finn* has been censored here and there ever since it was published—but the reasons for the censorship have changed over the years. The following selections illuminate the book's checkered history with the censors.]

BANNED IN CONCORD

The Concord (Mass.) Public Library committee has decided to exclude Mark Twain's latest book from the library. One member of the committee says that, while he does not wish to call it immoral, he thinks it contains but little humor, and that of a very coarse type. He regards it as the veriest trash. The librarian and the other members of the committee entertain similar views, characterizing it as rough, coarse and inelegant, dealing with a series of experiences not elevating, the whole book being more suited to the slums than to intelligent, respectable people.

Boston *Transcript*, March 17, 1885.

NO BAD PUBLICITY?

The Committee of the Public Library of Concord, Mass., have given us a rattling tip-top puff which will go into every paper in the country. They have expelled Huck from their library as "trash & suitable only for the slums." That will sell 25,000 copies for us, sure.

Mark Twain, letter to his publisher, Charles L. Webster, March 18, 1885.

LOW MORAL LEVEL

The Concord public library committee deserves well of the public by their action in banishing Mark Twain's new book, *Huckleberry Finn*, on the ground that it is trashy and vicious. It is time that this influential pseudonym should cease to carry into homes and libraries unworthy productions. Mr. Clemens is a genuine and powerful humorist, with a bitter vein of satire on the weaknesses of humanity which is sometimes wholesome, sometimes only grotesque, but in certain of his works degenerates into a gross trifling with every fine feeling. The trouble with Mr. Clemens is that he has no reliable sense of propriety.... These Huckleberry Finn stories ... are no better in tone than the dime novels which flood the blood-and-thunder reading population. Mr. Clemens has made them smarter, for he has an inexhaustible fund of "quips and cranks and wanton wiles," and his literary skill is, of course, superior; but their moral level is low, and their perusal cannot be anything less than harmful.

Springfield *Republican*, March 1885.

OUR PURE-MINDED LADS AND LASSES

"If Mr. Clemens cannot think of something better to tell our pure-minded lads and lasses," said Louisa May Alcott, with the moral weight of a lifetime of well-loved books behind every word, "he had best stop writing for them."

Louisa May Alcott, quoted in Justin Kaplan, *Mr. Clemens and Mark Twain*, 1966.

A SEARCH FOR THE HUMOROUS QUALITIES

Mark Twain is a humorist or nothing. He is well aware of this fact himself, for he prefaces the *Adventures of Huckleberry Finn* with a brief notice, warning persons in search of a moral, motive or plot that they are liable to be prosecuted, banished or shot. This is a nice little artifice to scare off the critics—a kind of "trespassers on these grounds will be dealt with according to law."

However, as there is no penalty attached, we organized a search expedition for the humorous qualities of this book with the following hilarious results:

A very refined and delicate piece of narration by Huck Finn, describing his venerable and dilapidated "pap" as afflicted with delirium tremens, rolling over and over, "kicking things every which way," and "saying there was devils ahold of him." This chapter is especially suited to amuse the children on long, rainy afternoons.

An elevating and laughable description of how Huck killed a pig, smeared its blood on an axe and mixed in a little of his own hair, and then ran off, setting up a job on the old man and the community, and leading them to believe him murdered. This little joke can be repeated by any smart boy for the amusement of his fond parents.

A graphic and romantic tale of a Southern family feud, which resulted in an elopement and from six to eight choice corpses.

A polite version of the "Giascutus" story, in which a nude man, striped with the colors of the rainbow, is exhibited as "The King's Camelopard; or, The Royal Nonesuch." This is a good chapter for lenten parlor entertainments and church festivals.

A side-splitting account of a funeral, enlivened by a "sick melodeum," a "long-legged undertaker," and a rat episode in the cellar.

Robert Bridges, *Life*, February 26, 1885.

"THE HUMOR OF THE FUTURE MUST BE CHASTE AND TRUTHFUL"

When the book appeared in the spring of 1885, most American critics received it very coldly. The guardians of the genteel tradition fumed over Twain's satirical handling of the bigots and hypocrites of the ante-bellum South and his audacious elevation of the rowdyish Huck Finn and the Negro runaway slave, Jim, into heroes....

The most vitriolic comments came from New England, seat of the genteel tradition, and were sparked by the action of the Public Library Committee of Concord, Massachusetts, which excluded the book as "a dangerous moral influence on the young." The *Literary World* of Boston hailed the committee's stand: "We are glad to see that the commendation given to this sort of literature by its publication in the *Century* has received a check by this action at Concord."...

Critical reaction to *Huckleberry Finn* all over the country followed this pattern. A Western Superintendent of Public Schools charged that the book proved once again that the writings of Mark Twain were "hardly worth a place in the columns of the average country newspaper which never assumes any literary airs." The reviewer in the Arkansas *Traveler* announced smugly: "This book is condemned, American critics say, because it is vulgar and coarse. The days of vulgar humor are over in this country. There was a time when a semi-obscene joke would find admirers, but the reading public is becoming more refined. Exaggerated humour will also pass away. The humor of the future must be chaste and truthful."

Philip S. Foner, *Mark Twain: Social Critic*, 1958.

A Vetoed Retort

Huckleberry Finn is not an imaginary person. He still lives; or rather, *they* still live; for Huckleberry Finn is two persons in one—namely, the author's two uncles, the present editors of the Boston *Advertiser* and the Springfield *Republican*. In character, language, clothing, education, instinct, and origin, he is the painstakingly and truthfully drawn photograph and counterpart of these two gentlemen as they were in the time of their boyhood, forty years ago. The work has been most carefully and conscientiously done, and is exactly true to the originals, in even the minutest particulars, with but one exception, and that a trifling one: this boy's language has been toned down and softened, here and there, in deference to the taste of a more modern and fastidious day.

Twain wrote this response to the newspaper attacks on *Huckleberry Finn* as a "Prefatory Remark" to be inserted in future printings, but it was never used. Quoted by Hamlin Hill, ed., *Mark Twain's Letters to His Publishers: 1867–1894*, 1967.

The Great Fault in American Character

The burlesque of the stage and the burlesque in literature have their common root in that spirit of irreverence, which . . . is the great fault in American character. In the cultivation of that spirit, Mark Twain has shown talents and industry which, now that his last effort [*Huckleberry Finn*] has failed so ignominiously, we trust he will employ in some manner more creditable to himself and more beneficent to his country.

Boston *Advertiser*, 1885, quoted in George Sanderlin, *Mark Twain as Others Saw Him*, 1978.

A Double Benefit

At the end of March [1885] a Concord group called the Free Trade Club proffered an amende honorable by electing [Clemens] to membership, and he immediately seized on this opportunity for publicity as well as public vindication by writing a graceful and ironic letter of acceptance, which was published in the New York *World* and other papers. His new membership, he said, "endorses me as worthy to associate with certain gentlemen whom even the moral icebergs of the Concord library committee are bound to respect." The excommunication of *Huckleberry Finn* was going to benefit him in several ways beyond doubling the sale:

For instance, it will deter other libraries from buying the book and you are doubtless aware that one book in a public library prevents the sale of a

sure ten and a possible hundred of its mates. And secondly it will cause the purchasers of the book to read it, out of curiosity, instead of merely intending to do so after the usual way of the world and library committees; and then they will discover, to my great advantage and their own indignant disappointment, that there is nothing objectionable in the book, after all.
Justin Kaplan, *Mr. Clemens and Mark Twain*, 1966.

NOT A CHILD'S BOOK

Tom Sawyer and *Huckleberry Finn* are prose epics of American life. The former is one of those books—of which *The Pilgrim's Progress, Gulliver's Travels* and *Robinson Crusoe* are supreme examples—that are read at different periods of one's life from very different points of view; so that it is not easy to say when one enjoys them the most— before one understands their real significance or after. Nearly all healthy boys enjoy reading *Tom Sawyer*, because the intrinsic interest of the story is so great, and the various adventures of the hero are portrayed with such gusto. Yet it is impossible to outgrow the book. The eternal Boy is there, and one cannot appreciate the nature of boyhood properly until one has ceased to be a boy. The other masterpiece, *Huckleberry Finn*, is really not a child's book at all. Children devour it, but they do not digest it. It is a permanent picture of a certain period of American history, and this picture is made complete, not so much by the striking portraits of individuals placed on the huge canvas, as by the vital unity of the whole composition. If one wishes to know what life on the Mississippi really was, to know and understand the peculiar social conditions of that highly exciting time, one has merely to read through this powerful narrative, and a definite, coherent, vivid impression remains.
William Lyon Phelps, *North American Review*, July 5, 1907.

DROPPED AS A TEXTBOOK

The Board of Education [of New York City] has quietly dropped Mark Twain's *The Adventures of Huckleberry Finn* from the approved textbook lists for the city's elementary and junior high schools.

The book can still be purchased for school libraries, but it can no longer be bought for wide distribution to pupils as a textbook, except in the high schools. Even in these schools, Huck Finn's days may be numbered.

Huckleberry Finn, which tells the story of boyhood in the Mississippi Valley in the Eighteen Forties, has been criticized by some Negroes as "racially offensive."
New York Times, September 12, 1957.

CHILDREN OFFENDED

WINNETKA, ILL. (AP)—Mark Twain's classic *The Adventures of Huckleberry Finn* has been removed from the required reading list at New Trier High School because of complaints from black parents that it includes the word "nigger."

The school board voted 4 to 2 to remove the novel after black parents complained that their children were offended by use of the word, and by relics of 19th century race relations depicted in the book.

The vote was recommended by Supt. Roderick Bickert, who said the book will remain on library shelves and be available for independent study and elective courses. A faculty committee also supported the change.

The Illinois division of the American Civil Liberties Union said the decision sets a dangerous precedent.

"In attempting to be sensitive to the feelings of some of their constituents, they have seriously undermined their greater obligation to academic freedom," the ACLU said.

Associated Press, June 30, 1976.

ACCLAIMED AND BANNED FOR THE SAME REASONS

The banning of *Huckleberry Finn* is a familiar sort of ironic anecdote whereby [Louisa May] Alcott and the cultural guardians of Concord reveal their moral timidity, their literary obtuseness, or both. But the story does not end here with the self-exposure of an ostensibly enlightened authority. *Adventures of Huckleberry Finn* did go on, of course, to become *the* American classic, and generations of children were duly made to read it. What makes this turnabout remarkable, and unlike the elevation of, for instance, *Madame Bovary* after it too was to be banned or, nearer home, the ascension of *Pierre* into a classic and a cult, is that the canonization of Twain's novel has not involved significant rereading. The *Huckleberry Finn* celebrated as the archetypal American novel is acclaimed precisely for being, as the Concord critics charged, "rough, coarse, and inelegant," and especially for featuring a hero who lies, uses profanity, and steals besides, a boy who everyone agrees is, as to class and culture, the "veriest trash." When Bernard DeVoto declared *Adventures of Huckleberry Finn* the preeminent American novel (maybe approached but certainly not surpassed by *Moby-Dick*), he took it as generally understood that jettisoning elegance and refinement through a vernacular narration was the novel's most spectacular achievement. "It is the one book in our literature," Leo Marx noted, "about which highbrows and lowbrows can agree.". . .

Twain's work *is* irreverent, and its lack of respectability is more precisely a lack of respect. It is perhaps only fair that its readers take their cue from it and treat *it* without reverence. No one feels compelled to grant *Huckleberry Finn* artistic license, as many do, for instance, *The Merchant of Venice*, with even Jews interpreting Shylock as an exposure of anti-Semitism rather than condemn Shakespeare.

Huckleberry Finn's lack of respect seems to have rendered it less sacrosanct than is common with classics; yet it has achieved, in Jonathan Arac's term, a state of "hypercanonization." Its banning is no surprise and not unreasonable, but simultaneously it is the country's official text. What does it say about America that is so telling, and how does its peculiar dissonant voice enter into what it tells?

Myra Jehlen, "Banned in Concord," in Forrest G. Robinson, ed., *The Cambridge Companion to Mark Twain*, 1995.

OUR MOST POWERFUL SECULAR BLASPHEMY

It's quite likely that if Mark Twain had merely used the word "slave" instead of the word "nigger," which appears more than two hundred times in the course of *Huckleberry Finn*, many of those who have recently attacked the book on the ground of racism would have been at least partially appeased. But "nigger" remains our most powerful secular blasphemy. Although a twelve-year-old Missourian would have had scant familiarity, in the eighteen-forties, with the word "slave"—a term that was generally confined to government proclamations, religious discussions, and legal documents—Huck's innocent vernacular usage appears to be one of the reasons for the panic that recently impelled the National Cathedral School, in Washington, to remove *Huckleberry Finn* from its tenth-grade curriculum, and to shift it from required to elective courses in the eleventh and twelfth grades. Only the nature of the school surprises: over the past decades, the book has been suppressed and banished from library shelves innumerable times.

In recent years, John H. Wallace, a black educator from Fairfax, Virginia, has campaigned to protect youth by insisting that *Huckleberry Finn* be taken away from school libraries, and has published what has to be an all-time curiosity in the annals of bowdlerization: a version of the text from which every use of the word "nigger" has been expunged. The crusade of Wallace, who has described his nemesis as "the most grotesque example of racist trash ever written," is an extreme example of the animus that has coalesced around the novel.

Huckleberry Finn reveals the mind of a writer with equivocal feelings about race. The wonder is that Twain's upbringing and experience (including a brief stint in the Confederate Army) should have left him so little tainted with bigotry. Although most of the book's millions of readers, including many black people, have found no racism in it (Ralph Ellison wrote admiringly of the author's grasp of the tormented complexity of slavery, his awareness of Jim's essential humanity), *Huckleberry Finn* has never really struggled up out of a continuous vortex of discord, and probably never will, as long as its enchanting central figures, with their confused and incalculable feelings for each other, remain symbols of our own racial confusion.

William Styron, *New Yorker*, June 26 & July 3, 1995.

A Classic of American Reform Literature

Charles L. Sanford

In *A Connecticut Yankee in King Arthur's Court*, Mark Twain both symbolically reenacted the American Revolution and examined the "utopian" character of the industrial revolution. His hero, Hank Morgan, is intended as an archetype of "hard, unsentimental common sense," but Twain suggests that the mechanical blessings of material progress have deprived Americans of imagination and a sense of heart. *A Connecticut Yankee* (1888) is compared with Edward Bellamy's *Looking Backward* (1887), a utopian novel concerned with industrial reform.

Reform may be defined broadly as the effort by words and deeds to change and improve upon existing conditions. In this sense, American reforming zeal is not confined to spasmodic social protest movements or eccentric experiments, but is characteristic of the American people generally, whatever their class or sectional interests. For some three centuries they have been enlisted in a "permanent revolution" dedicated to progress, to social and individual betterment, variously interpreted.

The American theme of progress underlying reform was initiated with the colonial mission to set up a "City on the Hill" as a beacon and example to unregenerate Europe of the Reformation's ideal holy commonwealth. The collective sense of mission became gradually translated into the more secular terms of Liberty, Equality, Prosperity, Civic Virtue. But Americans have continued to act, in the words of Logan Pearsall Smith, "as if America were more than a country, were a sort of cause ... which it is dishonorable to desert." At the same time, after the pattern of the Puritan jeremiad [prolonged lament], they have held it an obligation of citizenship

Excerpted from "Classics of American Reform Literature" by Charles L. Sanford, *American Quarterly*, Fall 1958, pp. 295-311. Copyright 1958, University of Pennsylvania. Reprinted by permission of the Johns Hopkins University Press.

to search the social conscience. Thus, the conservative James Fenimore Cooper believed that it was "the duty of the citizen to reform and improve the character of his country." Mark Twain, long a hallmark of Americanism, once wrote that "the citizen who thinks he sees that the commonwealth's political clothes are worn out, and yet holds his peace and does not agitate for a new suit, is disloyal; he is a traitor.". . .

FACING THE FALLOUT FROM THE INDUSTRIAL REVOLUTION

By 1888 American writers faced a *fait accompli*. Industrial capitalism was triumphant. Yet widespread industrial unrest, the growth of labor unions, agrarian discontent and the formation of reform movements with large popular followings all testified to the belief that something hoped for in American life, whether the holy commonwealth or the material paradise, was not being realized. Against this background appeared Edward Bellamy's *Looking Backward*, a novel concerned with industrial reform. . . . Bellamy held before Americans a realistic vision of a middle-class paradise based on the concept of Equality, to be fully realized by the year 2000 A.D. (when the hero awakes from his century-long hypnotic sleep).

The polar contrast in his book is between a past state of social and economic inequality centering in the city of Boston of 1887 and a future state of social and economic equality in the same city some one hundred years later. . . .

NATURE AND NATURAL LAW

Although Bellamy finds his solution to social problems entirely within the framework of an industrial society, the concept of nature and natural law is never far from his mind. Thus, in answer to the charge that the compulsory features of his industrial army are an abridgment to freedom he argues that people in the new society are freer in all respects, except for the fundamental law of work, which is a "codification of the law of nature—the edict of Eden." The functions of government under his system are reduced, since the machinery of production and distribution is so "logical in its principles and direct and simple in its workings, that it all but runs itself." Most important for Bellamy, the natural man is by nature good. Without the old institution of property (Henry David Thoreau also made this point) men are not tempted to lie and cheat and steal. Bellamy discards social Darwinism in favor of reform Darwinism and the older, sentimental view of nature. . . .

Bellamy's proposal is a middle-class paradise because it

incorporates most of the middle-class ideals. He accepts the dream of material abundance as being desirable and shows that it need not be incompatible with the dream of innocence. ... He is insistent that economic democracy, or nationalization, retain and extend the libertarian features of the old society. He has the middle-class faith in the power of reason at the dictates of the heart to shape human destiny. He embraces the middle-class philosophy of gradualism. His is a *peaceful* transformation which cooperates with the direction of industrial evolution toward larger and larger units and which is led by the middle class. He rejects the Marxist formula and class analysis completely. It is no wonder that his program gained so many ardent supporters and was regarded not as Utopian, but as a blueprint for Reality.

A Connecticut Yankee

The publication of Bellamy's book was followed in the next year [1889] by Mark Twain's *A Connecticut Yankee in King Arthur's Court,* a book which represented the other side of the same coin, a middle-class utopia already realized in the actual achievements of nineteenth-century American civilization, but projected back into sixth-century, feudal England. The resulting sharp contrast unwittingly exposed the psychological basis for the conservative claim to being progressive, to being already enlisted in the cause of a "permanent revolution." The measure of social progress was not the inherent conditions or contradictions of American society, but the reverse image of Europe. Mark Twain was essentially an innocent who grew up to great expectations in the Midwest, often called "the Garden of the World." He early succumbed to the bonanza fever of gold-rush days and accepted material progress as a great good. But emotional frustrations, crushing business disasters in the East, the loss of loved ones and a growing sense of guilt for having surrendered to material success tended to embitter him. His *Connecticut Yankee* was written in that period of soul-searching and doubt which preceded the bleak pessimism of his old age. In this period he combined a nostalgia for the halcyon days of youthful innocence in pre-industrial Hannibal, Missouri, with savage criticism of the social order and the materialistic morality upon which it was founded. Against this background the *Connecticut Yankee* may be regarded, I think, as a symbolic attempt to persuade himself that all was right in the American garden after all. (This statement takes into account both those critics who interpret

The Connecticut Yankee as a veiled attack upon American business practices and those who take his praise of modern times at face value.)

THE YANKEE IS NOT JUST AN OBSERVER—HE ACTS

The form of *A Connecticut Yankee* is what may be called an inverted Utopian fantasy. A graphic way to see the inversion is to compare it with Edward Bellamy's *Looking Backward*, which appeared in 1887 and was a best-seller by the time the *Yankee* was ready for publication. Mark Twain himself was extremely fond of Bellamy's book, though he apparently did not read it until after the *Yankee* was completed. In Bellamy's dream fantasy Julian West is precipitated into the future, where, faced with the material and ideological evolution evident in the year A.D. 2000, his own nineteenth century appears meager and startlingly inadequate. Through all his experience, West remains the observer, the listener, the interrogator who assimilates the persuasive criticism which the imaginary age affords. Bellamy's central achievement is to realize the terms of the Utopian fantasy, which is to say he conveys the notion of a dream of reason. Thus his hero finds himself being constantly persuaded that truths he had believed, values he had held, and causes he had supported are nothing more than outworn attitudes and trappings of a dead age. Being reasonable in the face of the disparity, he submits to the superior argument and assents to the promise of the strange new world.

Mark Twain, however, instead of sending his hero into an imaginary future territory outside history where the terms of criticism could operate freely to create the dream of reason, plunged him into history as if to invade and reform the past. The Yankee is not the innocent interlocutor but the chief actor of his chronicle.

James M. Cox, *Mark Twain: The Fate of Humor*, 1966.

In this book his missionary zeal finds an outlet in the traditional polarity of Europe and America, past and future, abundance and poverty, freedom and authority, democracy and aristocracy. It is significant that he does not attempt the conversion of modern England, which has led the world in scientific, industrial progress as well as in democratic, humanitarian reforms and which set an example for America in ending slavery. Rather, he loads the dice in his favor. Here he is still concerned, as he was, on the whole, during his travels abroad, with the intensely Protestant American stereotype of Europe as a priest-ridden, backward land, dominated by the same wicked nobility which the colonists had left behind. His book, therefore, symbolically re-enacts the American Revolution. His hero, Hank Morgan, the superintendent in a Bridgeport Colt factory, is suddenly transported into sixth-century Camelot by a blow on the head. There, his modern knowledge enables him to work miracles greater than those of Merlin, the king's magician, and he becomes Sir Boss of all England. The rest of the story concerns his attempt to bring the downtrodden masses to accept the blessings of American industrial progress thirteen centuries too soon. One of the ironies growing out of Mark Twain's divided state of mind is that although the inhumanity of the ruling hierarchies of feudal England is symbolized by the metallic qualities of armor suits—about which Mark Twain writes some of his funniest passages—the compulsive effect of the myth of America as a veritable Eden requires Mark Twain to call his hero's factories "*iron* and *steel* missionaries of future civilization."

Hank Morgan, the composite, archetypal American (Yankee) of the machine age, combines the qualities of a Benjamin Franklin and [James Fenimore Cooper's] Leatherstocking. Although he is an industrial type, he was raised on a farm and has learned to use the lariat and revolver in western fashion. Mark Twain styles him a "Unique," as if he came from a race newly sprung from God and were truly regenerate. His typically American missionary zeal to reform society, it is hinted, derives from his early proximity to American soil. While these features of Hank's character draw upon American nature as the source of divinity and moral superiority, the standard of nature is also implied in Hank's faith in the youth of England as a means of accomplishing his mission. Hank's assumptions, it must be said, are basically those of Edward Bellamy: that man is at heart good and that a peaceful revolution can be achieved through education and the ballot. The Hobbesian concept of the state of nature is also present in this book, but in general it is reserved for the degenerate state of English society, inhabiting the Garden after the Fall, from which only the youths of England are exempt.

A Moral Monster

But Hank Morgan early encounters a problem which Bellamy blithely ignores. Hank's system of education reaches the minds, but not the hearts of these people. He finds it almost impossible, except with youths, to eradicate the deep-seated loyalties and inherited prejudices which support the *ancien régime* [former political and social system]. He concludes that all successful revolutions must begin in blood: "What this folk needed ... was a Reign of Terror." Whereupon he sets himself up as a dictator and slaughters 30,000 of the flower of English knighthood in cold blood, thereby becoming the kind of moral monster so often portrayed by Nathaniel Hawthorne. Hank and material progress are finally bested by Merlin, representing the Church. Now this conclusion may indeed have been dictated by the need to end the story in such a fashion as to get Hank Morgan back to Bridgeport and to prevent the Industrial Revolution from humming thirteen centuries too soon, but it is certainly inconsistent with the story's underlying assumption of an identity between material and moral progress. If Mark Twain does not directly question the supposed blessings of material progress, he at least suggests that the industrial order lacks the symbols to captivate the imagination and that the new American may have lost the sense of heart which characterized the simpler, agrarian past. He calls Hank Morgan at the end the "champion of hard, unsentimental common sense."

Mark Twain's tentative identification of material prosperity with democratic progress, an identity underlying both Andrew Carnegie's "Gospel of Wealth" and the Horatio Alger success story, has, in the twentieth century, become the basic premise of the two major political parties, making a choice between them often difficult and defections from one party to the other a rather easy matter. Mark Twain's theory of revolution, on the other hand, was meaningful only in those countries, as in feudal England, where an *ancien régime* was firmly entrenched. Professor Louis Hartz has shown that it was almost unthinkable in the United States, where the *ancien régime* had never had a foothold, except as fictions in the mind, where the major parties largely agreed in principle and where any kind of social progress was thought of as part of a continuing revolution.

Clemens, Twain, and Morgan Are Not the Same Man

Lewis A. Lawson

Some have argued that Hank Morgan, the protagonist of *A Connecticut Yankee in King Arthur's Court*, expresses the views of Samuel L. Clemens/Mark Twain, the author. But a complex superstructure built around Morgan's tale of his visit to Arthurian England and other, internal clues suggest that Mark Twain did not endorse his hero or his hero's ideas—and that Sam Clemens remained yet a further step removed from Morgan.

There is no generally accepted reading of Samuel L. Clemens' *A Connecticut Yankee in King Arthur's Court* (1889). ... One chief reason is that the complexity of the novel's structure has not been emphasized. The novel begins with an "Author's Preface," signed on July 21, 1889, by Mark Twain. But he speaks as Clemens, acknowledging that he is the creator of all that follows. There then appears "A Word of Explanation," written by Mark Twain, speaking as the narrator, describing the circumstances under which he obtained "The Tale of the Lost Land," the book written by Hank Morgan, which follows. "The Tale" is followed by "A Postscript by Clarence," Hank Morgan's trusted subordinate. Last is a "Final P.S. by M.T.," which joins "A Word of Explanation" to create a frame for "The Tale" and "A Postscript." All too often, readers have assumed that Hank Morgan speaks for Samuel L. Clemens and that the frame is without significance.

The two problems are not entirely separate, of course. For the arrangement of parts is as much a statement of intention by an author as is his direct comment. ...

In this reading, several assumptions about the structure

Excerpted from Lewis A. Lawson, "Samuel L. Clemens: Gnosis in Camelot," *Modern Age*, Fall 1993; ©1993 by Intercollegiate Studies Institute. Reprinted by permission.

will be followed. First, that Clemens would not have employed a frame unless he wished to place the views of Mark Twain and of Hank Morgan in some kind of opposition. Second, that despite all the dream imagery in "A Word of Explanation," the reader is to accept Mark Twain as a truthful and rational narrator of an actual event, his experience with Hank Morgan. Third, that despite all the dream imagery in "The Tale of the Lost Land," the reader is to accept Hank Morgan's "transposition" to Camelot as an actual event. Fourth, that the reader is to accept Morgan's account of his experience in Camelot as a "book," crafted after the fact from his "journal" and thus meant to satisfy his feeling of success or failure. Fifth, that sometime after his visit by Morgan, Twain wrote his "Explanation," carefully implying certain clues to his mood at the time of Morgan's visit, but masking his post-reading judgment of the man and his book. Sixth, that Twain's response to Morgan in his "Final P.S." is designed to affect the reader's interpretation of the entire novel.

CONTRASTING THE MIDDLE AGES WITH MODERN CIVILIZATION

A Connecticut Yankee in King Arthur's Court was an attempt to imagine, and after a fashion set forth, the hard conditions of life for the laboring and defenseless poor in bygone times in England, and incidentally contrast these conditions with those under which the civil and ecclesiastical pets of privilege and high fortune lived in those times. I think I was purposing to contrast that English life, not just the English life of Arthur's day but the English life of the whole of the Middle Ages, with the life of modern Christendom and modern civilization—to the advantage of the latter, of course. That advantage is still claimable and does creditably and handsomely exist everywhere in Christendom—if we leave out Russia and the royal palace of Belgium.

Mark Twain, *The Autobiography of Mark Twain*, Charles Neider, ed., 1959.

This study acknowledges several themes that previous readers have identified as crucial problems in the tale. Some critics have from the very beginning argued that Morgan represents an American condemnation of the perquisites that nineteenth-century England still allowed aristocracy and an established church. Some readers have seen the novel as a satire directed against bumptious Americanism. It has been argued that technology is viewed favorably or unfavorably. There have been opposed views of Clemens' philosophy of history. There have also been widely differing views of Clemens' religious belief. One of the most energetic disagreements has been about the degree to which Clemens was steadfast to his original conception. And these represent but part of the lively critical effort....

THE CURIOUS STRANGER

In "A Word of Explanation," Twain first describes his introduction to a "curious stranger," during a tour of Warwick Castle. The stranger, Twain admits, had a profound effect upon him:

> As he talked along, softly, pleasantly, flowingly, he seemed to drift away imperceptibly out of this world and time, and into some remote era and old forgotten country; and so he gradually wove such a spell about me that I seemed to move along the spectres and shadows and dust and mold of a gray antiquity, holding speech with a relic of it! Exactly as I would speak of my nearest personal friends or enemies, or my most familiar neighbors, he spoke of Sir Bedivere, Sir Bors de Ganis, Sir Launcelot of the Lake, Sir Galahad, and all the other great names of the Table Round—and how old, old, unspeakably old and faded and dry and musty and ancient he came to look as he went on!

There is none of the reserve commonly attributed to Americans here, rather a leaping willingness to trust the appearance of things and a propensity to punctuate with exclamation points. When the stranger asserts that he had lived in the sixth century, Twain has been so bewitched that he is shocked into "electric surprise." When he recovers, the stranger has disappeared. Twain does not add that he had suspected the man to be a lunatic or an impostor.

That evening Twain's romantic mood lingers on:

> I sat by my fire at the Warwick Arms, steeped in a dream of the olden time, while the rain beat upon the windows, and the wind roared about the eaves and corners. From time to time I dipped into old Sir Thomas Malory's enchanting book, and fed at this rich feast of prodigies and adventures, breathed-in the fragrance of its obsolete names, and dreamed again. Midnight being come at length, I read another tale, for a night-cap.

Two implications are possible here. It could be argued that Twain possesses the deteriorationist view of history so very popular among certain groups in the late nineteenth century, for example, English literary folk and Southern mythmakers. It could also be argued—from the imagery—that Twain is fueling his reading with alcohol.

His "night-cap" is *"How Sir Launcelot Slew Two Giants, And*

Made A Castle Free," the text of which, Twain must think, is sufficiently important to warrant inclusion. After having read the tale Twain—so he is later asserting—had experienced the following event, whose strangeness goes unnoted:

> As I laid the book down there was a knock on the door, and my stranger came in. I gave him a pipe and a chair, and made him welcome. I also comforted him with a hot Scotch whiskey; gave him another one; then still another—hoping always for his story. After a fourth persuader, he drifted into himself, in a quite simple and natural way.

The lack of surprise by Twain, the lack of any speech between the two, the swift fluidity of the scene—all suggest that Twain is by now pretty tipsy.

At this point Twain inserts *"The Stranger's History,"* spoken to him that night, but actually constituting the crafted introduction to "The Tale of the Lost Land." Since Twain equates *"The Stranger's History,"* with *"How Sir Launcelot"* by typography and proximity, he seems to be implying that he was equally enchanted by them. He could be eager to see what two giants are vanquished in *"The Stranger's History"* (and by extension in the full story).

CONNING AN EASY MARK?

Considering the easy mark that he has chosen, the stranger offers impeccable credentials:

> I am an American. I was born and reared in Hartford, in the State of Connecticut—anyway, just over the river, in the country. So I am a Yankee of the Yankees—and practical; yes, and nearly barren of sentiment, I suppose—or poetry, in other words. My father was a blacksmith, my uncle was a horse doctor, and I was both, along at first. Then I went over to the great arms factory and learned my real trade; learned all there was to it; learned to make everything; guns, revolvers, cannon, boilers, engines, all sorts of labor-saving machinery. Why, I could make anything a body wanted—anything in the world, it didn't make any difference what; and if there wasn't any quick new-fangled way to make a thing, I could invent one—and do it as easy as rolling off a log. I became head superintendent; had a couple of thousand men under me.

This Yankee's history recapitulates the history of the Yankee race. Coming from the country, he first personifies Longfellow's "Village Blacksmith," that paean to pre-industrial America. Going to the city, he personifies the kind of industrialization initiated by such men as Samuel Colt. His boasting about his inventiveness is probably a looser allusion to Ben Franklin, the original Yankee of Yankees. Probably tipsy and perhaps nostalgic, Twain would seem to be vulnerable to any kind of con game the stranger could be playing.

Earlier that afternoon, in Warwick Castle, the stranger had asked Twain: "You know about transmigration of souls; do you know about transposition of epochs—and bodies?" He now purports to explain how one body was transported. One day in 1879, in a fight with one of his workmen, Hercules (does the stranger perhaps exaggerate?), he was brained with a crowbar. When he regains consciousness, he discovers that he is in Camelot.

Although he has apparently been asleep for over thirteen hundred years, the stranger grows sleepy after talking to Twain for only a few minutes. But, in a burst of trust and generosity whose motivation and strangeness go unnoted, he takes Twain to his room, to lend him the book that records his adventures in Camelot. Twain returns to his room, to share with his reader his reading:

> The first part of it—the great bulk of it—was parchment, and yellow with age. I scanned a leaf particularly and saw that it was palimpsest. Under the old dim writing of the Yankee historian appeared traces of a penmanship which was older and dimmer still—Latin words and sentences: fragments from old monkish legends, evidently.

Twain's description of this reading process is loaded with possible readings. Is the stranger a "Yankee historian" simply because he hails from Hartford or because Twain, writing after the fact, considers that the stranger shares a historical outlook typical of Yankee historians, such as an exclusive concern with New England as the last phase of God's unfolding progressive plan? Is it simply an accident that the stranger hails from Hartford, Twain's domicile, or is it a part of his cozenage [trickery]? Beyond those questions, does Twain mean to intimate that the stranger's version of history will be more enduring than the "old monkish legends"—once accepted as history—which it overlays? . . .

ULTIMATELY UNSEDUCED

It is to Twain's credit that he remains unseduced by "The Tale of the Lost Land" or by the melodramatic death scene staged by the "stranger." As he is apparently dying Morgan apparently hallucinates a scene of a great battle back in Camelot, as if to authenticate all that Twain has read. Rejecting the bait, Twain employs cool detachment:

> He lay muttering incoherently some little time; then for a time he lay silent, and apparently sinking away toward death.

Presently his fingers began to pick busily at the coverlet, and by that sign I knew that his end was at hand. With the first suggestion of the death-rattle in his throat he started up slightly, and seemed to listen; then he said:

"A bugle? ... it is the king! the drawbridge, there! Man the battlements!—turn out—"

He was getting up his last "effect"; but he never finished.

Apparently Morgan is dying. Twain must really appreciate the flocculation—like that great fraud Falstaff, Morgan is no doubt babbling of green fields. Is the death scene the effect, or is his response to Arthur's approach the effect to which Twain refers? Whatever the reference, the result is the same: Twain has rejected Morgan's lure, to sympathize and believe. . . .

And, too, the reading of Morgan's "Tale" would have taken long enough for Twain to get over his tipsiness and sentimentality that night in Warwick Arms. By daylight he must have known it is one thing to get drunk and dream a millennial dream about discovering America and hanker after a world certain and perfectible, but it is another thing to believe it sober in the morning. He would have shared Pudd'nhead Wilson's sentiments:

October 12, the Discovery. It was wonderful to find America, but it would have been more wonderful to miss it.

The Power of the Mysterious in *A Connecticut Yankee*

Kurt Vonnegut Jr.

The ending of *A Connecticut Yankee in King Arthur's Court* suggests some secrets about its author, Mark Twain.

Mark Twain was an autodidact, of course. His schoolbooks were steamboats and mining camps and newspaper offices and so on. His eventual greatness might almost be taken as an insult to formal education in America. It begs this question: "What good is school?"

This is the best reply, I think: "School is for people who are not nearly as gifted as was Mark Twain, who need lessons in counterfeiting gifts they do not have." It is an unfair world. Twain was as unfairly endowed with literary talent at birth as descendants of John D. Rockefeller, his contemporary, would be endowed with mountains of money a little later on.

Yes, and Twain was as shrewd and puritanical in managing his literary talent as Rockefeller was in managing money, it seems to me. He squandered almost none of it. His collected works are, among other things, a monument to nineteenth-century ambition, single-mindedness, and efficiency—like Standard Oil.

They are a good deal funnier than Standard Oil.

Rockefeller was a devout Christian, given to supposing out loud that God must have wished him to be as rich as he was. Twain, on the other hand, had almost nothing to say about God and His possible intentions. God does not make an appearance even in the Garden of Eden, in "Eve's Diary," and not even in Paradise itself, in "Captain Stormfield's Visit to Heaven."

Excerpted from Kurt Vonnegut Jr.'s "Opening Remarks" to *The Unabridged Mark Twain* (Philadelphia: Running Press, 1976). Copyright © 1976 by Kurt Vonnegut Jr. Reprinted by permission of Donald C. Faber, attorney for Mr. Vonnegut.

The Power of the Mysterious in A Connecticut Yankee

Although he was raised in what has been called the country's "Bible Belt," Twain found church services, especially the praying, to be downright comical. Why? Because, in an age of steam engines and dynamos and the telegraph and so on, praying seemed so *impractical*, I think.

Twain himself had had tremendously satisfying adventures with the most glamorous conglomerations of machinery imaginable, which were riverboats. So praying, as opposed to inventing and engineering, was bound to seem to him, and to so many like him, as the silliest possible way to get things done.

He was what would later be called "a technocrat."

He wished to sweep away superstitions and romantic illusions with laughter—because they were so *useless*. Connecticut Yankees should run the world, because they kept up with scientific discoveries and they had no illusions. They knew what would *really* work. They knew what was *really* going on.

Hi ho.

I have heard it said that the ending of *A Connecticut Yankee* was a prophecy of the World Wars Twain did not live to see. Superstitious knights fight technocrats, and both armies become parts of a pestilential mulch of corpses. This seems to me a better description of the war between the Confederacy and the Union than of the World Wars, which pitted technocrats against technocrats, and in which no one could have any illusions any more.

It is my belief that Twain was less interested in prophecy than ending his tale some way—almost any *which* way. So he did what Herman Melville did in *Moby-Dick*. He killed everybody, except for one survivor to tell the tale.

It is such a clumsy ending, in my opinion, that it destroys the balance of the author himself. It causes him to suggest some things about himself which he would have preferred not to see the light of day.

For instance: Merlin, the personification of contemptible superstititions, is present at the end. All through the book, Merlin has been a transparent fraud. But then he casts a spell which is more astonishing than anything the Connecticut Yankee has done. Merlin puts the Yankee to sleep for thirteen centuries. He can work miracles after all.

Not only that, but Merlin comes on his wicked errand *disguised as a woman.*

Imagine that.

Is it possible that Twain, the clear-eyed technocrat, could not help believing in magic after all? I think maybe so.

Is it possible that he suspected that women and their praying, from whom Huck Finn fled in such a frenzy, had mysterious powers superior to those of scientists and engineers? I think maybe so.

Camelot's Castle in Connecticut

Hamlin Hill

In *A Connecticut Yankee in King Arthur's Court*, Hank Morgan wakes up to the sight of a knight and soon spies a castle—yet he believes he is still in Connecticut. Twain's contemporaries would have understood: P.T. Barnum, the famous circus showman, had built a castle in Bridgeport, Connecticut, and stocked it with colorful circus leftovers. The connection with Barnum, a friend of Twain's, also suggests certain parallels between him and Morgan.

In the opening pages of *A Connecticut Yankee in King Arthur's Court*, Hank Morgan receives "a crusher alongside the head that made everything crack"; and when he awakens, he finds "a fellow fresh out of a picture-book" challenging him to "just." Hank suggests that the knight "get along back to your circus," and as the two march along Hank is puzzled because "we did not come to any circus or sign of a circus." Then follows the passage which Bernard De Voto claimed no one before Mark Twain could have launched a novel with:

> At the end of an hour we saw a far-away town sleeping in a valley by a winding river; and beyond it on a hill, a vast gray fortress, with towers and turrets, the first I had ever seen out of a picture.
>
> "Bridgeport?" said I, pointing.
>
> "Camelot," said he.

To my knowledge, no one has questioned why Hank should take a knight in armor so matter-of-factly, why he should refer three times to a circus or why a vast gray fortress with towers and turrets should not seem out of place in Bridgeport, Connecticut.

If Twain's allusion is obscure to modern readers, it was not to his contemporaries. Bridgeport was the headquarters of P.T.

Hamlin Hill, "Barnum, Bridgeport, and *The Connecticut Yankee*," *American Quarterly*, Winter 1964, p. 615. Copyright 1964, University of Pennsylvania. Reprinted by permission of the Johns Hopkins University Press.

Barnum, whose path Twain had first crossed when he described the Museum in an *Alta California* letter of April 9, 1867, and burlesqued Barnum's political aspirations in another letter the next day. The two later became friends, and Barnum attempted in the mid-1870s to persuade Twain "to write something that would help to popularize 'The Greatest Show on Earth.'"

Directly to the point, in 1848 Barnum constructed his "castle" Iranistan on the hills overlooking Bridgeport. Perhaps the best description of Iranistan is Constance Rourke's:

> The extravagant house ... arose, with serried balconies, wide wings, shining domes, spires, minarets, and a lacy fretwork wherever fretwork could be introduced, along the balconies, above the windows, at the cornices. Everything glittered; the edifice might have been washed with gold or silver; a huge fountain played outside; bronze deer appeared in clusters on the grounds; and beyond, lay the fair semblance of an English park.

Woodcuts of Iranistan appear in almost every edition of Barnum's *Struggles and Triumphs* (a book that was among Mark Twain's favorites), and it is towered and turreted enough for anyone to understand Hank Morgan's confusion about Bridgeport and Camelot.

In addition, Barnum collected at Iranistan all the rejects and leftovers from his museums and menageries, including Rocky Mountain elk on the grounds and an elephant with a keeper in Oriental costume who hitched a plow to the animal and dug furrows whenever a train appeared on the adjacent New York and New Haven railroad track. In such a setting, why expect Hank to be nonplused at a knight in armor?

When Iranistan burned in October 1852, Barnum built a succession of smaller, less palatial homes in Bridgeport—Lindencroft, Waldemere and Marina; but it is undoubtedly Iranistan, patterned on George IV's Brighton Pavilion, which provides the gloss for Hank's mention of Bridgeport.

There are, further, some tantalizing parallels between Hank Morgan and P.T. Barnum. Both were Connecticut Yankees, both shrewd entrepreneurs; both were interested in dazzling "effects" of showmanship and humbug, and both were amateur inventors. Perhaps it strains the indebtedness too far to suggest that Mark Twain had Barnum in mind when he created the character of Hank Morgan, but it does seem certain that the opening passage of *The Connecticut Yankee*, which refers to circuses and a castle in Bridgeport, can be read properly only in the context of Barnum's career.

The Absurdity of Man-Made Differentials

Langston Hughes

In *Pudd'nhead Wilson*, Mark Twain's basic theme is a serious treatment of slavery—and of the absurdity of any artificial differentiation made between people, such as caste or race. In presenting Negroes as developed human beings, Mark Twain stands above most writers of his time. That Twain was a man ahead of his time is also shown by his use of fingerprinting in his story (two years before the international chiefs of police decided to study the use of fingerprints) and his understanding of behavioristic psychology.

Mark Twain's ironic little novel, *Pudd'nhead Wilson*, is laid on the banks of the Mississippi in the first half of the 1800s. It concerns itself with, among other things, the use of fingerprinting to solve the mystery of a murder. But *Pudd'nhead Wilson* is not a mystery novel. The reader knows from the beginning who committed the murder and has more than an inkling of how it will be solved. The circumstances of the denouement, however, possessed in its time great novelty, for fingerprinting had not then come into official use in crime detection in the United States. Even a man who fooled around with it as a hobby was thought to be a simpleton, a puddenhead. Such was the reputation acquired by Wilson, the young would-be lawyer in the Missouri frontier town of Dawson's Landing. But Wilson eventually made his detractors appear as puddenheads themselves.

Although introduced early, it is not until near the end of the book that Wilson becomes a major figure in the tale. The novel is rather the story of another young man's mistaken identity—a young man who thinks he is white but is in reality colored; who is heir to wealth without knowing his claim is false; who lives as a free man, but is legally a slave; and who,

Langston Hughes, Introduction to *Pudd'nhead Wilson* by Mark Twain (New York: Bantam Books, 1959). Copyright © 1959 by Bantam Books; renewed 1987 by George Houston Bass. Reprinted by permission of Harold Ober Associates.

when he learns the true facts about himself, comes to ruin not through the temporarily shattering knowledge of his physical status, but because of weaknesses common to white or colored, slave or free. The young man thinks his name is Thomas à Becket Driscoll, but it is really Valet de Chambre—a name used for twenty-three years by another who is held as a slave in his stead, but who, unknown to himself, is white—and therefore legally free.

Puddn'head Wilson is the man, who, in the end, sets things to rights. But for whom? Seemingly for the spectators only, not for the principals involved, for by that time to them right is wrong, wrong is right, and happiness has gone by the board. The slave system has taken its toll of all three concerned—mother, mammy, ward and child—for the mother and mammy, Roxana, matriarch and slave, are one. Roxy is a puppet whose at first successful deceits cause her to think herself a free agent. She is undone at the climax by the former laughing stock of the town, Pudd'nhead Wilson, whose long interest in the little swirls at the ends of the fingers finally pays off.

SLAVERY, SERIOUSLY TREATED

Years before he published *Pudd'nhead Wilson* Mark Twain had been hailed as America's greatest humorist. From *The Celebrated Jumping Frog of Calaveras County* in 1865 to *The Adventures of Huckleberry Finn* in 1884, most of his fiction—and his spoken words on the lecture platform—had been sure sources of laughter. But in this work of his middle years (Twain was 59) he did not write a humorous novel. Except for a few hilarious village scenes, and a phonetic description of a baby's tantrums, the outloud laughs to be found in *Tom Sawyer* or *Huckleberry Finn* are not a part of *Pudd'nhead*. In this book the basic theme is slavery, seriously treated, and its main thread concerns the absurdity of man-made differentials, whether of caste or "race." The word *race* might properly be placed in quotes for both of Mark Twain's central Negroes are largely white in blood and physiognomy, slaves only by circumstance, and each only "by a fiction of law and custom, a Negro." The white boy who is mistakenly raised as a slave in the end finds himself

> rich and free, but in a most embarrassing situation. He could neither read nor write, and his speech was the basest dialect of the Negro quarter. His gait, his attitudes, his gestures, his bearing, his laugh—all were vulgar and uncouth; his manners were the manners of a slave. Money and fine clothes could not mend these defects or cover them up, they only made them the more

glaring and pathetic. The poor fellow could not endure the terrors of the white man's parlour, and felt at home and at peace nowhere but in the kitchen.

On the other hand, the young dandy who thought his name was Thomas à Becket, studied at Yale. He then came home to Dawson's Landing bedecked in Eastern finery to lord it over black and white alike. As Pudd'nhead Wilson, who had the habit of penning little musings beneath the dates in his calendar, wrote, "Training is everything. The peach was once a bitter almond; cauliflower is nothing but cabbage with a college education." It took a foreigner with no regard for frontier aristocracy of Old Virginia lineage to kick Thomas à Becket right square in his sit-downer at a public meeting. In the ensuing free-for-all that breaks out, the hall is set afire. Here the sparkle of Twain's traditional humor bursts into hilarious flame, too, as the members of the nearby fire department— "who never stirred officially in unofficial costume"—donned their uniforms to drench the hall with enough water to "annihilate forty times as much fire as there was there; for a village fire company does not often get a chance to show off." Twain wryly concludes, "Citizens of that village ... did not insure against fire; they insured against the fire-company."

Against fire and water in the slave states there was insurance, but none against the devious dangers of slavery itself. Not even a fine old gentleman like Judge Driscoll "of the best blood of the Old Dominion" could find insurance against the self-protective schemes of his brother's bond servant, Roxy, who did not like being a slave, but was willing to be one for her son's sake. Roxy was also willing to commit a grievous sin for her son's sake, palliating her conscience a little by saying, "white folks has done it." With "an unfair show in the battle of life," as Twain puts it, Roxy, as an "heir of two centuries of unatoned insult and outrage," is yet not of an evil nature. Her crimes grow out of the greater crimes of the slave system. "The man in whose favor no laws of property exist," Thomas Jefferson wrote in his *Notes on Virginia*, "feels himself less bound to respect those made in favor of others."

THE STRUCTURE OF SLAVE SOCIETY

Roxy's fear of eventually receiving the same punishment as that threatened other servants for the thieving of a few dollars from their master, Percy Driscoll, was enough to start a chain of thought in her mind that led eventually to disaster. Even though her master was "a fairly humane man towards slaves and other animals," was he not a thief himself? Certainly he was, to one in bondage, "the man who daily robbed him of an inestimable treasury—his liberty." Out of the structure of slave society itself is fashioned a noose of doom. In *Pudd'nhead Wilson* Mark Twain wrote what at a later period might have been called in the finest sense of the term, "a novel of social significance." Had Twain been a contemporary of Harriet Beecher Stowe, and this novel published before the War between the States, it might have been a minor *Uncle Tom's Cabin*. Twain minces no words in describing the unfortunate effects of slavery upon the behavior of both Negroes and whites, even upon children. The little master Thomas, and the little slave, Chambers, were both born on the same day and grew up together. But even in

> babyhood Tom cuffed and banged and scratched Chambers unrebuked, and Chambers early learned that between meekly bearing it and resenting it, the advantage all lay with the former policy. The few times his persecutions had moved him beyond control and made him fight back had cost him ... three such convincing canings from the man who was his father and didn't know it, that he took Tom's cruelties in all humility after that, and made no more experiments. Outside of the house the two boys were together all through their boyhood.... Tom staked him with marbles to play "keeps" with, and then took all the winnings away from him. In the winter season Chambers was on hand, in Tom's worn-out clothes ... to drag a sled up the hill for Tom, warmly clad, to ride down on; but he never got a ride himself. He built snow men and snow fortifications under Tom's directions. He was Tom's patient target when Tom wanted to do some snowballing, but the target couldn't fire back. Chambers carried Tom's skates to the river and strapped them on him, then trotted around after him on the ice, so as to be on hand when wanted; but he wasn't ever asked to try the skates himself.

A MODERN NOVEL

Mark Twain, in his presentation of Negroes as human beings, stands head and shoulders above the other Southern writers of his times, even such distinguished ones as Joel Chandler Harris, F. Hopkins Smith, and Thomas Nelson Page. It was a period when most writers who included Negro characters in their work at all were given to presenting the slave as ignorant and happy, the freed men of color as ignorant and miserable, and all Negroes as either comic servants on the one hand or dangerous brutes on the other. That Mark Twain's characters in *Pudd'nhead Wilson* fall into none of these categories is a tribute to his discernment. And that he makes them neither heroes nor villains is a tribute to his understanding of human character. "Color is only skin deep." In this novel Twain shows how more than anything else environment shapes the man. Yet in his day behavioristic psychology was in its infancy. Likewise the science of fingerprinting. In 1894 *Pudd'nhead Wilson* was a "modern" novel indeed. And it still may be so classified.

SHARING IMPIOUS ATTITUDES

Why, I asked myself, has the lawyer or the judge seldom appeared in our literature, serious or popular, in heroic roles?

One answer is that the presentation of the law in an unfavorable light allows for the formal expression and sharing of attitudes which are impious and irreverent, and that given such attitudes, they must be socially controlled, made visible, and socialized; otherwise they might be a force for the destruction of social order. . . .

I am not going to burden you with recounting the legal climate of 1894, when Mark Twain published *Pudd'nhead Wilson*. I will just remind you that it was a period of great theft, of much legal skulduggery, and no doubt this had something to do with the presentation. But if we think a little bit about Mark Twain as a humorist, and think about literary form as having a social function, then perhaps Twain was being far more than irreverent when he presented men of the legal profession in a comic light, because by so presenting them he allowed people who were very upset by some of the legal goings-on in the society to reveal their feelings, to laugh at themselves, and most impious of all, to laugh at the courts and perhaps at the Constitution itself.

Ralph Ellison, *Going to the Territory*, 1976.

Although knowledge of fingerprinting dates back some two thousand years, and fingerprints are found as signatures on ancient Chinese tablets and Babylonian records, it was not until 1880 that the first treatise on the possible use of fingerprinting in criminal identification appeared in English. And it was sixteen years later (two years after the appearance of *Pudd'nhead Wilson*) before the International Association of Chiefs of Police meeting in Chicago in 1896 decided to set up a Bureau of Criminal Identification and, as a part of its program, study ways and means whereby fingerprinting might supplement or perhaps supplant the Bertillon system of bodily measurements as a means of identifying criminals. So Mark Twain was well ahead of the international keepers of law and order when he devoted several pages in his novel to a description of how fingerprints might be used for the positive identification of a criminal who has neglected to put on gloves before committing a crime.

"Every human being," Twain has Pudd'nhead Wilson inform the court, "carries with him from his cradle to his grave certain physical marks which do not change their character, and by which he can always be identified—and that without shade of doubt or question. These marks are his signature, his physiological autograph, so to speak, and this autography cannot be counterfeited, nor can he disguise it or hide it away, nor can it become illegible by the wear and the mutations of time. . . . This autograph consists of the delicate lines or corrugations with which Nature marks the insides of the hands and the soles of the feet. If you will look at the balls of your fingers—you that have very sharp eyesight—you will observe that these dainty curving lines lie close together, like those that indicate the borders of oceans in maps, and that they form various clearly defined patterns, such as arches, circles, long curves, whorls, etc., and that these patterns differ on the different fingers."

Curiously enough, as modern as *Pudd'nhead Wilson* is, its format is that of an old-fashioned melodrama, as if its structure were borrowed from the plays performed on the riverboat theatres of that period. Perhaps deliberately, Twain selected this popular formula in which to tell a very serious story. Moving from climax to climax, every chapter ends with a teaser that makes the reader wonder what is coming next while, as in Greek tragedy, the fates keep closing in on the central protagonists. And here the fates have no regard whatsoever for color lines. It is this treatment of race that makes *Pudd'nhead Wilson* as contemporary as Little Rock [Arkansas: Gov. Orval Faubus unsuccessfully defied federal orders to desegregate public schools, 1957–1958], and Mark Twain as modern as William Faulkner, although Twain died when Faulkner was in knee pants.

The first motion picture was made in the year in which Twain wrote *Pudd'nhead Wilson*. As if looking ahead to the heyday of this medium, the author begins his story with a sweeping panorama of the river and Dawson's Landing, then briefly poses by name the cast of characters against it. Thereafter, he continues his tale in a series of visualizations, most of them growing logically one from another, but some quite coincidentally. A common dictum in Hollywood is, "Simply picture it on the screen, and the audience will believe it—because *there it is*." The advent of two handsome Italian twins in Dawson's Landing is pictured so vividly that the reader believes the men are there, and only briefly wonders *why*—although these two fellows immediately begin to figure prominently in the frightful march of events leading toward the novel's climax. But, to tell the truth, we do not need to know exactly why these ebullient twins came to Dawson's Landing. And they do brighten up the story considerably.

Additional, and what seem at first to be extraneous flashes of amusing brilliance in the novel (and at other times sober or ironic comment) are the excerpts that serve as chapter headings from *Pudd'nhead Wilson's Calendar.* "Few things are harder to put up with than the annoyance of a good example." And another: "It is often the case that the man who can't tell a lie thinks he is the best judge of one." And an observation that would have almost surely, had there been a McCarthy Committee in Twain's day, caused the author to be subpoenaed before it: *"October 12—The Discovery—*It was wonderful to find America, but it would have been more wonderful to miss it." And a final admonition that might almost be Mark Twain himself concerned with the tight and astringent style of this smallest of his novels: "As to the Adjective: when in doubt, strike it out." *Pudd'nhead Wilson* marches along much too rapidly to be bothered with a plethora of adjectives.

Chronology

For names and dates of more of Twain's works, see "Works by Mark Twain."

1835
November 30—Samuel Langhorne Clemens (who will become Mark Twain) is born in Florida, Missouri.

1838
Frederick Douglass escapes from slavery. Race riots and lynchings have been increasing for three years. The Underground Railroad, which helps slaves escape and tries to protect them from violent pursuers, is established.

1839
The Clemens family moves to Hannibal, Missouri, on the Mississippi River.

1842
British author Charles Dickens tours the United States, crusading for international copyright laws and attacking the institution of slavery.

1843
Sojourner Truth, a freed slave who saw most of her thirteen children sold as slaves, speaks out against slavery around the country.

1845
Editor John L. O'Sullivan writes that the nation has a "Manifest Destiny"—that it is the will of God that the United States expand and control the entire North American continent.

1847
March—Sam's father, John Marshall Clemens, dies.

1848
Sam is apprenticed to the Hannibal *Courier* to learn the newspaper trade. Gold is discovered near Sutter's Mill in California; gold rush begins. Political and social revolutions and rebellions sweep Europe.

1850
September—Orion Clemens, Sam's brother, begins publishing the weekly Hannibal *Western Union*. In the same month, Congress adopts the Compromise of 1850 in an attempt to prevent

the dissolution of the Union over the issue of slavery.

1851
January—Sam begins working on the *Western Union*.

1852
Harriet Beecher Stowe's *Uncle Tom's Cabin* is published. On July 4, Frederick Douglass states that Negroes should not celebrate Independence Day, since so many of them are slaves. Daniel Webster and Henry Clay, who helped hold the Union together while clashing on most other issues, both die this year.

1854
Abraham Lincoln calls for the gradual emancipation of slaves; "No man is good enough to govern another man without that other's consent," he asserts.

1855
Walt Whitman pays to have his book *Leaves of Grass* printed, and sets ten of its ninety-five pages into type himself.

1856
October 18—Sam's first letter signed "Thomas Jefferson Snodgrass" appears in the Keokuk, Iowa, *Daily Post*.

1857
Overspeculation in railroads and real estate leads to national financial panic. Sam begins training as a riverboat pilot.

1858
June 13—The steamer *Philadelphia* explodes; victims include Sam's brother Henry, who dies six days later.

1859
April 9—Sam Clemens receives his pilot's license.

June—The Comstock silver lode is discovered in Nevada.

1860
November 6—Abraham Lincoln is elected president.

December 20—South Carolina votes to secede from the Union.

1861
April 14—Fort Sumter, South Carolina, is captured by Confederate forces.

April 15—Lincoln declares a state of "insurrection." The American Civil War begins.

June—Ten more states have seceded to join South Carolina in the Confederacy.

January 21–March 30—Sam's "Quintus Curtius Snodgrass" letters are published in the New Orleans *Crescent.*

February 28—The Nevada Territory (known then as the Washoe) is created from land taken from Mexico.

June—Sam sees brief service with the Confederate Marion's Rangers ("The Campaign That Failed").

July—Sam and Orion go to Carson City, Nevada, where Orion is to take up his post as the secretary of the Nevada Territory.

1862

February–July—Sam's "Josh" letters are published in the Virginia City *Territorial Enterprise.*

August—Sam joins the Enterprise staff.

1863

January 1—Lincoln signs the Emancipation Proclamation.

February 3—Sam first uses "Mark Twain" byline.

November 20—Lincoln delivers the Gettysburg Address.

1864

May—Twain leaves Virginia City for San Francisco.

October 31—Nevada becomes a state; cynics suggest that the timing—just before the November presidential election—is intended to help Lincoln's chances for reelection.

1865

March 4—Lincoln is sworn in for his second term as president.

April 9—Confederate general Robert E. Lee surrenders to Union general Ulysses S. Grant at Appomattox, Virginia, bringing the Civil War to an end.

April 14—Lincoln is assassinated.

November 18—"The Celebrated Jumping Frog of Calaveras County" is printed in the New York *Saturday Press.* Relief at the end of the war has many Americans looking for light-hearted fare; the "Frog" is an immediate success.

1866

Twain spends four months in the Sandwich Islands (Hawaii). On his return to San Francisco he begins giving lectures, earning enough by December to pay for his passage to New York.

1867

May—*The Celebrated Jumping Frog of Calaveras County and Other Sketches* is published.

June 8—As travel correspondent for the San Francisco *Alta California*, Twain sails on the *Quaker City* for a tour of the Mediterranean and the Holy Land. This tour will become the basis of *The Innocents Abroad*.

December 27—Twain meets Olivia ("Livy") Langdon.

1869

February 4—Sam becomes engaged to Livy.

1870

February 2—Sam marries Livy.

November 7—Their first child, Langdon Clemens, is born.

1872

March 19—Olivia Susan (Susy) Clemens is born.

June 2—Langdon Clemens (Sam and Livy's only son) dies.

1873

December—*The Gilded Age* is published. The title of this tale of rampant greed and financial chicanery will be used to describe the entire period from 1870 to 1898.

1874

June 8—Clara Clemens is born.

1880

July 26—Jean Clemens is born.

1884

Twain campaigns for Grover Cleveland for president.

1885

Fall—Twain publishes the memoirs of Ulysses S. Grant.

1890

Twain begins investing in the Paige typesetting machine.

1891

March 4—The International Copyright Act Twain and Dickens lobbied for is passed, protecting foreign authors from piracy at the hands of American publishers. (Twain, who has suffered piracy from publishers around the world, hopes other countries will follow suit.)

1892

King Leopold II of Belgium, who rules the Congo Free State, imposes forced labor on the natives. His personal rule of the region will become so scandalous that on October 18, 1908, the Belgian parliament will take over the country, renaming it the Belgian Congo (today called Zaire).

1893

A stock-market crash in June leads to a national financial panic; by the end of the year, the country is in what is being called the worst depression in its history.

July 12—Frederick Jackson Turner declares that the American "frontier has gone, and with it has closed the first period of American history."

1894

April 18—With the failure of his publishing company and other financial difficulties, Twain is bankrupt.

June—Coal miners end a bloody two-month strike, undertaken to protest wage cuts and dangerous working conditions. Unrest in the coal industry has decimated Livy's income from coal stocks.

1895

July—Twain begins world lecture tour to pay off debts.

1896

August 18—Susy Clemens dies.

1898

The Twains' last debts are paid off in late 1898 or early 1899. In winning the Spanish-American War, the United States establishes itself as a world power. The Anti-Imperialist League objects to the growing drive to claim American colonies. Twain, reformer Jane Addams, philosopher William James, industrialist Andrew Carnegie, labor leader Samuel Gompers, and thirty thousand other members of the league object to U.S. conquests to build an empire.

1901

February—*To the Person Sitting in Darkness* is published (the publisher is the Anti-Imperialist League of New York).

1904

June 5—Livy Clemens dies.

1905

King Leopold's Soliloquy: A Defense of His Congo Rule, about Leopold II's ill-treatment of his subjects in the Congo (see 1892 above), is published.

1909

December 24—Jean Clemens dies.

1910

April 21—Mark Twain dies.

WORKS BY MARK TWAIN

Since many volumes and many different editions and combinations of Mark Twain's work have been made available over the years (and previously unpublished material still appears occasionally), the following is not a complete listing. Short stories and essays are generally included only when they have been collected into books; dates are for first U.S. publication.

1867

The Celebrated Jumping Frog of Calaveras County and Other Sketches.

1869

The Innocents Abroad, or The New Pilgrims' Progress.

1871

Mark Twain's (Burlesque) Autobiography and First Romance.

1872

Roughing It.

1873

The Gilded Age: A Tale of To-day [with Charles Dudley Warner].

1874

Mark Twain's Sketches.

1875

Sketches, New and Old.

1876

The Adventures of Tom Sawyer.

1877

Ah Sin [with Bret Harte].

A True Story and the Recent Carnival of Crime. [*The Facts Concerning the Recent Carnival of Crime in Connecticut.*]
Punch, Brothers, Punch! and Other Sketches.

1880

A Tramp Abroad.

"1601" or Conversation at the Social Fireside as It Was in the Time of the Tudors.

1882
The Prince and the Pauper.
The Stolen White Elephant, Etc.

1883
Life on the Mississippi.

1885
The Adventures of Huckleberry Finn (Tom Sawyer's Comrade).

1888
Mark Twain's Library of Humor. Edited by Samuel Langhorne Clemens, William Dean Howells, and Charles Hopkins Clark. [Contains works by Twain, "Anonymous," and forty-six other authors.]

1889
A Connecticut Yankee in King Arthur's Court.

1890
The Man That Corrupted Hadleyburg.

1892
The American Claimant.
Merry Tales.

1893
The £1,000,000 Bank-note and Other New Stories.
The Niagara Book [by W.D. Howells, Mark Twain, Prof. Nathaniel S. Shaler, and others].

1894
The Tragedy of Pudd'nhead Wilson and the Comedy of Those Extraordinary Twins [by 1899 called *Pudd'nhead Wilson and Those Extraordinary Twins*].
Tom Sawyer Abroad ["by Huck Finn, edited by Mark Twain"].

1896
The Personal Recollections of Joan of Arc.
Tom Sawyer Abroad, Tom Sawyer Detective, and Other Stories.

1897
How to Tell a Story and Other Essays.
Following the Equator.

1900

The Man That Corrupted Hadleyburg and Other Stories and Essays.

1901

To the Person Sitting in Darkness.

1902

A Double Barrelled Detective Story.

1903

My Debut as a Literary Person with Other Essays and Stories.

The Jumping Frog in English, Then in French, Then Clawed Back into a Civilized Language Once More by Patient Unremunerated Toil.

1904

Extracts from Adam's Diary, Translated from the Original MS.

A Dog's Tale.

1905

King Leopold's Soliloquy: A Defense of His Congo Rule.

Editorial Wild Oats.

1906

Eve's Diary, Translated from the Original MS.

What Is Man?

The $30,000 Bequest and Other Stories.

1907

Christian Science.

A Horse's Tale.

1909

Extract from Captain Stormfield's Visit to Heaven.

Is Shakespeare Dead? From My Autobiography.

PUBLISHED POSTHUMOUSLY

1910

Mark Twain's Speeches. Compiled by F.A. Nast. Introduction by W.D. Howells.

1913

Death-Disk.

1916

The Mysterious Stranger.

1917

Mark Twain's Letters. Edited by Albert Bigelow Paine.

Who Was Sarah Findlay? With a Suggested Solution of the Mystery by J.M. Barrie.

1919

The Curious Republic of Gondour and Other Whimsical Sketches [by Samuel L. Clemens].

1920

Mark Twain, Able Yachtsman, Interviews Himself on Why Lipton Failed to Lift the Cup.

1922–1925

The Writings of Mark Twain. 37 vols. Edited by Albert Bigelow Paine. [Includes *Mark Twain's Autobiography*, 2 vols., 1924.]

1928

The Adventures of Thomas Jefferson Snodgrass. Edited by Charles Honce.

1930

A Champagne Cocktail and a Catastrophe: Two Acting Charades.

1935

Mark Twain's Notebook. Edited by Albert Bigelow Paine.

1938

Letters from the Sandwich Islands Written for the Sacramento Union *by Mark Twain.* Edited by G. Ezra Dane.

1940

Mark Twain in Eruption: Hitherto Unpublished Pages About Men and Events. Edited by Bernard De Voto.

Mark Twain's Travels with Mr. Brown. Edited by G. Ezra Dane.

1941

Mark Twain's Letters to Will Bowen: "My First & Oldest & Dearest Friend." Edited by Theodore Hornberger.

1942

Mark Twain's Letters in the Muscatine Journal. Edited by Edgar M. Branch.

1946

The Letters of Quintius Curtius Snodgrass.

1949

The Love Letters of Mark Twain. Edited by Dixon Wecter.

Mark Twain to Mrs. Fairbanks. Edited by Dixon Wecter.

1953

Mark Twain to Uncle Remus [Joel Chandler Harris]. Edited by Thomas H. English.

1957

Mark Twain of the Enterprise. Edited by Henry Nash Smith with Frederick Anderson.

1959

The Autobiography of Mark Twain. Edited by Charles Neider. [Quotations from the *Autobiography* in the present work were taken from this version.]

1960

Mark Twain–Howells Letters: The Correspondence of Samuel L. Clemens and William Dean Howells, 1872–1910. 2 vols. Edited by Henry Nash Smith and William M. Gibson. [Cover says "1869–1910."]

1961

Mark Twain's Letters to Mary. Edited by Lewis Leary.

1962

Letters from the Earth. Edited by Bernard De Voto.

1979

Early Tales and Sketches, vol. 1 (1851–1864). Edited by Edgar Marquess Branch and Robert H. Hirst with Harriet Elinor Smith.

1987

The Outrageous Mark Twain: Some Lesser-Known but Extraordinary Works, with "Reflections on Religion" Now in Book Form for the First Time. Edited by Charles Neider.

1991

Mark Twain's Aquarium: The Samuel Clemens Angelfish Correspondence, 1905–1910. Edited by John Cooley.

FOR FURTHER RESEARCH

Frederick Anderson and Kenneth M. Sanderson. *Mark Twain: The Critical Heritage.* New York: Barnes and Noble, 1971.

Van Wyck Brooks. *The Ordeal of Mark Twain.* New York: Dutton, 1920. Revised edition, 1933.

Louis J. Budd, ed. *Critical Essays on Mark Twain, 1867–1910.* Boston: G.K. Hall, 1982.

Louis J. Budd, ed. *Critical Essays on Mark Twain, 1910–1980.* Boston: G.K. Hall, 1983.

Louis J. Budd, ed. *A Listing and Selection from Newspaper and Magazine Interviews of Samuel Clemens: 1874–1910.* Arlington, TX: American Literary Realism, 1977.

Clara Clemens. *My Father, Mark Twain.* New York: Harper & Brothers, 1931.

Cyril Clemens. *Young Sam Clemens.* Portland, ME: Leon Tebbetts, 1942.

James M. Cox. *Mark Twain: The Fate of Humor.* Princeton, NJ: Princeton University Press, 1966.

Sherwood Cummings. *Mark Twain and Science.* Baton Rouge: Louisiana State University Press, 1988.

Bernard De Voto. *Mark Twain at Work.* Cambridge, MA: Harvard University Press, 1942.

Bernard De Voto. *Mark Twain's America.* Boston: Little, Brown, 1932.

Margaret Duckett. *Mark Twain and Bret Harte.* Norman: University of Oklahoma Press, 1964.

Everett Emerson. *The Authentic Mark Twain: A Literary Biography of Samuel Clemens.* Philadelphia: University of Pennsylvania Press, 1984.

Shelley Fisher Fishkin. *Was Huck Black? Mark Twain and African-American Voices.* New York: Oxford University Press, 1993.

Philip Foner. *Mark Twain, Social Critic.* New York: International Publishers, 1958.

Walter Francis Frear. *Mark Twain and Hawaii.* Chicago: Lakeside Press, 1947.

Dewey Ganzel. *Mark Twain Abroad: The Cruise of the Quaker City.* Chicago: University of Chicago Press, 1968.

Susan Gillman. *Dark Twins: Imposture and Identity in Mark Twain's America.* Chicago: University of Chicago Press, 1989.

Susan Gillman and Forrest G. Robinson, eds. *Mark Twain's Pudd'nhead Wilson: Race, Conflict, and Culture.* Durham, NC: Duke University Press, 1990.

William Dean Howells. *My Mark Twain: Reminiscences and Criticisms.* New York: Harper & Brothers, 1910.

M. Thomas Inge, ed. *Huck Finn Among the Critics: A Centennial Selection.* Frederick, MD: University Publications of America, 1985.

Justin Kaplan. *Mark Twain and His World.* New York: Simon and Schuster, 1974.

Justin Kaplan, *Mr. Clemens and Mark Twain: A Biography.* New York: Simon and Schuster, 1966.

Sydney J. Krause. *Mark Twain as Critic.* Baltimore, MD: Johns Hopkins University Press, 1967.

John Lauber. *The Making of Mark Twain: A Biography.* New York: American Heritage Press, 1985.

James S. Leonard, Thomas A. Tenney, and Thadious Davis, eds. *Satire or Evasion? Black Perspectives on Huckleberry Finn.* Durham, NC: [Duke University Press], 1992.

E. Hudson Long. *Mark Twain Handbook.* New York: Hendricks House, 1957.

Fred Lorch. *The Trouble Begins at Eight: Mark Twain's Lecture Tours.* Ames: Iowa State University Press, 1968.

Kenneth S. Lynn. *Mark Twain and Southwestern Humor.* Boston: Little, Brown, 1959.

Effie Mona Mack. *Mark Twain in Nevada.* New York: Scribner's, 1947.

William R. Macnaughton. *Mark Twain's Last Years as a Writer.* Columbia: University of Missouri Press, 1979.

Bruce Michelson. *Mark Twain on the Loose: A Comic Writer and the American Self.* Amherst: University of Massachusetts Press, 1995.

Albert Bigelow Paine. *Mark Twain: A Biography. The Personal and Literary Life of Samuel Langhorne Clemens.* 3 vols. New York: Harper & Brothers, 1912.

George Sanderlin. *Mark Twain: As Others Saw Him.* New York: Coward, McCann & Geoghegan, 1978.

Henry Nash Smith. *Mark Twain: The Development of a Writer.* Cambridge, MA: Harvard University Press, 1962.

Edward Wagenknecht. *Mark Twain: The Man and His Work.* New Haven: Yale University Press, 1935.

Samuel C. Webster. *Mark Twain, Business Man.* Boston: Little, Brown, 1946.

Dixon Wecter. *Sam Clemens of Hannibal.* Boston: Houghton Mifflin, 1952.

James D. Wilson. *A Reader's Guide to the Short Stories of Mark Twain.* Boston: G.K. Hall, 1987.

INDEX

Addams, Jane, 100
African Americans. *See* blacks
Ah Sin, 84
Alcott, Louisa May
  on *Huckleberry Finn*, 136, 162, 166
Alta California, 34, 35, 53, 138, 184
America
  changes in, 119
  Great Valley, 46-48, 50, 53
  literature of
    classical influence, 45
    and democracy, 47, 126
    disdains Europe, 49, 133
    effect of *Huckleberry Finn* on, 143-44
    and heartland culture, 46-49
    and oral storytelling, 122
    reform, 168-73
  politics in, 98-99, 118
  Revolution, 171-72
  view of Europe, 48, 67, 116-17, 133, 171-72
America's Coming of Age (Brooks), 107
Angelou, Maya, 155, 156
Arac, Jonathan, 167
art, Twain's opinion of, 116
Arthurian England, 175-76, 178, 179, 183
A.T. Lacey (steamboat), 27
Atlantic Monthly, 39, 79, 135
Autobiography of Mark Twain, The, 175

Babcock, C. Merton, 124
banned books, 144, 155-56, 160-61
Barnum, P.T., 59, 183-84

Bellamy, Edward, 169-72
Bellamy, Gladys Carmen, 139
Bennett, Arnold, 96, 109
bible
  allusions to, 136-37
  influence on Twain's writing, 137
Bierce, Ambrose, 118
Billings, Josh, 130
Bixby, Horace, 26
blacks
  dialect of, 161
  object to *Huckleberry Finn*, 156, 165-67
  Southern portrayal of, 188
  and Twain, 15, 17-18, 160-61
  Twain's portrayal of, 188
Blair, Walter, 140, 145
Bliss, Elisha, 79
Boston Advertiser, 164
Boston Transcript, 143, 161, 162
Branch, Edgar Marquess, 78
Brashear, Minnie M., 114, 138
Bridges, Robert, 163
Brooks, Van Wyck, 91, 99, 108-14, 119
Brown, William, 26
Browning, Robert, 80
Buffalo Express, 77
Bunyan, John, 85, 86

Calverton, V. F., 111
"Captain Stormfield's Visit to Heaven," 180
Catcher in the Rye, The (Salinger), 155
Celebrated Jumping Frog of Calaveras County, The
  first book, 36, 53, 78

first success, 77, 89, 102, 115
labels Twain as humorist, 89, 115, 119, 186
origins of, 33-34
censorship, of books, 144, 155-56, 160-61
Cervantes, 137
characters, 138
Chinese, 56, 57
Civil War, 27-29, 46-47, 51, 52, 76, 98-99, 107, 181
Clare, Ada, 53
Clemens, Benjamin (brother), 14, 16
Clemens, Clara (daughter), 38, 42, 43
Clemens, Cyril (cousin), 85, 114
Clemens, Henry (brother), 14, 16, 24-27, 41, 95
Clemens, Jane Lampton (mother)
character of, 18, 19, 108
death of, 42
early married life, 13-14, 49
empathy for slaves, 18
influence on Sam, 18, 19, 108, 109, 111
poverty of, 19, 24, 102
and Sam's mischievousness, 16, 63
Clemens, Jean (daughter), 38, 42, 91
Clemens, John Marshall (father)
character of, 20, 62
death of, 19, 20, 63, 109, 112
early married life, 13-14, 49
moves family, 14-15, 19
as poor businessman, 14, 15, 19, 102
poverty of, 19, 40, 102
Clemens, Langdon (son), 38, 41
Clemens, Margaret (sister), 14, 15, 16
Clemens, Olivia Langdon (wife), 95, 110
death of, 41, 42
as editor of Twain's work, 98, 103, 112-13
influence on Twain, 37, 40, 103-104, 108, 111
marriage to Twain, 37-38
Clemens, Olivia Susan (Susy, daughter)
biographer of father, 27
death of, 38, 41, 42, 81, 95
Clemens, Orion (brother)
as abolitionist, 27
appointment to Nevada, 29, 34, 40, 52
apprentice to printer, 19-20
birth, 14
death, 42
newspaper work, 21-22, 24-25
work with brothers, 24-25, 29
Clemens, Pamela (sister), 14, 16, 20, 21, 26, 34, 42
Clemens, Pleasants Hannibal (brother), 14, 16
Clemens, Samuel Langhorne. *See* Twain, Mark
Clemens, Will, 62
Comstock Lode, 55-56, 58-59
Connecticut Yankee in King Arthur's Court, A, 67, 80
Author's Preface, 174
Camelot in, 175, 176, 178, 183
ending of, 181
"Final P.S. by M.T.," 174-75
Hank Morgan, 168, 172-73, 174-75, 179, 183-84
Merlin, 172, 173, 181-82
"Postscript by Clarence, A," 174
as reform literature, 168-73
social criticism in, 89, 112

stranger, 176-78
"Stranger's History, The," 177
structure of, 174-75
"Tale of the Lost Land, The," 174-75, 177, 179
technology in, 170-73, 175, 177, 181
as Utopian fantasy, 171-72
women in, 182
"A Word of Explanation," 174-76
Conrad, Joseph, 153
Coolbrith, Ina, 53
Cooper, James Fenimore, 126, 169, 172
Cox, James, 131, 171
Crompton, Charles H., 114

Daggett, Rollin, 58
Dahl, Roald, 155
Deerslayer (Cooper), 126
Defoe, Daniel, 85, 86
Democracy in America (de Tocqueville), 47
De Quille, Dan, 30, 55, 58, 59
De Voto, Bernard
  on continental American literature, 45-54
  on how frontier shaped Twain, 30, 36, 112-14
  on growth of Twain's work, 36
  on *Huckleberry Finn*, 166
  refutes Brooks's theory of Twain, 30, 112-14
  on Twain's birth, 14
Dickens, Charles, 80
Dos Passos, John, 144
Douglass, Frederick, 160
Dreiser, Theodore, 125, 131, 144
Dunne, Finley Peter, 100

Eastman, Max, 114, 124
Eliot, T.S.
  on *Huckleberry Finn*, 144, 151-54

Ellison, Ralph, 141, 157, 167, 189
Emerson, Ralph Waldo, 45, 49, 122, 161
Europe
  American view of, 48, 49, 67, 116-17, 133, 171-72
  literature of, 45, 116, 122
Europe and Elsewhere, 117
"Eve's Diary," 180

Fatout, Paul, 139, 140
Fairbanks, Mary Mason, 36
Faulkner, William, 131, 157, 190
"Fenimore Cooper's Literary Offenses," 43
Fishkin, Shelley Fisher, 157, 160-61
Fitzgerald, F. Scott, 144
Foner, Philip S., 89, 107, 127, 164
Frank, Waldo, 107-108
Freudianism, 43, 91-97, 107, 109, 111
Frost, Robert, 122

Garland, Hamlin, 72
Geismar, Maxwell, 133
geography, effect on literature, 46-51
Gibson, William M., 122
Gilded Age, The, 62
  Laura Hawkins's death, 72-73
Gillis, Steve, 57, 60-61
Gillman, Susan, 131
Going to the Territory (Ellison), 189
Golden Era, 53
Goldsmith, Oliver, 138
Goodman, Joe, 57, 58
Gorky, Maxim, 100-102
Grant, Ulysses S., 99
Grattan, C. Hartley, 114
Guild of Authors, 77

Halley's Comet, 42-43

Hannibal, Missouri
  influence on Twain, 15-20, 50-52, 62-63, 108, 113, 121, 161
  slavery in, 17-19
Hannibal Journal, 20-22
Harris, Frank, 111
Harte, Bret, 33, 34, 53, 84, 118
Hawthorne, Nathaniel, 45, 139, 173
Hemingway, Ernest, 144
  on *Huckleberry Finn*, 143, 157
Henry, O., 144
Herndon, William Henry, 47
Hicks, Granville, 111
Hill, Hamlin, 183
Hinckle, Warren, 55
Hinton, J.T., 22
Hirst, Robert H., 78
Hobbs, Fredric, 55
Howells, William Dean
  and Gorky, 100-101
  on Hannibal, Missouri, 62
  influence on Twain, 39, 93, 108, 111, 112-13
  on Twain, 90, 91, 131
  on Twain's use of words, 85-86
  Twain takes as mentor, 116, 119
"How I Escaped Being Killed in a Duel," 57
Huckleberry Finn, The Adventures of
  as adventure story, 145-46, 151, 159
  alcoholism in, 145, 157, 163
  Aunt Sally, 154, 157
  banning of, 144, 156, 162-67
  based on Twain's childhood, 15, 22, 28, 50, 63, 64, 67, 74, 137, 140-42
  beginning notice, 159, 163
  best work, 107, 111, 119
  blacks object to, 156, 165-67
  Boggs, 145, 160
  characterization in, 64, 145, 140, 157
  child abuse in, 145, 157
  Colonel Sherburn, 145, 160
  duality theme, 131-32
  Duke, 145, 147, 152
  editing of, 103
  ending of, 146, 153-54
  evil in, 51
  flaws in, 73, 109
  flight-to-freedom theme, 145-48
  Grangerford-Shepherdson feud, 145, 147, 152
  as great American novel, 127, 144, 153, 157, 165-66
  Huck, as symbol, 153-54
  Huck's character development, 145-49
  Huck's moral dilemma, 29, 147-49, 158
  humor in, 125, 126, 130, 153-54, 157-58, 186
  Injun Joe, 132
  is not for children, 136, 162-63, 165-67
  is not racist, 156, 159, 167
  Jim's flight to freedom, 145-48
  King, 145, 147, 152
  Miss Watson, 145, 147, 148
  moral values in, 158-59
  Mrs. Loftus, 146
  paired with *Tom Sawyer*, 157
  Phelps, 146, 147
  plot in, 73
  racial themes, 48, 133, 144, 147, 159, 167
  religion in, 149, 158
  reviews of, 143-44, 161-67
  river controls, 151-54
  social satire in, 145-50, 152, 153, 157
  story development, 146
  switched-meanings in, 159
  Tom Sawyer in, 29, 142, 153
  use of dialect in, 84, 161
  violence in, 145, 157, 160,

163
Widow Douglas, 145
Hughes, Langston, 157, 185
humor
  and *Celebrated Jumping Frog*, 89, 115, 119, 186
  dark, 125-27
  and deception, 134-35
  gravity of, 49
  "higher goofyism," 124-30
  in *Huckleberry Finn*, 125, 126, 130, 153-54, 157-58, 186
  innocent, 71-72
  in *Innocents Abroad*, 48-49, 67, 74, 88, 89, 92
  journalistic, 52, 58-59
  oral, 52
  in *Pudd'nhead Wilson*, 187, 191
  purposes of, 124, 126, 127, 135
  tradition in America, 122-23
  Twain excels at, 88-90, 124-30
  Twain fails at, 65-66
  in view of Europe, 67, 116
  warm, 124-25

I Know Why the Caged Bird Sings (Angelou), 155
Indians, 50-51, 56, 58
Industrial Revolution, 169, 172-73
Innocents Abroad, 36, 54
  disdains European culture, 48
  humor in, 48-49, 67, 74, 88, 89, 92
  money from, 102
  and moral conflict, 150
  popularity of, 77, 79
  seriousness in, 89, 115
Irving, Washington, 139

James, Henry, 126
Jehlen, Myra, 167
"Jim Smiley and His Jumping Frog," 34, 53
Jungle, The (Sinclair), 100

Kaplan, Justin, 100, 132, 162, 165
Keller, Helen, 70
Kipling, Rudyard, 92, 118
Kreymborg, Alfred, 111

Laguna, Theodore de, 69
Laird, James, 57, 60-61
Lamb, Charles, 80
Lang, Andrew, 144
Langdon, Jervis, 36-37
language
  American, 84-86
  spoken, 85-87
  used in characterization, 122-23
  use of dialect, 84, 123
  vernacular, 69-70, 74, 123, 127-28, 144, 157, 161, 167
Lardner, Ring, 144
Lauber, John, 16, 19, 56, 110
Lawson, Lewis A., 174
Leacock, Stephen, 64
Lewis, Sinclair, 144
Life magazine, 163
Life on the Mississippi
  as autobiographical, 26, 64, 67, 68, 76, 79
  as great writing, 115
  theme of duality in, 133
Lincoln, Abraham, 45-49, 66, 85, 86, 99
literature
  and democracy, 47, 49, 126
  geographical effects on, 46-51
  realism in, 143
  romanticism in, 138-39, 143
  see also America, literature of; Europe, literature of
Lohengrin (Wagner), 116
London, Jack, 107, 144
London Spectator, 111
London Times, 59
Looking Backward (Bellamy),

169, 171
Lynn, Kenneth, 139

Macy, John, 114
Malory, Thomas, 139
Man Who Corrupted Hadleyburg, The, 119
"Mark the Double Twain" (Dreiser), 132
Mark Twain (Leacock), 64
Mark Twain: An American Prophet (Geismar), 133
Mark Twain Laughing (Zall), 86
Mark Twain's America (De Voto), 107, 112, 113, 121
Mark Twain: Social Critic (Foner), 164
Mark Twain: The Fate of Humor (Cox), 171
Mark Twain—The Man and His Work (Wagenknecht), 114
Marx, Leo, 166
Masters, Edgar Lee, 111
Matthews, Brander, 83, 93, 127
McComb, John, 78
Melville, Herman, 45, 181
Mencken, H.L.
  compared with Twain, 124-30
  on Twain, 126, 127
Mississippi River, 52, 63-64, 152-54
Moby-Dick (Melville), 166, 181
Moffett, Annie, 14
Moffett, William, 26, 34
Moore, Olin H., 137
Moos, Malcolm, 125
Morrow, Lance, 155
Mr. Clemens and Mark Twain (Kaplan), 132, 162, 165
Mulford, Prentice, 53
Mumford, Lewis, 111
My Cousin Mark Twain (Clemens), 85

My Mark Twain (Howells), 131
Mysterious Stranger, The, 106, 119

Narrative of the Life of Frederick Douglass (Douglass), 160
New York Saturday Press, 34
New York Times, 165
New York Tribune, 53
New York World, 143
North American Review, 100, 165
Nye, Bill, 116, 129

Of Mice and Men (Steinbeck), 155, 156
Ordeal of Mark Twain, The (Brooks), 99, 107, 108, 110, 121
Our America (Frank), 107

Paige, James W., 39, 40
Paine, Albert Bigelow
  on death of Twain's father, 109
  on Gorky affair, 101
  on Twain and Halley's Comet, 42
  on Twain returns to Hannibal, 119-20
  on Twain's success, 92, 108
  on Twain's temperament, 91, 94, 95
Parrington, Vernon L., 111
Parshall, Gerald, 143
Pattee, Fred Lewis, 111
Pennsylvania (steamboat), 26-27
"Personal Habits of the Siamese Twins," 134
Personal Memoirs of Joan of Arc, 72, 80
"Petrified Man," 30, 31
Phelps, Elizabeth Stuart, 139
Phelps, William Lyon, 144, 165

Philadelphia Inquirer, 23
Pochmann, Henry A., 136
Poe, Edgar Allan, 45, 49, 93, 140
politics, American, 98-99
  Twain's involvement in, 118
Prejudices (Mencken), 126
Prince and the Pauper, The
  humor in, 74
  lookalike theme, 131, 133, 134
  social criticism in, 112
"Private History of a Campaign That Failed, The," 28, 52
Pudd'nhead Wilson
  on America, 179, 191
  autobiographical types in, 68
  behavioristic psychology of, 189
  evil in, 51
  fingerprinting in, 185-86, 189-90
  humor in, 64, 187, 191
  Percy Driscoll, 197
  Pudd'nhead Wilson, 186-87, 190
  Roxana, 186, 187
  slavery theme in, 186-88
  and storytelling art, 73
  theme of duality in, 131, 133, 185-86
  Thomas à Becket Driscoll, 186-88
  Valet de Chambre, 186, 188

Quarles, Patsy and John (aunt and uncle), 15
Quentin Durward (Scott), 116

racism, 133, 149-50, 156-57, 166-67
realism, 143
religion, 89-90, 111, 112, 115, 119, 180-81
Rice, Clement T., 30

Rockefeller, John D., 180
Rogers, Henry H., 40, 104, 118, 119
romanticism, 143
Roughing It
  as autobiographical, 29, 32, 57, 67, 76
  humor in, 115, 126
Ruskin, John, 126

Sacramento Union, 35
Salinger, J.D., 155, 156
Sanford, Charles L., 168
San Francisco Californian, 33, 53
San Francisco Chronicle, 34
San Francisco Morning Call, 32, 78
satire, 53, 110, 145
Saturday Press, 53
Saturday Review of Literature, 111
science fiction, 59
Scott, Sir Walter, 116
Shaw, George Bernard, 93
Shelley, Harriet, 118
Schönemann, Friedrich, 138
Sinclair, Upton, 98, 111
slavery
  Frederick Douglass on, 160
  in *Huckleberry Finn,* 133, 147-50, 156, 166-67
  in *Pudd'nhead Wilson,* 133, 186-88
  Twain grew up with, 17-18, 62
  Twain on, 17-18
Smart Set (Mencken), 126, 127
Smith, Henry Nash, 121, 145
society
  class system, 132-33, 169-70, 175
  reform of through literature, 186-73
Spectator, The, 138
Springfield Republican, 162, 164

Steinbeck, John, 155
St. Louis, Missouri, 50-51
Stoddard, Charles Warren, 53
Stowe, Harriet Beecher, 188
Struggles and Triumphs (Barnum), 184
Strunsky, Simeon, 88
Styron, William, 167
Sumner, Charles, 86

Territorial Enterprise, 30-32, 34, 52-53, 55, 57-60, 109
themes, in Twain's work
  duality, 131-35, 185-86
  freedom and slavery, 145-48, 185-89
  gender, 131
  imposters, 134
  lookalikes, 131, 133, 134
  mistaken identity, 185-87
  racial, 133, 144, 147-48, 159, 167, 186-88
    prejudice, 133, 149-50, 156-57, 166-67
  rivers, 151-54
  social classes, 133, 157
  technology, 170-73, 175, 177, 181, 185
  twins, 131, 133, 191
Thompson, Charles Miner, 62, 127
Thoreau, Henry David, 45, 49
Those Extraordinary Twins, 73, 131
Tocqueville, Alexis de, 47
Tom Hood's Comic Annual for 1873, 57
Tom Sawyer, The Adventures of
  based on Twain's childhood, 15, 22, 28, 51, 62, 63, 67, 74, 140
  description in, 72
  duality theme in, 131-32
  flaws in, 109
  humor in, 74
  influence of *Don Quixote*

on, 138
  as masterpiece, 165
  Muff Potter, 132, 134
  paired with *Huckleberry Finn*, 28, 29, 153, 157
  plot in, 73
  poor characterization in, 64
  as portrait of period, 115
  as typically American, 67
Tramp Abroad, A, 84
Transcendentalism, 161
"Travelling Stones of Pahrangat Valley" (De Quille), 59
Trevelyan, George Macaulay, 85
Trilling, Lionel, 144
Tri-Weekly Journal, 24
Turner, George, 58, 61
Twain, Mark
  autobiographical works, 13, 67-68, 74, 76, 79, 104, 132
  autobiography of, 135, 137, 175
  birth of, 13, 47, 49, 51, 62, 102
  and blacks, 15, 17-18, 160-61
  and book publishing, 39-41
  boyhood experiences, 16-20, 117-18
  business ventures, 39-41, 104
  champions causes, 100-102, 118
  character of, 89, 92-94, 110, 130
  childhood of, 15-20, 49-51, 62-63, 117-18, 161, 170
  children of, 27, 81, 91, 95
  and Civil War, 27-29, 52, 102, 181
  as clown, 99, 102, 108, 110, 129
  compared with Mencken, 124-30
  and death,

of family, 16, 27, 38, 41-42, 81, 91, 95
murders, 18, 19, 41, 102, 118
war, 28, 117
death of, 42-43
disillusionment of, 105-106, 115-20
duality of, 104-105, 131
duel with Laird, 32, 57, 60-61, 118
education of, 16, 20, 52, 63, 64, 78, 80, 180
honorary degrees, 64, 81, 125
fails as writer, 65-66, 73, 95-97, 107-11
con, 112-14
father of. *See* Clemens, John Marshall
first stories, 21-22
Freudian analysis of, 43, 91-97, 108-109, 111
genius was repressed, 98-106
as great humorist, 88-90, 106, 124-30, 135, 186
con, 64-65
and Halley's Comet, 42-43
Hannibal's influence on, 15-20, 50-52, 62-63, 108, 113, 121, 161
historical view of, 175-76, 178
illness of, 16, 119
influences on writing, 136, 138, 139, 140-42
as journalist, 21-24, 30-34, 52-53, 58, 60, 64-65, 76-78, 109, 118
as lecturer, 35-36, 40, 53, 77
letters by, 81, 162, 164
marriage of, 36-38, 77, 102-103
as Mississippi River pilot, 26-52, 76, 152
Mississippi River's influence on, 63-64, 152-53
as misunderstood, 48-49
money earned, 99, 102
mother of. *See* Clemens, Jane Lampton
on music, 116
occupations of, 29, 52, 118
opinion of art, 116
opinion of other writers, 126
pen names of, 21-22, 30-32, 48, 52, 55, 58, 109, 131-32
personifies Americans, 67-68, 113
pessimism of, 25-26, 40-42, 91, 93-96, 105-106, 109-11, 170
philosophy of, 95-97
and politics, 118
poor style of, 64, 69-70, 74
popularity of, 39, 75, 77, 92-93, 99, 118, 120, 127, 133
printing jobs of, 20-22, 25
and religion
Calvinist upbringing, 19, 41, 108, 111, 115, 118-19, 181
didn't believe in, 89, 90, 95, 180
siblings, 14
similarities to Lincoln, 49, 66, 67, 86
as social satirist, 53, 71, 106, 108-14, 125-29, 145, 170-71
as storyteller, 70, 73, 122
as technocrat, 39, 181, 185-86, 189-90
travels of, 23, 29-36, 52-53, 118
use of American English, 83-87
use of common language, 69-70, 74, 122, 127, 144, 157, 160, 167
Twichell, Joseph, 76, 81, 119

Uncle Tom's Cabin (Stowe), 188

Van Doren, Carl, 111
Verne, Jules, 139
Virginia City, Nevada, 52-53, 55-61
Virginia City Union, 30-32, 60
Vonnegut, Kurt, Jr., 180

Wagenknecht, Edward, 110, 114, 136
Walker, Alice, 157
Wallace, John H., 167
Ward, Artemus, 34, 53, 130
"War-Prayer, The," 105, 117
Was Huck Black? Mark Twain and African-American Voices (Fishkin), 160-61
Webb, Charles H., 36, 53, 89
Webster, Charles L., 42
Webster, Samuel Charles, 20
Webster & Company, 39
Weekly Courier, 63
Wendell, Berrett, 127
Western Union, 21
What Is Man?, 96, 105
White, E.B., 129
Whitman, Walt, 45, 48, 72, 107, 122
Wister, Owen, 115
Wolf, Jim, 117
women
  effect on Twain, 37, 38, 40-42, 103-104, 108, 111
  in Twain's work, 145, 147, 148, 182
Wright, William. *See* Dan De Quille

Zall, Paul M., 86